T0196211

TRANSGENDER FAMILY LAW

A GUIDE TO EFFECTIVE ADVOCACY

Edited by

JENNIFER L. LEVI

&

ELIZABETH E. MONNIN-BROWDER

authorHOUSE®

AuthorHouse™
1663 Liberty Drive
Bloomington, IN 47403
www.authorhouse.com
Phone: 1-800-839-8640

Published by AuthorHouse   4/13/2012

ISBN: 978-1-4685-5214-0 (sc)
ISBN: 978-1-4685-5453-3 (e)

Library of Congress Control Number: 2012902284
Cover design by Robbii.
Photography courtesy of Jess Dugan, Tony Scarpetta and Susan Symonds

This book is printed on acid-free paper.

Contents

Chapter 2: Recognition of Name and Sex
Janson Wu and Kylar W. Broadus

Chapter 3: Relationship Recognition and Protections
Elizabeth E. Monnin-Browder

Chapter 4: Protecting Parental Rights
Shannon Price Minter and Deborah H. Wald

Chapter 5: Divorce and Relationship Dissolution
Jennifer L. Levi

Chapter 6: Parental Rights After Relationship Dissolution
Patience Crozier

Chapter 7: Custody Disputes Involving Transgender Children
Shannon Price Minter and Deborah H. Wald

Chapter 8: Legal Protections for Transgender Youth
Zack M. Paakkonen

Chapter 9: Intimate Partner Violence
Morgan Lynn, Terra Slavin, and Wayne A. Thomas Jr.

Chapter 10: Estate Planning and Elder Law
Michelle B. LaPointe

Preface

Gay & Lesbian Advocates & Defenders (GLAD) is a Boston-based non-profit legal organization that works throughout the six New England states on cases of discrimination involving LGBTQ clients and those with HIV/AIDS. The heart of GLAD's work is impact litigation—bringing cases of first impression (that is, cases typically involving facts not heard by a court before) in which a favorable impact will benefit the entire community in addition to the parties before the court.

In June 2008, GLAD launched the Transgender Rights Project. The move to create a separate transgender-focused project reflects a deep commitment on the part of the organization to broaden and protect the rights of transgender people. Although GLAD has worked on behalf of transgender people throughout its thirty-five-year history, the creation of a separate project has enabled the organization to bring that work to a new and higher level.

Throughout its history, GLAD has brought lawsuits that successfully challenged transgender bias: a middle school's mistreatment of a transgender student, a prison system's denial of essential health care for a transgender inmate, a government agency's denial of insurance coverage for a transgender person's medically necessary care, the federal government's unequal treatment of a transgender taxpayer, among others. Throughout the same period of time, GLAD has received calls from people throughout New England, and beyond, about serious challenges they faced across a range of family law contexts.

In discussion with the other GLAD attorneys, I realized that one of the challenges in bringing family law impact cases on behalf of transgender clients is the dearth of knowledge among family law attorneys—even those deeply committed to advocating on behalf of their transgender clients—about how to best and most effectively represent them. As a result, many transgender clients have been negotiating away family law protections out of fear, often well-founded, that they will fare worse in the courts than if they strive to reach some negotiated agreement with someone seeking to restrict their familial rights. In addition, many transgender clients who have taken the risk of going to court have found themselves in front of tribunals influenced by the widespread community and social bias against transgender people generally.

One example of the bias transgender people and their families face in the legal system comes from a corporate lawyer who told me about a case she had worked on nearly thirty years ago, when she was doing family law work. She had represented a transgender woman who, prior to her gender transition, had been in an otherwise lawful different-sex marriage and was being divorced by her wife of many years. The couple had a child with whom the attorney's client had a close, loving relationship. However, the wife said the transgender client would never see the child again and quickly turned to poisoning the relationship between the parent and child. The transgender client chose not to challenge the wife's legal custodial status but asked that she be allowed to retain her parental status and maintain an obligation of child support. The transgender parent wanted to be sure that her child always knew that she had never stopped financially supporting her, no matter how effectively the other parent worked to destroy their relationship, and even though she could not enjoy visitation with the child with whom she had been so close.

Thirty years later GLAD's legal information line continues to receive calls from people whose family relationships suffer because of legal bias and discrimination. Many parents who undergo divorce and relationship dissolution at or around the time of their gender transition have diminished or no relationships with their kids. In addition, I have witnessed a disturbing recent trend of courts reversing custody arrangements because a parent has supported a child's cross-gender identification. In such cases, courts have ignored the predominant perspective offered by medical and mental health professionals, preferring instead to credit testimony offered by bigoted, biased, and uncredentialed professionals.

These stories are heartbreaking and remind us how essential it is to reverse the course of negative legal precedent, rampant bias, and discrimination against transgender people that infuses our legal system.

Reversing bad precedent, establishing favorable outcomes, and changing public attitudes regarding transgender people is especially critical in the area of family law because it presses so deeply on the most intimate of human relationships. Those are the goals of this book.

I am proud of the Transgender Rights Project's many accomplishments that have brought about structural and systemic changes benefitting transgender people. Reversing precedent and changing attitudes requires knowledge, information, and resources. This book is the effort of GLAD's Transgender Rights Project to provide the essential tools for building strong law to protect all families, including those formed by transgender people.

— Jennifer L. Levi

Acknowledgments

Writing this book has been a labor of passion shared by many individuals and organizations who are committed to transgender equality and to ensuring that transgender people have access to high quality, culturally competent, effective legal services. There are many people to thank for bringing it to fruition.

We wish to thank all of the contributing authors, many of whom are in small and solo law practices or working for non-profit legal organizations and who have little or no spare time. We are incredibly grateful to them for contributing their time, wisdom, and expertise to this project. Thanks to Kylar W. Broadus, Patience Crozier, Benjamin L. Jerner, Michelle B. LaPointe, Morgan Lynn, Shannon Price Minter, Zack M. Paakkonen, Terra Slavin, Wayne A. Thomas Jr., Deborah H. Wald, and Janson Wu.

In addition to the contributing authors, a number of GLAD and former GLAD employees and interns worked tirelessly to see this book to completion. Many thanks to Gary Buseck, Carisa Cunningham, Jonah Fabricant, Katusha Galitzine, Laura Kiritsy, Anna Kurtz, Karen Loewy, Matt Redovan, Raymond Rodriguez, and Robbie Samuels. Very special thanks to Amanda Johnston and Joseph Wildey for their attention to detail, thoughtfulness, and thoroughness in editing and proofreading. A huge thanks to Ashley Dunn, who offered unparalleled technical reviews and continued contributing to the project long after she had completed her one-year fellowship with GLAD. Thanks also to Robin Maltz for her contribution to the editing and review of this book.

Several individuals provided crucial feedback and perspective as the chapters were being developed, including M. Barusch, Hyman Darling, Sara M. Fleming, Bri Lacy, Karen Loewy, Jody Marksamer, Victoria Neilson, Catherine E. Reuben, Erika Rickard, Elizabeth Roberts, Melanie Rowen, Cathy Sakimura, Hema Sarang-Sieminski,

Jennifer L. Levi & Elizabeth E. Monnin-Browder

Gunner Scott, and Ilona Turner. Thanks also to Spencer Bergstedt, Erin Buzuvis, Beth Cohen, MJ Edwards, Kathie Gummere, Leora Harpaz, Joyce Kauffman, Hilary J. Libka, Maureen Murphy, and Wendy Haller Verlander for their invaluable contributions.

Special thanks to June, Diego Sanchez, Nancy Nangeroni, Gordene MacKenzie, Sarah Blanchette, Tre'Andre Valentine, and Ruben Hopwood for generously allowing us to use their images on the book cover.

A number of individuals and law firms also stepped up to support this book, again, because of their recognition and appreciation of the importance of ensuring that family law attorneys are equipped to defend the familial rights of their transgender clients. Special thanks to A.M. Clark; Diane Ellaborn, LICSW; Miriam & Ralph Freidin; Rachel Goldberg, Esq.; Anne Guenzel & Frances Pieters; Joanne Herman & Terry Fallon; Charlotte Kinlock & Anne Stanback; Dianne R. Phillips of Holland & Knight LLP; and Shipman & Goodwin LLP for their extraordinary support of this project.

CHAPTER 1: CULTURALLY COMPETENT REPRESENTATION

Benjamin L. Jerner

Introduction

Representing transgender clients presents attorneys with work that is often unique, challenging, and rewarding. A bit of preparation and a few changes to office policies and procedures can go a long way toward providing representation that is effective and makes the experience as comfortable as possible for transgender clients.

An important first step is for the attorney to establish a welcoming and respectful environment at the firm or legal services office before the client's initial contact. To be an effective advocate the attorney may have to educate herself/himself about transgender people's lives as well as about some new legal issues in the area of domestic relations. The attorney must also be prepared, where a client's transgender status is relevant, to educate the court, opposing counsel, and other interested parties about transgender issues and, where the client's transgender status is not relevant, to shield the client from attacks or bias based on it. Finally, in the emerging and constantly changing area of transgender law, the attorney must be mindful that particular legal positions and tactics may impact not only the transgender client, but also the larger community.

1.1 Key Terms Defined

Attorneys should be familiar with the terminology generally used to describe transgender individuals and other terms related to gender identity and transition, while also being aware that most of these are not legal terms of art and may be used variously depending on a client's age, race, ethnicity, socioeconomic status, geography, personal preference, and other demographic and individual considerations. As a result, each attorney needs to take into account her/his client's preferences as well as the local legal and political climate in determining how best to frame such issues during the course of representation.

While this chapter is intended to be a resource and an introduction to key terms that are used in this publication and that an attorney may encounter in representing transgender clients, an attorney should ask her/his client open-ended questions and respect and mirror the language s/he uses to self-identify and to explain her/his life experiences. Where the attorney determines that use of the client's post-transition name, sex, and/or pronoun—with a court, with opposing counsel, or with experts—may compromise the client's claim, the attorney should advise the client regarding the attorney's determination but should respect the client's decision about which language to use.

"Gender identity" refers to one's internal sense of being male, female, both, or neither.

"Gender expression" is the way in which a person expresses her/his gender identity through mannerisms, behavior, dress, or appearance.

"Sexual orientation" is the term typically used to describe the direction of a person's romantic and physical attractions. People may be attracted to others of the same sex, others of a different sex, or some combination of those two. Gender identity and sexual orientation are different components of one's identity. A transgender person (or a person who has a transgender partner) may identify her/his sexual orientation as heterosexual, gay, lesbian, bisexual, or queer.

"Transgender" is a term used to refer to individuals whose gender identity or gender expression does not, in some way, match stereotypical expectations based on the sex they were assigned at birth. For example, most persons assigned the sex of female at birth are expected to and do grow up looking, behaving, feeling, and living like a girl and then a woman. Most persons assigned the sex of male at birth are expected to and do grow up looking, behaving, feeling, and living like a boy and then a man. A person who identifies as transgender often does not match this stereotypical paradigm, and/or may live as a different sex from the one assigned to that individual at birth.

"Transsexual" typically refers to someone whose body and gender identity do not match and who transitions by undergoing medical treatment. This includes living full-time consistent with her/his gender identity, taking cross-gender hormones, undergoing a range of surgeries, or any combination of these three therapeutic modalities, to bring her/his body and gender identity more in line. "Transsexual" has historically been the term most frequently used in case law to describe transgender people, although the use of "transgender" has become increasingly common in case law in recent years. When searching for family law cases involving transgender people, an attorney should be sure to include the search terms "transgender" and "transsexual."

"Gender identity disorder" (GID) is the underlying diagnosis used by psychological and medical professionals to identify persons who experience "**gender dysphoria**," the clinically significant distress associated with the incongruencies of assigned birth sex, physical body, and gender identity. Treatment for GID is tailored to an individual's medical needs and desires and can range from psychotherapy to physical transition, which may include support for living full-time in the desired gender, hormone therapy, sex reassignment surgery, or any combination of these. It is important to note that the feeling that one's gender is inconsistent with one's birth sex is not, in and of itself, considered to be a mental disorder. It is only considered to be a mental disorder if those feelings cause substantial and clinically significant emotional distress or impairment in the person's functioning.

"Gender transition" or just **"transition"** is the process by which a transgender person begins to live in accordance with her/his gender identity. This is often done under the supervision of medical and mental health professionals.

"Intersex" is a general term used for a variety of conditions in which a person is born with reproductive or sexual anatomy that doesn't fit the typical definition of male or female. **"Disorders of sex development"** (**DSD**) is increasingly being used to refer to intersex persons.

"Crossdresser" is a term that refers to people who sometimes or often dress, behave, and/or present in ways that do not meet stereotypical expectations associated with their birth sex. They may or may not have a gender identity consistent with the sex associated with their dress or behavior.

"Genderqueer," "gender nonconforming," or **"gender variant"** are terms that refer to people whose gender identity is either both male and female, is neither male nor female, or are in some ways identified with a sex different than that assigned to them at birth. Some, but not all, people who identify as genderqueer, gender nonconforming, or gender variant consider themselves transgender.

"Female to male" (**FTM**) are those who are assigned the female sex at birth, but whose gender identity is male. Such individuals may identify as "FTM," "transgender man," "transman," "transgender," or simply as a "man."

"Male to female" (**MTF**) are those who are assigned the male sex at birth, but whose gender identity is female. Such individuals may identify as "MTF," "transgender woman," "transwoman," "transgender," or simply as a "woman."

"Cisgender" are non-transgender people. This term has emerged in social and cultural realms to highlight the point that everyone has a gender, but that people whose gender identity is consistent with their assigned sex at birth and their physiology tend to give very little thought to their gender. In this publication, cisgender people will be referred to as "**non-transgender**."

The ***Diagnostic and Statistical Manual of Mental Disorders***, (**DSM**), published by the American Psychiatric Association, categorizes mental disorders. The most recent edition, the *Diagnostic and Statistical Manual of Mental Disorders, 4ᵗʰ Edition, Text Revised* (DSM-IV-TR) includes diagnoses for GID, transvestic fetishism, and Gender Identity Disorder Not Otherwise Specified. The DSM-IV-TR is currently undergoing comprehensive revision. Future versions may significantly modify or even remove certain diagnoses that affect transgender people.

The **World Professional Association for Transgender Health (WPATH),** formerly known as the Harry Benjamin International Gender Dysphoria Association, has developed internationally accepted **standards of care (SOC)** for the health of transsexual, transgender, and gender nonconforming people. The standards provide recommendations for diagnosis and best practices for care and treatment of gender dysphoria and GID. They also affirm that treatment must be individualized, with no single medical protocol required for all persons to satisfy requirements for gender transition.

Pronouns typically reflect a person's gender identity. A transgender person may prefer to be identified using third-person singular gendered pronouns (e.g., she or he and her or him), third person plural pronouns (e.g., they and them), or alternative pronouns (e.g., ze and hir). S/he and her/him are the pronouns used in this publication.

1.2 Practice Recommendations

1.2.1 Education and Training

To be an effective advocate for a transgender client, an attorney should have a general understanding about the social and legal issues pertaining to transgender people and must be able to advocate for her/his transgender client without reservation or discomfort about the client's gender identity or expression.[1] Given the longstanding societal misunderstandings about and disapproval of transgender people, even well-meaning attorneys may hold prejudices and unexamined preconceptions about transgender clients that could undermine representation. Therefore, each attorney has a special responsibility to educate herself/himself about transgender law and transgender people's lives in order to ensure zealous advocacy for transgender clients.

The best way for an attorney to educate herself/himself is to attend trainings or presentations by transgender people. There are also many informative autobiographies and memoirs that provide insight into transgender people's experiences.[2] In addition, there are helpful resources online, from handbooks about how to work with transgender clients or staff, to blogs and videos by transgender people sharing information about their lives.[3] It may also be helpful to look at some of the social and cultural literature on this topic.

Effective advocacy does not require the attorney to eradicate every vestige of bias; however, it is vital that an attorney representing a transgender client be aware of any internal bias or prejudice and consciously work to keep any such bias from affecting the representation. At a minimum, the attorney must be sure s/he consistently refers to the client using the client's preferred gender, name, and pronoun.[4] Even small inconsistencies can prejudice a court against the client and strengthen the other side's legal position.

1.2.2 How to Make a Law Office a Safe, Respectful, and Welcoming Place for Transgender Clients, Visitors, and Staff

Before accepting transgender clients, it is important to establish transgender-friendly office policies and implement basic education and training of all employees. A list of ten things to do to make a law office safe, respectful and welcoming for transgender clients, visitors, and staff is included in Appendix 1A.

1.2.2.1 Educating Office Staff and Colleagues

Once the attorney has acquired a basic understanding of transgender people's experiences, it is important to educate all office colleagues and staff about transgender people. Where the service is available, have someone who specializes in cultural competency training relating to transgender people come in to the office. At a minimum, colleagues and staff must come away from the training understanding that some clients may be transgender and that all clients' gender identities must be respected. They should understand that it is imperative to use a client's preferred name in all client interactions, including phone calls and other correspondence to the client, and when calling the client's name in the waiting room. They should also understand that a client may prefer to have a different name and pronoun used in different contexts and this must be respected. Other options for educating colleagues and staff are to share useful reading materials, attend an event that specifically relates to gender identity and the transgender community, or watch and discuss a movie about transgender people.

Additionally, all law office employees must understand the need for confidentiality (such as not disclosing the client's transgender status, prior legal name, or legal issues, to those outside the firm or legal services office) and discretion (such as using the client's birth name and pronoun when contacting the client at the client's workplace if the client has not disclosed her/his transgender status to her/his employer). Although important for every client, confidentiality and discretion are particularly important for many transgender clients. Given the lack of legal protections in many areas of the country, the transgender person's housing and job may be at risk if her/his transgender status is disclosed. And, because of persistent prejudice against this population, disclosure may even put a transgender person's physical safety in danger.

Staff should also be made aware of any logistical issues or circumstances associated with a particular law office that might create barriers for transgender clients and visitors. For example, if a law office is in a building with a security policy that requires clients and visitors to present identification prior to admission, it may be necessary to communicate with the security staff when a transgender client, potential client, or visitor is expected to visit the office or, better yet, to negotiate a plan with security personnel that permits transgender people with mismatched identity documents to proceed unimpeded. The security staff should not be informed that the client or visitor is transgender, but they should be instructed to allow an individual to check-in and enter the office even if the name or gender on her/his identification does not appear to "match" the individual's gender identity or expression.

Employees should also be made aware if the state/locality has protections against gender identity discrimination. Law offices are generally considered places of public accommodation, so overt discrimination on the part of employees risks exposure to liability.

1.2.2.2 Client Intake Forms

One of the ways to signal that a law office is welcoming and respectful of transgender clients is to modify client intake forms. A more inclusive intake form will include open-ended questions about gender and relationship status.

Intake forms should allow space for a client's current legal name, name given at birth, and name the client prefers to be called. If the form includes a question about the client's sex or gender, instead of checkboxes for "male" or "female," simply list "gender" or "self-identified gender" and provide space for the client to respond. The form can also include a question about which pronoun the client prefers.

In addition, if the intake form includes questions about a client's relationship status and her/his partner, these questions should be asked in an open-ended way to allow clients to provide the most accurate information possible, and to communicate to clients that the law office does not expect or require her/his relationship to fit into a limited set of options. For example, an intake form can state, "Relationship status: _____," rather than the standard checkboxes. This open-ended format allows a client to indicate if s/he is single, married, unmarried but in a civil union or domestic partnership, or unmarried but with a life partner even though their relationship is not legally recognized. In addition, the intake form should use "partner" rather than "spouse" where the intake form seeks information regarding the name and gender of the client's partner, which also shows that the law office appreciates relationships other than marriage.

Similarly, if the intake form includes questions about a client's parental status and her/his children, these questions should be asked in such a way that captures full and complete information, but does not presuppose a "traditional" family structure and anticipates the possibility of transgender parents and transgender children.

Making these changes to a law office's intake form immediately communicates respect to clients by allowing space for self-identification and by not forcing a transgender client to fit her/his personal information onto a form that ignores or insults her/his life experience. These simple modifications will also enable the law office to collect more complete information from all clients, not just transgender clients, and may result in more productive initial client meetings by assisting attorneys in asking better questions to more efficiently understand the client and her/his needs. In addition, making these changes provides an attorney with an opportunity to have important conversations about how and why the language on the intake form is being changed, which is a vehicle for educating colleagues. A sample intake form is included in Appendix 1B.

1.2.2.3 Restroom Policies

The law office or firm should also evaluate its restroom policies to ensure that they are welcoming to transgender clients, visitors, and staff, and, if they are not, make modifications. Often, one of the most difficult and stressful parts of a transgender person's day is dealing with sex-segregated restrooms. For those who "pass" well, the person's use of a gendered restroom matching her/his gender identity may not present any challenge. However, for many transgender individuals who are either early in transition or who simply do not "pass" well regardless of method or stage of transition, use of a gendered restroom can pose real difficulty, anxiety, and even safety risks.

One way to avoid discomfort and anxiety for transgender clients, visitors, and staff is to have a single-stall, gender-neutral restroom that is available to all. If a single-stall bathroom is not available or feasible, a multi-stall bathroom may be designated with signage stating that it is a "family restroom" that can be used by all. Family restrooms have added benefits in that people with disabilities who have different-sex helpers can enter the restroom together, as well as parents and children of different sexes.

Whether or not the provision of a single-stall or family restroom can be implemented, any restroom should be made available to clients, visitors, and staff based on their gender identities, not their physiology or assigned sex at birth. Successful implementation of such a policy requires that all office staff be knowledgeable about the policy. For example, if clients and other visitors to the office have to request a key to use the restroom, it is important that the person from whom they seek the key—such as a receptionist or security guard—be informed about the office restroom policy.

1.2.2.4 Office and Employee Policies

Another way to signal that a law office is welcoming of transgender clients, visitors, and staff is to include sexual orientation and gender identity and expression in the office's nondiscrimination policy and, where possible, offer benefits to lesbian, gay, bisexual, transgender, and queer (LGBTQ) employees, including health insurance for domestic partners and health insurance coverage for transition-related treatment. The law office may publicize its nondiscrimination policy and/or insurance benefits on the firm's website and in promotional literature.

1.2.3 Preliminary Contact with a Potential Client

1.2.3.1 Initial Client Contact

The attorney or staff person in charge of initial client contact or client intake should not assume that s/he knows the client's gender identity and should avoid using gendered language (e.g., "sir" or "ma'am") until the client makes it clear how s/he identifies. Additionally, the staff member conducting the initial intake should inquire as to the client's preferred name and preferred pronoun, as well as the client's current legal name, if this information was not already collected on the client intake form. Once the potential client identifies that s/he is transgender, the person conducting the intake should inquire as to the potential client's need for discretion in communication, including the best way to contact the potential client and the name to be used when emailing, writing, and either calling to speak with a potential client or leaving a message for her/him. The law office or firm should implement procedures whereby any special instructions regarding potential client contact can be easily found to prevent inadvertent use of the incorrect name or pronoun.

1.2.3.2 Initial Attorney Meeting

When initially meeting with a transgender client, it is critical for the attorney to respect the client's privacy and to be respectful of her/his gender identity and expression. Early on in the representation, an attorney should learn how the client identifies her/his sexual orientation and how the client categorizes her/his relationship (i.e., as a relationship with someone of a different sex or of the same sex). Knowing the answer to these questions is fundamental to building a respectful, collaborative attorney-client relationship and, specifically, understanding a transgender client's needs and priorities.

As with all clients, an attorney should not make assumptions about a client's sexual orientation based on her/his gender identity or expression or transgender identity. Asking open-ended questions about how a client identifies her/his sexual orientation and categorizes her/his relationship communicates respect for the client and elicits useful information. In addition, it is important for an attorney to use the same language that the client uses to describe her/his identity and her/his relationship, at least in interactions with the client.

In addition to other case-specific information that must be solicited from a client in the initial meeting, an attorney may need to ask particular questions of a transgender client. It is entirely appropriate to ask whether the client has obtained a court-ordered name and/or sex change. It may also be necessary for an attorney to elicit information about the specifics of a client's gender identity and expression and/or gender transition. For example, it may or may not be necessary for an attorney to ask a transgender client questions about her/his medical transition. Where the details about a client's gender identity and expression and/or transition are not relevant to the legal case, it is inappropriate for an attorney to inquire about them.

When questions regarding a client's gender transition are relevant, it is important to pose these extremely personal questions with sensitivity and respect. For instance, the attorney should ask a transgender client about her/his medical transition in an open-ended way, such as: "what steps have you taken to transition?" Only if legally relevant, and only if the client does not volunteer the information in response to an open-ended question, should the attorney ask directed questions about specific medical treatment or surgical procedures.

To determine what information, if any, the attorney needs to know about a client's gender identity or transition, it may be helpful for the attorney to research the relevant jurisdiction's legal definition of what constitutes a male or female; whether the jurisdiction allows and/or recognizes a legal change of sex and, if so, what is required for a legal change of sex; and for many family law matters, whether a change of sex has an impact on an existing or contemplated marriage.[5] The answers to these questions will guide an attorney in determining what information s/he needs from a transgender client and ensure that the attorney is asking questions because the information is relevant to the representation, and not to satisfy her/his own curiosity.

The initial client meeting is also a good time to discuss the law office's policies with respect to confidentiality and discretion in communications from the law office to the client and to confirm any specific needs the client may have in this area.

Finally, transgender clients, like all clients, often have legal needs beyond the issue presented to the attorney. For instance, a transgender client may come in for consultation regarding a child custody matter but also need assistance with a legal name change, a legal sex change, and/or changes to identity documents. If it seems appropriate under the circumstances, an attorney should inquire about whether the client has a need for legal representation in these other areas. Where the client presents with legal needs beyond the scope of counsel's expertise, counsel should provide the client with appropriate referrals.

1.2.4 Client Communications, Court Documents, and Court Appearances

If a client has not yet obtained a court-ordered name change, the representation agreement between an attorney's law office and the client should indicate the name the client prefers, but should be signed by the client using her/his current legal name. The attorney should ask the client whether s/he wants the current legal name and pronoun or the post-transition name and pronoun used on subsequent correspondence, and the attorney should make this known to relevant staff.

Where the decision has been made to use the client's post-transition name and pronoun during the course of litigation, correspondence with opposing counsel, pleadings, and references to the client in court should consistently refer to the client using the client's post-transition name and pronoun.

1.2.5 Role of Transgender Client's Transgender Status in the Case

A transgender client's transgender status generally should not be legally relevant in most domestic relations disputes, but it may nevertheless be central to the decision maker's analysis and the outcome of the case. As a result, an attorney may be well-advised to proactively educate the court about transgender people, even if the client's transgender status has not yet been raised by opposing counsel.

Conversely, it may be inadvisable to disclose a client's transgender status when the primary objective of the representation (such as seeking custody of the client's child) may be compromised by the client's need to honestly express her/his gender identity in the litigation process. Attaining both of these goals may not always be possible due to factors such as the conservative leanings of the court that will hear the matter, or the existence of discriminatory statutes or bad case law. For example, in some cases it may advance the client's goal of obtaining custody of her/his child for the client to minimize the outward expression of her/his gender identity and to appear in court using her/his pre-transition name (if the client has not legally changed her/his name), pronoun, and presentation. An attorney should be prepared to assist a client in assessing the need for discretion about her/his transgender identity after considering all of the pertinent factors of the case.

These are sensitive strategic decisions that will depend upon the circumstances of the case, the relationship between the parties, the client's goals, the culture of the court, and what is known about the particular judge. Ultimately, these are decisions that should be made by the client after the client is advised of all relevant considerations and possible risks. (See the other chapters in this publication for more guidance on this topic.)

1.2.6 How to Address Bias and Educate Opposing Counsel, Judge, Jury, and Court Personnel

Transgender individuals comprise a small percentage of the population and are widely misunderstood. They are often sexualized, pitied, and/or seen as mentally ill. Such stereotypes are often used to maximum advantage by opposing counsel in contested domestic relations matters. For instance, because certain gender identities and expressions are recognized as mental disorders, a client's diagnosis of GID or "transvestic fetishism" may be used by a divorcing spouse to attack the client's fitness as a parent.

In these cases, it is critical to disabuse the trier of fact of stereotypes they may hold about transgender people. Educating the court and opposing counsel can be accomplished in several ways. One of the most effective strategies is to use expert witnesses. Examples of such experts may include psychological professionals who can educate the court about a client's parental fitness and psychological or medical professionals who can educate the court about the appropriateness of, and need for treatment of, GID. In child custody cases, it may also be necessary to have a professional specializing in child psychology who can testify about the benign effect of a parent's gender expression and/or transition on a child.

Other approaches to education include citing social science research in briefs and, in those jurisdictions that allow jury trials for family law cases, educating the jury through voir dire.

1.2.7 Impact of Legal Tactics and Appeals

Family law disputes can be difficult for the parties involved and can generate strong emotions that sometimes result in clients (and attorneys) behaving badly. While it is always important to try to advance a client's interests, accomplishing those goals while advancing certain legal theories can be damaging to the collective interests of the transgender community.[6] Likewise, the decision to appeal a case that may have bad facts, or where the chance of success is slim because of a particularly conservative appellate court, can have significant negative ramifications for the larger transgender community. Therefore, it is important for an attorney to consider the broader implications of legal positions and tactics taken during litigation involving a transgender client.

An attorney representing a client in a family law dispute that involves a transgender person should find ways to achieve her/his client's objectives without using legal theories that challenge a transgender person's legal sex. Additionally, an attorney should not use legal theories that challenge marriage validity, parental rights, or parental fitness solely on the basis of transgender status.

When considering a questionable legal tactic or an appeal of an issue that is related to the client's transgender status, it is advisable to consult with legal organizations that have experience with impact litigation for the LGBTQ community (see Appendix 1C). The attorney can then discuss these implications with the client as the attorney and client decide on the next course of action.

---

1   MODEL RULES OF PROF'L CONDUCT R. 8.4 (2007) (prohibiting a lawyer from "engag[ing] in conduct that is prejudicial to the administration of justice").

"A lawyer who, in the course of representing a client, knowingly manifests by words or conduct, bias or prejudice based upon race, sex, religion, national origin, disability, age, sexual orientation or socioeconomic status, violates paragraph (d) when such actions are prejudicial to the administration of justice." MODEL RULES OF PROF'L CONDUCT R. 8.4 cmt. (2007).

2   *See, e.g.*, HELEN BOYD, MY HUSBAND BETTY: LOVE, SEX, AND LIFE WITH A CROSSDRESSER (2003); JENNIFER FINNEY BOYLAN, SHE'S NOT THERE: A LIFE IN TWO GENDERS (2003); JAMISON GREEN, BECOMING A VISIBLE MAN (2004); JOANNE HERMAN, TRANSGENDER EXPLAINED FOR THOSE WHO ARE NOT (2009); JULIA SERANO, WHIPPING GIRL: A TRANSSEXUAL WOMAN ON SEXISM AND THE SCAPEGOATING OF FEMININITY (2007); MAX WOLF VALERIO, THE TESTOSTERONE FILES: MY HORMONAL AND SOCIAL TRANSFORMATION FROM FEMALE TO MALE (2006).

3   *See, e.g.*, Massachusetts Transgender Political Coalition, I AM: TRANS PEOPLE SPEAK, http://www.transpeoplespeak.org (last visited Sept. 1, 2011).

4   It can sometimes be difficult to remember to use a client's preferred pronoun or name, especially if the attorney has known the client prior to gender transition. One of the most effective ways to ensure use of the proper pronoun and name is to use them consistently and exclusively, subject to the needs of the client regarding discretion in communications and subject to the constraints of the litigation strategy. It may take some effort initially, but over time use of the client's "new" name and pronoun becomes quite natural.

5   Answers to these questions are rarely straightforward and it may help to consult legal organizations that focus on LGBTQ and/or transgender law for resources and support.

6   For example, while it might benefit a client financially if his marriage were to be declared void due to his transition from female to male before the marriage, the implications of such a court ruling could be devastating for the larger transgender community because of the likelihood that it could undermine the security of other transgender people's marriages.

CHAPTER 2: RECOGNITION OF NAME AND SEX

Janson Wu and Kylar W. Broadus

Introduction

Two of the most basic legal needs of transgender individuals are obtaining legal recognition of their post-transition name and sex. For transgender people, the ability to live fully in their post-transition name and sex can be vitally important to their safety, gender transition, and family security. For example, having a driver's license that still contains a person's assigned name or sex at birth, or having inconsistent names and/or sex designations on various identity documents, exposes that person to unnecessary risks to her/his physical safety and emotional well-being each time s/he must show her/his driver's license or other identity document to a third party.[1] In addition, for many transgender individuals, changes in name and gender marker on identity documents can help alleviate gender dysphoria, according to the World Professional Association for Transgender Health (WPATH).[2] Finally, legal recognition of a person's sex may be important for access to appropriate sex-segregated facilities, such as prisons, shelters, or bathrooms, as well as in the family law context.[3]

That being said, simply changing one's name or sex designation on one's identity document may not be sufficient to have that name or sex recognized for all purposes, such as, for example, a person's sex for purposes of marriage.[4] Although birth certificates may offer more certainty in establishing a person's legal sex, there have been cases where courts have refused to recognize an amended birth certificate as evidence of a person's legal sex.[5] Moreover, no single standard exists for changing a person's name or sex designation across different identity documents.[6] For those reasons, it is advisable for a transgender client to change her/his name and sex designation on as many legal and identity documents as possible, as well as seek a court order when such an option exists, in order to provide the most certainty.

2.1 Change of Legal Name

There are two ways for a person to change her/his name legally: (1) through common law usage—meaning that through usage and passage of time, a person's preferred name is recognized as her/his legal name, or (2) through a statutory (usually judicial) process that in almost all states results in a court order establishing the new legal name.[7] Currently, all fifty states and the District of Columbia provide a statutory, and usually a judicial, process for changing a person's name legally,[8] while many states also still provide a common law option.[9] Given that to change one's name on most government-issued identity documents, some form of legal or official documentation of a person's new name usually is required, it is best for an attorney to advise her/his transgender clients to obtain a statutory name change in order to change most readily their names on all identity documents.[10]

Although statutes vary from state to state, many states share similar procedural requirements,[11] including:

- a public notice requirement, often in a local newspaper;[12]
- hearing requirements;[13]
- information required to be included within the petition, including petitioner's criminal history, financial history, etc.;[14] and
- a good and sufficient reason for the petition to be granted.[15]

The general purpose of these procedural requirements is to ensure that the petitioner is not seeking to change her/his name for any fraudulent purposes, such as to evade a creditor, as well as to protect third party interests, if any.[16]

Beyond these procedural requirements, most states' statutes

regarding name changes are either silent or grant broad discretion to the judge regarding the standard for granting a name change petition.[17] In the absence of specific statutory criteria, most state courts have developed some standards to apply to name change petitions.[18] The two most common criteria are: (1) "some substantial reason must exist for [the denial]," and (2) the "denial is limited to a showing of an 'unworthy motive, the possibility of fraud on the public, or the choice of a name that is bizarre, unduly lengthy, ridiculous or offensive to common decency and good taste.'"[19]

However, these standards developed by the courts still do not provide much guidance to judges, who continue to have broad discretion in granting name change petitions. This discretion has resulted in some judges denying petitions for a variety of improper reasons, including bias against the petitioner.[20] While denials of name change petitions by trial court judges are technically reviewed under an abuse of discretion standard,[21] a number of appellate courts have demonstrated their willingness to reverse such denials, especially in instances where the trial court has failed to provide findings of fact or reasons for its denial. [22] Specifically, there have been a handful of appellate courts that have reversed a trial court's denial of a name change petition to a transgender individual, where anti-transgender bias was alleged and/or suspected. [23]

Transgender individuals may wish to seek a waiver of the publication requirements so as not to publicize their transgender status and to accelerate the approval of their name change. Many states explicitly provide for such exemption, specifically if such notification may jeopardize the safety of the petitioner.[24] In making such an argument for waiver, it will be important to point to any past instances of discrimination or harassment due to a person's transgender status, or, if no specific instances exist, general statistics showing the increased incidence of violence and discrimination against transgender people.[25]

2.2 Change of Legal Sex

There is a common misconception that everyone has one "legal sex" that is consistently recognized by the government and that can be changed for all purposes by meeting one legal standard. The reality is more complicated. First, it is not guaranteed that a person will be recognized as the sex designation on an identity document (including a driver's license or even a birth certificate) for a specific legal purpose (such as marriage or access to sex-segregated facilities). In addition, a person can have inconsistent sex designations on different identity documents, given differing standards for various identity documents.

Generally, transgender individuals have successfully relied on two items to establish their legal sex: a birth certificate and a court order. As will be discussed further below, each option has its advantages and disadvantages. For example, while a court order may more likely be recognized for purposes of establishing a person's legal sex, an amended birth certificate may be more readily obtained. For some individuals, pursuing both options will provide the most certainty in having that individual's post-transition sex recognized. For other individuals, one or both of these options may not even be available.

2.2.1 Amended Birth Certificates

The requirements and procedure to change a person's sex designation on her/his birth certificate vary from state to state. Forty-seven states, the District of Columbia and New York City allow a person to amend the sex designation on her/his birth certificate.[26] While the majority of states authorize such amendments through statute or regulation, many states have no written rule in place and do so according to local practice.[27]

Of those states that allow a person to change the sex designation on her/his birth certificate, most states require that a person show proof of having undergone surgery, whether by statute, regulation, or informal practice/policy.[28] For most of those states, that surgical requirement is contained within the relevant statute or implementing regulation. Some states will require "complete" or "genital" surgery,[29] while others will leave the type of surgery unspecified.[30] Finally, some states require that the person also have changed her/his name in order to change the sex designation on her/his birth certificate.[31]

States also vary as to what type of documentation, proof, and/or process is required. Some states will change a birth certificate as a matter of administrative process upon submission of a letter from a physician attesting that the individual has met the requisite standard.[32] Other states require an individual to obtain a court order indicating that the individual has met the requisite standard.[33] For individuals who were born in a state that requires a court order to amend their birth certificate and who still live in that state, they should not have difficulty in obtaining such a court order.[34]

However, if that same individual has moved to another state, and especially if s/he has moved to a state that does not have any statute contemplating the issuance of a court order to amend a birth certificate, that individual may have more difficulty obtaining such a court order. Her/his only options may be to seek a court order from her/his state of birth or to ask a court in her/his state of residence to exercise its equitable jurisdiction to issue an order finding that the person has met the standard and authorizing, to the extent possible, the issuing state to amend the birth certificate.

It is recommended first to make efforts to seek a court order from the issuing state, assuming that the individual has the financial resources to travel to her/his home state and/or hire an attorney in her/his home state. Otherwise, that individual's only other option is to ask a court in her/his state of residence to issue an order that is sufficient to authorize an amendment to a birth certificate issued from a different state. Only Connecticut specifically contemplates such a situation within its statutes, though a number of states anticipate court orders being issued by out-of-state courts.[35] In every other state, the individual will need to ask the court with general equity jurisdiction in her/his state of residence to issue such an order pursuant to its equitable powers. Such equitable court orders are discussed further in Section 2.2.2.

Assuming that a client is successful in changing the sex designation on her/his birth certificate, some states will issue a new birth certificate with the new sex designation entirely replacing the old one.[36] Other states will only cross out the prior sex designation, leaving it still readable,[37] and still others will leave that decision to the discretion of the court.[38] For transgender individuals, having any evidence of their past sex designation on their birth certificate effectively reveals their transgender status and leaves them at risk of discrimination and prejudice in any context where birth certificates are used. For that reason, it is important to seek a new birth certificate without any visible amendments whenever such an option is available.

Practice Tip: It is important to pay attention to the specific language of the standard for amending a birth certificate. If only "sex reassignment surgery" or "sex change surgery" is specified, then any type of transition-related surgery should suffice, including bilateral mastectomy and male chest reconstruction for transgender men, as well as facial feminization surgery and breast augmentation surgery for transgender women.[39] Only in those states that specifically require "genital surgery" should an individual be required to provide proof of such.

In addition, if the standard requires a letter or affidavit from a physician or surgeon, it is important to note whether that physician or surgeon must be the treating surgeon. If it does not, then often it is simpler for transgender individuals to obtain a letter from their current primary care physician than reestablish contact with a physician or surgeon with whom they do not have a present relationship. That primary care physician can then attest to her/his patient having undergone surgery based upon the medical history or observation.

2.2.2 Equitable Court Orders Establishing Legal Sex

There are a number of situations where an amended birth certificate may not be sufficient or even an option, and an individual may want to obtain a court order establishing her/his legal sex. For example, in some states, it is impossible for any person to change the sex designation on her/his birth certificate. Tennessee and Idaho, by statute and regulation, respectively, do not allow changes to the sex designation on birth certificates.[40] In Ohio, a probate court held that Ohio's birth certificate statute only authorizes corrections if there was an error in the original entry.[41] Transgender individuals who are born in a foreign country may also be unable to amend their birth certificate, whether because of legal prohibitions or because it would be prohibitively expensive and difficult for that individual to travel back to her/his home country in order to process the request. In addition, as described above, an individual may have been born in a state that requires a court order to amend the birth certificate, but have moved out of the state.

Even if a person is successful in amending her/his birth certificate, such birth certificate is not always recognized for purposes of establishing a person's legal sex. For example, some courts have refused to recognize a person's amended birth certificate for purposes of establishing her/his legal sex—most often in the context of marriage in those states that only license and recognize as valid marriages of different-sex individuals.[42] The question of recognition of an amended birth certificate is further complicated if a person moves out of her/his birth state. In contrast to the almost unqualified interstate respect that court orders and judgments receive under the Full Faith and Credit clause, the "records and acts" of a state (which include birth certificates) are entitled to recognition from another state only if they do not violate the forum state's strong public policy.[43] While this public policy exception is rarely invoked, some courts have taken advantage of it in refusing legal recognition of a person's sex designation on an amended birth certificate from another state.[44]

For these reasons, attorneys in an increasing number of states, including Alaska, Maine, Maryland, Massachusetts, and Washington, have sought to obtain equitable court orders establishing a person's legal sex (whether or not specifically tied to a birth certificate amendment request), even though the laws of her/his state of residence may not contemplate the issuance of such an order. To obtain such an order, given that there are no statutes establishing a right to such an order, a petitioner must convince a court that it has equitable jurisdiction and power to issue such an order. While the law of equity varies from state to state, a court's equitable power typically extends to provide relief that is necessary to remedy a wrong but not explicitly provided by law.[45] In those situations where a petitioner cannot receive adequate relief through law, courts have the power and the discretion to grant such relief through equity and have done so in the context of a person's change of sex.[46] A sample petition for change of legal sex, proposed order for change of legal sex, and supporting memorandum for change of legal sex and affidavits[47] of an individual born in New Hampshire but residing in Maine are provided in appendices 2A, 2B, 2C, 2D, 2E, and 2F.

> **Practice Tip**: An attorney who is contemplating seeking such an order is well-advised to reach out to one of the LGBTQ legal organizations, including Gay & Lesbian Advocates & Defenders (GLAD), LAMBDA Legal, the National Center for Lesbian Rights, and the ACLU's National LGBT and AIDS Project, for further advice.[48]

2.3 Changing Name and/or Sex Designation on Identity Documents

2.3.1 Driver's License or State Identification Card

Each state has its own requirements and procedures for changing a person's name or sex designation on her/his driver's license or state identification card. These requirements and policies are often difficult to find, as they usually are not established by statute or regulation, but rather are set forth in policy manuals and handbooks, or sometimes not at all.

In addition, many front-desk clerks at motor vehicle departments do not actually know the correct policy or may have a misunderstanding of the policy. As such, the policy as enforced can vary even from office to office within the same state or jurisdiction. This is more often the case when attempting to change the sex designation on a driver's license as opposed to a name change, which is a more common request.

In the case of changing a person's name, most states require official documentation indicating a name change, such as court order, marriage license, or civil union certificate.[49] See Section 2.1, Change of Legal Name.

In the case of changing a person's sex designation on a state-issued driver's license or identification card, the situation can be challenging for transgender individuals. Many states require that a person have undergone surgery before being able to change the sex designation on her/his driver's license. A few states have amended their policies to reflect better current medical and scientific understanding of how sex is determined. In those states, including Colorado, Connecticut, Maine, Massachusetts, New Jersey, New Mexico, Nevada, Ohio, Pennsylvania, and Vermont, as well as the District of Columbia, what is required is a letter or affidavit from a qualified healthcare provider that a person has undergone medical transition of sex and is now the stated sex.[50]

2.3.2 Passport

2.3.2.1 Change of Name

A passport is generally issued in the name shown on the documentary evidence that every applicant must produce to prove citizenship and identity (e.g., prior passport, driver's license, birth certificate).[51] If a person has obtained a legal name change and that name change is not reflected in these documents, s/he can submit an original or certified copy of the court order, adoption decree, divorce decree, or marriage certificate showing a legal change of name in order to have the correct name recorded on her/his passport.[52] If the person's passport was issued less than a year ago, s/he will not need to pay a fee for a new passport issued in her/his new name.[53]

There is also a procedure by which a person can change her/his name through a "customary name change."[54] To do so, an applicant must present original or certified copies of three or more public documents, one of which must be a government-issued identification with photograph, evidencing that s/he has used the acquired name generally for five years or longer.[55] Such document must show the acquired name and one other piece of identifying data (such as date of birth, place of birth, age, or Social Security number), and may include but is not limited to: driver's license, military records, employment records, tax records, school records, census records, hospital birth record, or baptismal certificate. If an applicant is unable to submit three such documents, the applicant must submit, in lieu of one of the documents, an affidavit from two or more individuals attesting that they have known the applicant by both the birth and adopted name, and that the applicant has used the adopted name for all purposes for at least five years.[56] Given these stringent requirements in conjunction with increasingly stricter standards for other supporting forms of identification, it may be difficult, if not impossible, to achieve a passport name change absent a statutory/court order for change of name. Accordingly, it is recommended that a person seek a statutory name change when possible. See Section 2.1.

2.3.2.2 Change of Sex Designation

If a transgender person is applying for a passport and s/he is able to provide sufficient evidence of identity (such as a prior passport, driver's license, birth certificate, etc.) that also reflects her/his post-transition sex, then there is no need to provide additional proof of sex. Instead, s/he should also be able to receive a new passport with the accurate sex designation.[57]

However if any of the requisite documentation does not match her/his post-transition sex designation, then s/he will have to provide additional evidence of her/his sex. In June 2010, the U.S. Department of State announced a change to its prior policy of requiring proof of sex reassignment surgery in order to obtain a change of a person's sex designation on a passport. The new policy allows individuals to change their sex designation on their passport provided that they submit certification from a physician confirming that they have had appropriate clinical treatment for gender transition.[58] Such clinical treatment is not limited to surgery only, but instead reflects WPATH's standards-of-care guidance as to what is appropriate transition-related healthcare for each individual, as determined by her/his physician.

Specifically, under the new policy, in order to receive a full, ten-year passport with a changed, post-transition sex designation, an individual must provide a "signed original statement, on office letterhead, from a licensed physician who has treated the applicant for her/his gender-related care or reviewed and evaluated the gender-related medical history of the applicant."[59] That statement must include:[60]

- the physician's full name;
- the physician's medical license or certificate number;
- the issuing state, country, or other jurisdiction of the medical license/certificate;
- the Drug Enforcement Administration (DEA) registration number or comparable foreign registration number;
- the address and telephone number of the physician;
- a statement that the physician has treated the applicant or has reviewed and evaluated the medical history of the applicant and that the physician has a doctor/patient relationship with the applicant;
- a statement that the applicant has had appropriate clinical treatment for gender transition to the new gender of either male or female;[61] and
- a statement that reads, "I declare under penalty of perjury under the law of the United States that the forgoing is true and correct."

Additional information regarding the specific type of transition-related medical treatment that an individual has undergone is not only unnecessary but unnecessarily invasive of a client's medical privacy.

2.3.3 Social Security Database

2.3.3.1 Name Change

In order to change one's name with the Social Security Administration (SSA), s/he needs to provide original or certified copies of the following documents to a local Social Security office:

- form SS-5, "Application For A Social Security Card;"

- one or more identity documents in her/his post-transition legal name (e.g., passport, driver's license, state-issued ID, etc.);

- one or more identity documents in her/his former name; and

- proof of legal name change (e.g., court order for legal name change, marriage document, divorce decree, or Certificate of Naturalization).[62]

For either a name change or change of sex designation, if a client is a United States citizen and has not previously established citizenship with Social Security, s/he needs to present a birth certificate, United States passport, or other proof of citizenship, although the birth certificate or other document establishing citizenship does not need to indicate the client's post-transition name or sex.[63] However, if the client's documentation of her/his citizenship is in a different name or sex than the client's post-transition name or sex, the client needs to provide proof that s/he is the same person, such as with a court order for legal name change. If a client is a noncitizen, s/he must also prove her/his immigration status and work eligibility. Given the many types of immigration scenarios that exist, an attorney should check the Social Security website for more information[64] and/or ask a local Social Security office to find out which documents are sufficient as proof. Finally, a transgender client may use one document for two purposes.

For example, s/he may use a United States passport as proof of both citizenship and identity.[65]

2.3.3.2 Change of Sex Designation

Social Security requires that a person have undergone sex reassignment surgery or amended her/his birth certificate in order to change the sex designation in the Social Security database.[66] With regard to Social Security benefits, a person's sex is relevant foremost for purposes of spousal and survivor benefits. Specifically, different-sex spouses and surviving spouses may be entitled to higher Social Security benefits based upon the earning history of their spouse or deceased spouse.[67] Such spousal or survivor benefits do not extend to same-sex married couples due to the Defense of Marriage Act (DOMA), and so a person's sex as recognized by Social Security may determine whether s/he is in a federally-recognized marriage for purposes of Social Security benefits.

In order to change one's sex designation with Social Security, a person must provide original or certified copies of the following documents to a local SSA office:

- form SS-5 "Application For A Social Security Card;"

- proof of identity: An acceptable document must be current (not expired) and show the applicant's name, identifying information (date of birth or age), and preferably a recent photograph. Acceptable documents include: United States driver's license, state-issued nondriver identification card, or a United States passport; and

- proof of sex (such as one's birth certificate, or a letter from a surgeon or attending physician stating that the surgeon/physician has completed the applicant's sexual reassignment surgery and that the applicant has transitioned to the new gender). [68]

2.3.3.3 No Match Letters

For transgender individuals, their sex designation and name on record with Social Security can have consequences with regard to their employment, because employers are required to submit employee information to Social Security whenever they hire a new employee. If there are inconsistencies between the information the employer sends and what is on record with Social Security, then Social Security will send what is commonly called a "no match letter," alerting the employer as to the inconsistency.

Such letters were originally designed to ensure that employees are using legitimate Social Security numbers and to police employment of nondocumented employees. For transgender individuals, however, Social Security may also send no-match letters when the sex designation or name of an employee in the employer's records does not match Social Security's records. Such letters can effectively disclose an employee's transgender status to her/his employer and thereby increase the risk of employment discrimination.

On September 15, 2011, Social Security announced that it would no longer issue gender no-match letters.[69] If a transgender employee's employer does receive a gender no-match letter, despite this new policy, it is important for the employer to understand that the employer is not required to do anything, nor is the employer subject to any penalties, unlike in the situation where an employee's name or Social Security number does not match. In addition, employers are not required to submit gender information regarding any employee to Social Security, and so a transgender employee may want to suggest to her/his employer that they resubmit the information to Social Security without her/his gender information. How a transgender employee decides to talk with her/his employer about the reason for the gender no-match letter and how s/he should handle the letter will depend on the individual's specific situation and how supportive the employer is of her/his transition.

In contrast, if an employer receives a name no-match letter, the transgender employee must resolve that discrepancy. If s/he has already changed her/his name legally but has not yet done so with the SSA, s/he needs to change her/his name with the SSA as well. If a transgender employee has not changed her/his name legally but uses a different name with her/his employer and wants to continue using that name on employment records, s/he needs to obtain a legal name change and then change her/his name with Social Security.

2.4 Practice Recommendations

2.4.1 Use Client's Post-transition Name and Pronouns in Legal Proceedings Unless Doing So Is Inconsistent with Client's Priorities

It is important to use a client's post-transition name and pronouns in legal proceedings, regardless of whether the client has obtained a legal name change or gender change, unless it is not possible to do so or doing so would be inconsistent with the client's priorities. Doing so not only respects the client's gender identity but also educates the court as to the reality of the client's lived experience. While the court or opposing party may object, it is important to inform the court and opposing party about how the use of a transgender person's post-transition name and sex is part of that person's transition process and is often a medically indicated and necessary component of treatment of gender identity disorder.[70]

---

1   For information and statistics relating to discrimination and violence against transgender individuals, see Jaime M. Grant et al., Nat'l Ctr. for Transgender Equal. & Nat'l Gay & Lesbian Task Force, Injustice at Every Turn: A Report of the National Transgender Discrimination Survey 100 (2011), *available at* http://www.thetaskforce.org/downloads/reports/reports/ntds_full.pdf.

2   World Prof'l Ass'n for Transgender Health, Standards of Care for Gender Identity Disorders 10 (7th ed. 2011) [hereinafter WPATH SOC], *available at* http://www.wpath.org/documents/Standards%20of%20Care%20 V7%20-%202011%20WPATH.pdf.

3   For example, who a person may marry in states that do not allow same-sex couples to marry is contingent upon a person's legal sex.

4   *See generally* Chapter 3 of this publication for guidance on assessing the validity of a transgender person's marriage.

5   *See, e.g., In re* Marriage of Simmons, 825 N.E.2d 303 (Ill. App. Ct. 2005).

6   Even when the standard for changing a person's name or sex on one form of identity document may be clearly laid out in a statute or regulation, there can be wide inconsistencies in how that standard is implemented on the ground. For example, it is not uncommon for different motor vehicle department offices in the same state to enforce different requirements for a person to change the sex designation on a driver's license.

7   *See generally* Julia Shear Kushner, *The Right to Control One's Name*, 57 UCLA L. Rev. 313 (2009).

8   Only Hawaii requires a petition to the lieutenant governor except in certain situations involving, *inter alia*, marriage, divorce, and adoption. Haw. Rev. Stat. § 574-5.

9   Kushner, *supra* note 7, at 325.

10   *Id.* at 327.

11   *Id.* at 329.

12   *See, e.g.*, Alaska R. Civ. P. 84; Ga. Code Ann. § 19-12-1.

13   *See, e.g.*, Alaska R. Civ. P. 84; Ga. Code Ann. § 19-12-1.

14   *See, e.g.*, N.J Stat. Ann. § 2A:52-1; N.Y. Civ. Rights Law § 61.

15   *See, e.g.*, Alaska Stat. § 09.55.010; Kan. Stat. Ann. § 60-1402(c).

16   *See, e.g.*, Mich. Comp. Laws § 711.1(1) ("If the individual who petitions for a name change has a criminal record, the individual is presumed to be seeking a name change with a fraudulent intent.").

17   Kushner, *supra* note 7, at 330. *See, e.g.*, Alaska Stat. § 09.55.010 ("A change of name of a person may not be made unless the court finds sufficient reasons for the change and also finds it consistent with the public interest."); Del. Code Ann. tit. 10, § 5904 ("Upon presentation of a petition for change of name under this chapter … and there appearing no reason for not granting the petition, the prayer of the petition may be granted."); La. Rev. Stat. Ann. § 13:4753 ("The judge to whom the application is made, either in open court or in chambers, may proceed to hear and determine the case and render such judgment as the nature of the relief and the law and the evidence shall justify.").

18   Kushner, *supra* note 7, at 319.

19   *Id.* at 332. *See also In re* Knight, 537 P.2d 1085, 1086 (Colo. App. 1975); *In re* Mokiligon, 106 P.3d 584, 586 (N.M. Ct. App. 2004).

20   Kushner, *supra* note 7, at 334–35, n.124 ("Policy denials include, for example, petitions of individuals trying to Americanize ethnic surnames, or vice versa, same-sex couples trying to acquire the same surname, and transgender petitioners' requests to change their names to reflect their changed gender.").

21   *Id.* at 333.

22   *See, e.g., In re* Porter, 31 P.3d 519, 522 (Utah 2001) (reversing trial court's denial of petitioner's request to change name to "Santa Claus").

23   *See, e.g., In re* A.M.B., 997 A.2d 754 (Me. 2010) (while the petitioner argued on appeal that the cause of the denial was the trial judge's bias against transgender individuals, the Maine Law Court based its decision on the fact that the Probate Court had failed to include any findings explaining how the petition was fraudulent or otherwise contrary to public policy, and remanded the case to the

trial court for judgment); *In re* Eck, 584 A.2d 859, 860–61 (N.J. Super. Ct. 1991) ("Absent fraud or other improper purpose a person has a right to a name change whether he or she has undergone or intends to undergo a sex change through surgery, has received hormone injections to induce physical change, . . . or simply wants to change from a traditional 'male' first name to one traditionally 'female,' or vice versa."); *In re* Winn-Ritzenberg, 891 N.Y.S.2d 220, 221 (N.Y. Sup. Ct. 2009) (reversing lower court's denial of transgender individual's name-change petition in the absence of evidence of fraud, misrepresentation, or interference with the rights of others, and holding that there was "no sound basis" to require that transgender petitioner present medical substantiation for desired name change); *In re* McIntyre, 715 A.2d 400, 403 (Pa. 1998) ("The details surrounding Appellant's quest for sex-reassignment surgery are not a matter of governmental concern. As the name change statute and the procedures thereunder indicate a liberal policy regarding change of name requests, we see no reason to impose restrictions which the legislature has not.") (internal citation omitted).

24   *See, e.g.*, N.Y. Civ. Rights Law § 64-a (authorizing waiver of notification requirement upon finding that publication for a name change would jeopardize the safety of the person whose name is changed).

25   *See, e.g.*, *In re* E.P.L., 891 N.Y.S.2d 619 (N.Y. Sup. Ct. 2009) (relying on national statistics and recent hate crimes legislation protecting transgender individuals as evidence that the petitioner had a reasonable fear for his personal safety).

26   Dean Spade, *Documenting Gender*, 59 Hastings L.J. 731, 767–68 (2008).

27   *Id.* at 768.

28   Only California, Iowa, Vermont, and Washington allow a person to change her/his sex designation on her/his birth certificate without necessarily having undergone surgery. *See* 2011 Cal. Legis. Serv. ch. 718 (recent legislation requiring "clinically appropriate treatment for the purpose of gender transition"); Iowa Code § 144.23 (requiring "surgery or other treatment"); Vt. Stat. Ann. tit. 18, § 5112 (requiring proof of "surgical, hormonal, or other treatment" for the purpose of gender transition).

29   *See, e.g.*, 410 Ill. Comp. Stat. 535/17(1)(d); New York, N.Y., R.C.N.Y. tit. 24, § 207.05(a)(5).

30   *See, e.g.*, Cal. Health & Safety Code § 103425; Mass. Gen. Laws ch. 46, § 13(e).

31   *See, e.g.*, Ala. Code § 22-9A-19(d); Colo. Rev. Stat. § 25-2-115(4); Me. Rev. Stat. tit. 22, § 2705.

32   *See, e.g.*, Ariz. Rev. Stat. Ann. § 36-337(A)(3); N.C. Gen. Stat. §§ 130A-118(b)(4), (e).

33   *See, e.g.*, Ala. Code § 22-9A-19(d); Ark. Code Ann. § 20-18-307(d); Colo. Rev. Stat. § 25-2-115(4); Me. Rev. Stat. tit. 22, § 2705.

34   Many courts in such states have standardized forms that are designed for

pro se petitioners requesting such orders. *See, e.g.,* CAL. DEP'T OF PUB. HEALTH, OBTAINING A NEW BIRTH CERTIFICATE AFTER GENDER REASSIGNMENT, *available at* http://www.cdph.ca.gov/certlic/birthdeathmar/Documents/GenderReassignmentPAMPHLET-(11-10)-MERGED.pdf.

35   *See* CONN. GEN. STAT. § 19a-42b (allowing residents born in out-of-state jurisdictions that require a court decree in order to amend the sex designation on a birth certificate to submit application for such a court decree in Connecticut probate court).

36   *See, e.g.,* CAL. HEALTH & SAFETY CODE § 103425; HAW. REV. STAT. § 338-17.7(a)(4)(b); VT. STAT. ANN. tit. 18, § 5112.

37   *See, e.g.,* ALA. CODE § 22-9A-19(d); MONT. CODE ANN. § 50-15-204; MONT. ADMIN. R. 37.8.106(6).

38   *See, e.g.,* MINN. STAT. § 144.218; WIS. STAT. § 69.15.

39   WPATH SOC, *supra* note 2, at 57–58.

40   IDAHO ADMIN. CODE r. 16.02.08.201; TENN. CODE ANN. § 68-3-203(d) ("The sex of an individual shall not be changed on the original certificate of birth as a result of sex change surgery.").

41   *In re* Ladrach, 513 N.E.2d 828, 831 (Ohio Prob. Ct. 1987). In addition, there is some question in Texas as to the ability of transgender individuals to amend the sex designation on their birth certificates since an appellate court in *Littleton v. Prange*, 9 S.W.3d 223, 231 (Tex. App. 1999), interpreted Texas's birth certificate amendment statute to only allow amendments to correct for inaccuracies at the time the certificate was recorded — i.e. at birth. While there are reports that certain judges will issue an order allowing amendments of sex designation on birth certificates for transgender individuals, there are also reports that some officials refuse to allow such amendments. One workaround is, when seeking orders of name change, to draft the proposed findings of fact for the court to include a finding declaring the petitioner's sex.

42   *See, e.g., In re* Simmons, 825 N.E.2d 303 (finding that the fact that a transgender person had changed his sex from female to male on his birth certificate was not sufficient to make him legally male for purposes of determining the validity of his marriage to a woman, where Illinois did not recognize marriages between persons of the same sex); *id.* at 310 ("[T]he mere issuance of a new birth certificate cannot, legally speaking, make petitioner a male").

43   Julie A. Greenberg & Marybeth Herald, *You Can't Take It With You: Constitutional Consequences of Interstate Gender-Identity Rulings*, 80 WASH. L. REV. 819, 851–55 (2005). Under the Full Faith and Credit Clause of the U.S. Constitution, states must honor judgments from other states, provided that the judgment is issued by a court of proper jurisdiction, the proceeding provides for a reasonable method of notification and a reasonable opportunity to be heard, and the parties comply with the formalities of the issuing state. *See id.* at 847–51. Any proceeding resulting in a court order establishing a person's legal sex should suffice to meet

these requirements. *Id.*

44   For example, in *In re Nash*, an Ohio court refused to recognize the legal sex of a transgender man as male for purposes of allowing him to marry his female fiancée, despite the fact that his Massachusetts birth certificate had been amended to reflect his sex as male. Nos. 2002-T-0149, 2002-T-0179, 2003 WL 23097095 (Ohio Ct. App. Dec. 31, 2003). The court argued that full faith and credit was not violated when granting full faith and credit to another state's record would violate Ohio's public policy against marriages of same-sex couples. *Id.* at *5. *See also In re* Estate of Gardiner, 42 P.3d 120 (Kan. 2002) (refusing to recognize transgender woman's legal sex as female for purposes of determining validity of marriage, despite her having amended the sex designation on her Wisconsin birth certificate to female).

45   "The absence of precedents, or novelty in incident, presents no obstacle to the exercise of the jurisdiction of a court of equity, and to the award of relief in a proper case. It is the distinguishing feature of equity jurisdiction that it will apply settled rules to unusual conditions and mold its decrees so as to do equity between the parties." 30 C.J.S. *Equity* § 12 (1965).

46   In *In re Heilig*, a Maryland resident sought a court order to change her "sexual identity" designation from male to female for the purpose of being able to amend her birth certificate from Pennsylvania, which requires a court order to amend a person's birth certificate. 816 A.2d 68 (Md. 2003). Maryland's highest court held that equitable jurisdiction existed to issue such an order declaring a change in sex, even though it recognized that it could not issue an order specifically ordering an official from another state to amend a birth certificate from that state. *Id.* at 84–85.

47   A primary care doctor affidavit, an LCSW affidavit, and a surgeon affidavit supporting change of legal sex are included in Appendices 2D, 2E, and 2F.

48   *See* ACLU AIDS Project, http://www.aclu.org/hiv-aids (last visited Nov. 14, 2011); ACLU LGBT Rts. Project, http://www.aclu.org/lgbt-rights (last visited Nov. 14, 2011); Gay & Lesbian Advocs. & Defenders, http://www.glad.org (last visited Nov. 14, 2011); Lambda Legal, http://www.lambdalegal.org (last visited Nov. 14, 2011); Nat'l Ctr. for Lesbian Rts., http://www.nclrights.org (last visited Nov. 14, 2011).

49   *See, e.g., Change of Name*, Conn. Dep't of Motor Vehicles, http://www.ct.gov/dmv/cwp/view.asp?a=805&Q=244738 (last visited Nov. 15, 2011); *Driver License and Identification Card Information*, Cal. Dep't of Motor Vehicles, http://dmv.ca.gov/dl/dl_info.htm#truename (last visited Nov. 15, 2011); *Required Identity Documentation for Driver License, Permit and ID Card Transactions*, Or. Dep't of Motor Vehicles, http://www.oregon.gov/ODOT/DMV/driverid/id-proof.shtml#LName (last visited Nov. 15, 2011).

50   For example, the District of Columbia requires that an applicant submit a form signed by a health care or social service provider attesting that in that per-

son's professional opinion, the applicant's gender identity is either male or female and can reasonably be expected to continue as such in the foreseeable future. *See Gender Identification on a License or Identification Card*, D.C. Dep't of Motor Vehicles, http://dmv.dc.gov/pdf/Gender_Change_Policies.pdf (last visited Nov. 15, 2011).

51   *See* 22 C.F.R. § 51.25.

52   *See* 22 C.F.R. § 51.25; Names to be Used in Passports, U.S. Dep't of State, 7 Foreign Affairs Manual 1300 Appendix C, *available at* http://www.state.gov/documents/organization/94676.pdf.

53   Names to be Used in Passports, *supra* note 52.

54   Change of Name Without Court Order (Customary Name Change), U.S. Dep't of State, 7 Foreign Affairs Manual 1330 Appendix C, *available at* http://www.state.gov/documents/organization/94676.pdf.

55   *See* 22 C.F.R. § 51.25. *See also* Change of Name Without Court Order, *supra* note 54. There is a discrepancy between the Foreign Affairs Manual and the regulations as to whether "an acceptable identification reflecting the acquired name" is required in addition to the other three documents evidencing use of the adopted name. Such a requirement is stated in the Foreign Affairs Manual but not the implementing regulations, which only require "three or more" public documents. However, given that the regulations require that one of those three public documents be a "government-issued identification with photograph," the only real difference may be the number of documents required in addition to an identification document in the adopted name. Given that the Foreign Affairs Manual is the resource that passport office employees consult, it is best to provide an identification document reflecting the acquired name, in addition to the three public documents showing the continued use of the adopted name for at least five years.

56   If the acquired name has been used less than five years, it may be included as a "known as" name if the same type of evidentiary evidence is submitted as for a "customary name change" request. *See* Change of Name Without Court Order, *supra* note 54.

57   *See* Nat'l Ctr. for Transgender Equal., Understanding the New Passport Gender Change Policy (2011), http://transequality.org/Resources/passports_2011.pdf.

58   *Id. See also* Gender Change, U.S. Dep't of State, 7 Foreign Affairs Manual 1300 Appendix M, *available at* http://www.state.gov/documents/organization/143160.pdf.

59   *See* Gender Change, *supra* note 58, § (b)(1).

60   *Id.* For a sample physician letter, see Documents to be Submitted With Passport Application, U.S. Dep't of State, 7 Foreign Affairs Manual 1320 Appendix M Exhibit B, *available at* http://www.state.gov/documents/organization/143160.pdf.

61   All transgender individuals who are living consistently in their desired

gender should be able to obtain such a statement from their physician, under the SOC's recognition that gender transition-related treatment should be individualized and need not require surgery. WPATH SOC, *supra* note 2, at 2, 9–10. Transgender clients who cannot meet this standard but have initiated transition can still obtain a two-year limited validity passport reflecting the new gender with a statement from the physician that the applicant is in the process of gender transition to the new gender of either male or female. *See* Gender Change, *supra* note 58, § (b)(2).

62   *Change a Name on a Social Security Card*, Soc. Secur. Online, http://ssa-custhelp.ssa.gov/app/answers/detail/a_id/315 (last visited Nov. 15, 2011). *See also* Changing Your Documentation, Nat'l Ctr. for Transgender Equal., http://transequality.org/Issues/federal_documents.html#ss_name (last visited Nov. 15, 2011).

63   *See U.S. Citizenship Documents Needed for a Social Security Card*, Soc. Sec. Online, http://ssa-custhelp.ssa.gov/app/answers/detail/a_id/2282 (last visited Nov. 15, 2011); *Federal Documents*, Nat'l Ctr. for Transgender Equal., http://transequality.org/Issues/federal_documents.html (last visited Nov. 15, 2011).

64   *See Immigration Status Documents Needed for a Social Security Card*, Soc. Sec. Online, http://ssa-custhelp.ssa.gov/app/answers/detail/a_id/2283 (last visited Nov. 15, 2011).

65   *See Identity Documents Needed for a Social Security Card*, Soc. Sec. Online, http://ssa-custhelp.ssa.gov/app/answers/detail/a_id/2281 (last visited Nov. 15, 2011).

66   *See Change Gender on Your Social Security Record*, Soc. Sec. Online, http://ssa-custhelp.ssa.gov/app/answers/detail/a_id/1667/kw/gender (last visited Nov. 15, 2011).

67   *See, e.g.*, 42 U.S.C. § 402(b)–(c), (e)–(f).

68   *See Change Gender on Your Social Security Record*, *supra* note 66.

69   Waymon Hudson, *Social Security Ends "Gender No-Match" Letters for Employees*, Huffington Post (Sept. 21, 2011, 1:05 PM), http://www.huffingtonpost.com/waymon-hudson/social-security-ends-gender-no-match_b_966654.html.

70   *See, e.g.*, O'Donnabhain v. Comm'r of Internal Revenue, 134 T.C. 34, 35 n.3 (2010) ("Reflecting petitioner's preference, we use the feminine pronoun to refer to her throughout this Opinion."); Manning v. Goord, No. 05-CV-850F, 2010 WL 883696, at *1 n.1 (W.D.N.Y. Mar. 8, 2010) ("Although Plaintiff remains anatomically male, the court uses female pronouns when referring to Plaintiff for consistency with the papers filed by the parties, who use female pronouns when referring to Plaintiff because Plaintiff considers herself a female.").

CHAPTER 3: RELATIONSHIP RECOGNITION AND PROTECTIONS

Elizabeth E. Monnin-Browder

Introduction

Some transgender people marry, enter into domestic partnerships or civil unions, or enjoy committed relationships without a legally recognized relationship status. Which of these options are available to a transgender client depends on the type(s) of relationship status available in a particular state for same-sex and different-sex couples, and how that state regards a transgender client's and her/his partner's legal sex for the purpose of marriage or a marriage equivalent. In addition, some states have case law that specifically addresses the validity of transgender people's marriages.

A transgender person's marriage can be "post-transition" or "pre-transition."[1] A post-transition marriage is a marriage in which a transgender person marries after having transitioned from her/his birth sex to a different sex. For example, a transgender man might transition from female to male and, after his transition, marry a woman. In contrast, in a pre-transition marriage a transgender person marries before transitioning from her/his birth sex to a different sex. For instance, a man marries a woman and later transitions from male to female.

Some courts have recognized the validity of post-transition marriages while other courts have invalidated such marriages. However, a pre-transition marriage—if valid at the time and in the jurisdiction where it was entered into—remains valid because of strong public policy favoring the validation of existing marriages and because there is no case law to the contrary.[2]

Marriage is the basis for numerous legal rights and responsibilities, including, in some instances, parental, property, immigration, and inheritance rights, in addition to spousal rights. Therefore, an attorney should counsel a transgender client about whether her/his marriage is likely to be recognized as valid if challenged, and about how to protect her/his collateral rights in case the marriage is invalidated. Even if a transgender person's marriage will most likely be considered valid, an attorney should still advise the client to execute any available supplemental documentation to support her/his relationship. The attorney should also formally record the intentions of the client and the client's spouse regarding parenting, property, and testamentary dispositions. This "belt and suspenders" approach helps ensure that the transgender spouse's relational interests will be protected if a reactionary court decision or legislation invalidates the marriage. Executing similar documentation is also an option for protecting the relational interests of a transgender client who is unable or chooses not to marry.

3.1 Building a Respectful Attorney-Client Relationship: Understanding the Client's Sexual Orientation

An attorney should learn how a client self-identifies by asking open-ended questions and should not presume to know a client's sexual orientation based on the client's gender identity or expression. The distinction between sexual orientation and gender identity is discussed in more detail in Chapter 1, which also offers guidance about culturally competent representation for transgender clients.

3.2 Pre-transition Marriages and Marriage Equivalents

There is no precedent in United States case law for invalidating a pre-transition marriage that was valid when and where it was entered into.[3] Therefore, a client's transition or a client's spouse's transition subsequent to a lawful marriage should not invalidate the marriage. In a state with marriage equality for same-sex couples, a transgender client and her/his (transgender or non-transgender) spouse can marry, regardless of whether the marriage is considered a same-sex or different-sex union, and a transition and legal change of sex after the marriage should not invalidate the marriage. In a state that prohibits same-sex couples from marrying, a marriage that becomes a same-sex union after a spouse's transition should still be valid if it was valid when entered into.

In addition, Section 3 of the Defense of Marriage Act (DOMA)—the federal law defining marriage as only between a man and a woman for purposes of federal recognition—does not invalidate a pre-transition marriage for federal purposes.[4] See Section 3.3 for more guidance regarding federal recognition of transgender people's marriages.

3.3 Post-transition Marriages and Marriage Equivalents

This section suggests a series of issues that a family law attorney should address in order to effectively represent a transgender client (or a client who has a transgender partner) who is seeking counsel relating to post-transition marriage or another form of legal relationship recognition.

3.3.1 Advising a Transgender Client About Marriage or Another Legally Recognized Relationship Status

The validity of a transgender person's post-transition marriage or marriage equivalent may come into question when a client is seeking counsel prior to entering into a marriage or another legally recognized relationship status, or when the validity of a client's pre-existing marriage is challenged either by her/his spouse or by a third party. In either situation, to determine whether the state recognizes the validity of a transgender client's marriage or marriage equivalent, an attorney should consider: (1) choice of law rules; (2) the relevant state's law pertaining to legal change of sex for the purpose of marriage and what form(s) of legal relationship recognition are available to same-sex and different-sex couples in the state; and (3) case law about the validity of transgender people's marriages.

> **Practice Tip**: An attorney should advise a client to defend the validity of her/his post-transition marriage and not agree to an annulment, even if the client wants

to terminate the marriage. In many circumstances, there could be adverse and unintended collateral consequences if a client stipulates that the marriage is invalid or agrees to an annulment. For example, a client's legal parentage or property rights may be contingent upon recognition of a valid marriage.[5] Thus, an attorney should advise a client to defend against any challenges to the validity of her/his marriage and refuse an annulment. If a client wants to terminate the marriage, an attorney may counsel the client regarding divorce. For guidance on advising a transgender client who wants to divorce, see Chapter 5.

3.3.1.1 Choice of Law: Which State's Law Governs?

All states have a strong interest in validating existing marriages because the parties expected that their marriage would be recognized and because invalidating a marriage may cause hardship to the parties and their children, if any.[6] The general rule is that a marriage is presumed to be lawful everywhere if it was lawful where entered into.[7] A public policy exception exists only where the marriage is against the strong public policy of, or expressly invalidated by the statute of, another state which had the most significant relationship to the spouses and the marriage at the time of the marriage.[8] This exception is extremely narrow and therefore rarely applicable.[9]

Thus, if a post-transition marriage was considered a valid marriage according to the law in the jurisdiction where the couple married, it should be recognized as a valid marriage in all other states. No state has a sufficiently strong public policy against transgender people marrying or a statute invalidating transgender people's marriages that are lawfully entered into elsewhere that would warrant invalidating the marriage. In other words, there is no basis for an exception of transgender people's marriages from the general choice of law rule governing marriage validity.

Moreover, if a post-transition marriage was considered a valid marriage between different-sex spouses under state law where the marriage was entered into, the marriage should be respected by all other states. Section 2 of DOMA—the federal law allowing states not to recognize marriages between same-sex couples that were lawfully entered into elsewhere—does not apply.[10] Congress did not contemplate transgender people's marriages when it enacted DOMA, and neither DOMA nor any other federal law defines or even relates to the sex of transgender individuals.[11] Therefore, DOMA does not apply to transgender people's different-sex marriages because DOMA relates only to federal and interstate recognition of marriages between couples who were the same sex when they entered into the marriage.[12]

3.3.1.2 Does the State Consider the Client's Relationship to be Between Same-Sex or Different-Sex Partners? What Options for Legal Relationship Recognition are Available in the State for Same-Sex and Different-Sex Couples?

The next question is how the state where a client was or will be married perceives the client's relationship *for the purpose of marriage*: as a relationship between same-sex or different-sex individuals. Whether the state perceives the client's relationship to be between two people of the same sex or of different sexes depends on what the state considers each partner's legal sex to be for the purpose of marriage. Chapter 2 focuses on the process by which a transgender person can legally change her/his sex, but legal change of sex does not fully answer the issue. For instance, attorneys should be aware that at least one state allows a transgender individual to change the sex designation on her/his birth certificate but, nevertheless, does not recognize, *for the purpose of marriage,* that the transgender individual has changed her/his sex.[13] And, in states that do recognize a person's legal sex based on a change in sex designation on a birth certificate or a court order, an attorney should consider making the argument that someone who meets the standard for changing her/his sex designation should have her/his sex recognized based on whether or not s/he meets the standard, not simply whether or not s/he took the formal steps to document the change of sex. In other words, as long as a person could have met the state standard for changing her/his sex, s/he should be recognized as that sex whether or not her/his documentation actually reflects it.

Whether the state considers the relationship to be between individuals of the same or different sexes affects a couple's marriage options.[14] If the transgender client's relationship will be categorized by the state as a same-sex relationship, the attorney should determine whether the state allows same-sex couples to marry; recognizes marriages between same-sex couples that are lawfully performed in other jurisdictions; or recognizes civil unions, comprehensive or limited domestic partnerships, or any other legal relationship protections for same-sex couples. If the state perceives the transgender client's relationship to be a different-sex relationship because the state recognizes her/his legal change of sex, the client should be able to marry her/his different-sex partner if s/he chooses to do so, unless there is case law to the contrary.

A married transgender client may seek counsel about whether her/his marriage is likely to be validated if challenged. If a transgender client married in a state that allows same-sex couples to marry, an attorney should determine whether the state where the marriage was entered into considered the marriage to be a union between a same-sex or different-sex couple because, pursuant to Section 2 of DOMA, other states are not required to afford full faith and credit to a marriage if it was considered a marriage between same-sex individuals where it was entered into.[15]

> **Practice Tip**: The state's perception of the legal sex of the client, and the client's partner, for the purpose of marriage, may or may not match their self-identification. Knowing how a client self-identifies and how the state perceives the client's relationship serve different purposes, and both pieces of information should inform an attorney's representation.

3.3.1.3 Does the State Recognize the Validity of Transgender People's Marriages?

Some state cases, discussed below, have addressed the validity of transgender people's post-transition marriages. All of these cases were decided in states that prohibited same-sex couples from marrying. Even if there is no applicable case law in the jurisdiction relevant to a particular client, family law attorneys should familiarize themselves with other jurisdictions' case law because a judge may find it to be persuasive.

Most states do not have express policies or case law addressing the validity of a post-transition marriage. If an attorney practices in such a state and the state does not recognize marriages between same-sex couples, the attorney should defend the validity of a transgender client's post-transition different-sex marriage by demonstrating that the client has changed sex and that the marriage is therefore a marriage between a different-sex couple. To do so, an attorney should consider producing the following, if applicable and available:

- evidence of a transgender client's legal change of sex, such as an amended or new birth certificate, license, passport, or Social Security card, or a court order for change of sex;

- marriage license and/or marriage certificate, especially if it documents the transgender spouse's post-transition sex;

- examples demonstrating that the client's legal change of sex is recognized for other purposes;

- medical evidence of the transgender client's transition, including testimony from physicians and therapists;

- non-transgender spouse's acknowledgment of her/his transgender spouse's transgender identity, or evidence that the spouse knew of the transgender spouse's transgender identity prior to the marriage; and

- testimony and evidence from the client and others supporting the transgender client's gender identity.

State statutes, regulations, and policies that set forth a standard for changing the sex designation on a birth certificate may be helpful to an attorney defending a client's legal change of sex. A state policy allowing a transgender person to change the sex designation on her/his birth certificate does not guarantee, however, that a state recognizes the validity of post-transition marriages. At least half of the states set forth such a standard in statutes while several other states do so through regulations or agency policies.[16] If a state has a process for changing or amending the sex designation on a birth certificate and the client has made this change, an attorney should use the statute, regulation, or policy that designates the process to support the argument that the state recognizes the transgender client's legal change of sex. If the transgender client has not changed her/his birth certificate but could meet the standard for doing so, s/he should be legally regarded as the sex to which the birth certificate could have been changed.[17]

> **Practice Tip**: Be aware that some courts have interpreted their state's birth certificate amendment statutes narrowly to only allow for amendments to information that was incorrect *at the time the birth certificate was issued*, and therefore do not allow amendments, or refuse to issue new birth certificates, to change a transgender person's sex.[18] An attorney should analyze the language of the relevant state's birth certificate amendment statute and, if it is unclear, find examples of analogous situations in which the statute has authorized changes to birth certificates based on changes that occurred after a child's birth (i.e., subsequent marriage of child's parents, determination of parentage different than that reported on the birth certificate).

There are two lines of cases that reach different conclusions regarding the validity of post-transition marriages. These cases were all decided in jurisdictions that prohibited same-sex couples from marrying, and involved challenges to marriages between a transgender person and a spouse who was a different sex from the transgender spouse's post-transition sex.

Cases Upholding Marriages

In one line of cases, most notably *M.T. v. J.T.*,[19] courts have upheld post-transition marriages, recognizing that a transgender individual can enter into a valid marriage with a different-sex spouse by legally changing her/his sex and then marrying her/his different-sex partner.

In contrast, the second line of cases have either concluded that birth sex is immutable,[20] or held that, in a particular instance, a legal change of sex had not been accomplished for the purpose of marriage. Cases in which the court concluded that birth sex is immutable generally follow the principles set forth in *Corbett v. Corbett*, an English case decided in the early 1970s that is no longer good law. As a result, these courts have treated the post-transition marriage as a marriage between persons of the same sex, and found the post-transition marriage to be invalid because marriage between same-sex couples was prohibited in their respective states (and foreign jurisdictions).

Some state courts have recognized that a transgender spouse legally changed her/his sex for the purpose of marriage and, as a result, have upheld a post-transition marriage as a valid marriage between different-sex spouses.

New Jersey:

In 1976, in *M.T. v. J.T.*, a New Jersey appellate court affirmed a trial court's decision that a transgender woman was female for the purpose of marriage and that her marriage to a man was thus a valid marriage.[21] The court expressly rejected *Corbett v. Corbett* and its conclusion that "for purposes of marriage sex is irrevocably cast at the moment of birth."[22] Instead, the court found that several criteria or standards may be relevant in determining the sex of an individual, including "an individual's gender, that is, one's self-image, the deep psychological or emotional sense of sexual identity and character."[23] The trial judge had ruled that the transgender spouse "was of the female psychic gender all her life and that her anatomical change through surgery required the conclusion that she was a female at the time of the marriage ceremony."[24] The appellate court agreed, concluding that "for marital purposes if the anatomical or genital features of a genuine transsexual are made to conform to the person's gender, psyche or psychological sex, then identity by sex must be governed by the congruence of these standards."[25] Thus, since the transgender spouse's "gender and genitalia are no longer discordant; they have been harmonized through medical treatment[,]" the court held that she was female for the purpose of marriage.[26]

California:

In *Vecchione v. Vecchione*, in 1997, a California trial court denied a petition to annul a post-transition marriage because "California recognizes the post-operative gender of a transgendered person."[27] In so ruling, the judge cited a California statute that allows a transgender person who has undergone sex reassignment surgery to receive a new birth certificate that reflects her/his legal change of sex.[28] Therefore, because the transgender spouse had transitioned, including having undergone sex reassignment surgery prior to his marriage, the court recognized the marriage as a valid marriage between different-sex spouses.[29] Significantly, the California trial court recognized that the transgender spouse had legally changed his sex—a necessary condition for the marriage to be valid—despite the fact that he had been unable to change the sex designation on his New York-issued birth certificate.[30]

New York:

On February 7, 2011, the City Clerk for New York City issued an interoffice memorandum articulating a policy that all staff must accept the sex listed on the identification documents individuals must present when applying for a marriage license, regardless of the applicant's gender identity or expression.[31] The City Clerk ordered that "[g]ender stereotypes or preconceived notions related to gender expression—including an applicant's physical appearance, dress, behavior, or name—may not be considered when deciding whether to issue a marriage license."[32] The practical result—which is expressly set forth in the memorandum—is that a transgender person who presents one of the enumerated forms of identification can apply for a marriage license consistent with the name and sex on the identification document, and the issuing clerk is not allowed to request additional proof of the applicant's sex.[33] Additionally, since July 2011, same-sex couples can marry in New York, so a transgender person can marry her/his partner, whether the partner is the same sex or a different sex.[34]

Department of Veterans Affairs:

In 1990, in a precedential opinion[35] titled "Benefit Determinations Involving Validity of Marriage of Transsexual Veterans," the Department of Veterans Affairs determined that a veteran who had changed the sex designation on his birth certificate in accordance with Texas law "should be treated [as a man] for all purposes under Texas law [including marriage]."[36]

International:

In 1994, in *Attorney-General v. Otahuhu Family Court*, New Zealand's High Court[37] held that "where a person has undergone surgical and medical procedures that have effectively given that person the physical conformation of a person of a specified sex, there is no lawful impediment to that person marrying as a person of that sex."[38] In addition, the court held that a pre-transition marriage is not void if one of the spouses transitions after marrying.[39]

In 2002, in *Goodwin v. United Kingdom*, the European Court of Human Rights held that prohibiting post-transition marriages violates the European Convention for the Protection of Human Rights and Fundamental Freedoms, and recognized the transgender plaintiff's post-transition sex as her marital sex, thereby reversing the ruling in *Corbett* which held that birth sex was immutable.[40]

In 2003, in *Attorney-General v. Kevin*, the Full Court of the Australian Family Court upheld the trial court's determination that the post-transition marriage was valid because the words "man" and "woman" as used in the Australian marriage statute include "post-operative transsexuals as men and/or women in accordance with their sexual reassignment"[41] and that sex for the purpose of marriage is determined as of the date of the marriage.[42]

Cases Invalidating Marriages

Some courts in the United States and internationally have found, however, that post-transition marriages between different-sex spouses are invalid. Some United States jurisdictions have relied upon *Corbett* to conclude that a person's birth sex is legally unchangeable and, therefore, a marriage entered into by a transgender person post-transition and her/his different-sex partner is invalid in jurisdictions that prohibit same-sex couples from marrying. Other courts have reached the same result by concluding that the transgender spouse had not accomplished a change of legal sex for the purpose of marriage. Because these courts did not recognize that the transgender partner had changed her/his legal sex for the purpose of marriage, the transgender partner was either precluded from marrying someone of the same sex as her/his birth sex or, in cases challenging the validity of an existing marriage, her/his marriage to someone of the same sex as her/his birth sex was deemed a nullity.

One practical outcome of the case law in these jurisdictions is that it allows for post-transition marriages that appear to be marriages between same-sex couples, despite the fact that these states do not allow same-sex couples to marry. Indeed, jurisdictions in which courts have held that a person's sex for the purpose of marriage is her/his birth sex, irrespective of whether the individual subsequently transitioned to a different sex, allow a transgender person to marry someone who is the same sex as her/his post-transition sex. This is not merely a theoretical possibility; there were reported examples of such marriages in Texas after the *Littleton v. Prange* decision.[43]

Florida:

In *Kantaras v. Kantaras*, in 2004, a Florida appeals court invalidated a post-transition marriage based on its conclusion that birth sex is immutable.[44] The court determined that it was the legislature's prerogative to decide whether scientific advances had changed the common meanings of "male" and "female" as used in Florida's marriage statute.[45] Thus, the court concluded that "[u]ntil the Florida legislature recognizes sex-reassignment procedures and amends the marriage statutes to clarify the marital rights of a postoperative transsexual person, we must … invalidate any marriage that is not between persons of the opposite sex determined by their biological sex at birth."[46]

Illinois:

In 2005, in *In re Marriage of Simmons*, an Illinois Appeals Court affirmed a trial court's decision holding that the transgender husband was legally a female, and therefore the marriage was invalid because it was a union between same-sex individuals.[47] The trial court determined that the transgender spouse's legal sex was female at the time of the marriage even though he had been transitioning for several years through the use of hormones, resulting in a male appearance.[48] Furthermore, even though Illinois law recognizes that a marriage that was prohibited when entered into is valid as of the date that the impediment to validity is removed if the parties cohabitate, the court denied that the "impediment" to marriage had been removed because the transgender spouse had not "completed" sex reassignment and "the mere issuance of a new birth certificate cannot, legally speaking, make petitioner a male."[49]

Kansas:

In 2002, in *In re Estate of Gardiner*, the Kansas Supreme Court invalidated a post-transition marriage based on its interpretation of a Kansas statute limiting marriage to different-sex couples.[50] The transgender woman's husband had died intestate and her husband's estranged son, arguing that he was his father's sole heir, challenged the validity of his father's marriage because his stepmother, a transgender woman, was assigned male at birth.[51]

The court concluded that the plain meanings of "male" and "female" do not include "post-operative transsexual[s,]" and interpreted the legislature's silence on post-transition marriages in the history of the Kansas marriage statute to mean that "transsexuals are not included."[52] As a result of the court invalidating her marriage, the transgender woman was denied the spousal share of her deceased husband's estate.

New York:

In 1971, in *Anonymous v. Anonymous*, a New York trial court declared that a marriage ceremony between a pre-operative transgender woman and her husband "did not in fact or in law create a marriage contract"[53] because "[t]he court [found] as a fact that the defendant was not a female at the time of the marriage ceremony" and, at that time, same-sex couples could not marry in New York.[54] Three years after the decision in *Anonymous*, a New York trial court denied a divorce claim in *Frances B. v. Mark B.* based on its determination that the underlying post-transition marriage was not a valid marriage and therefore could not serve as the basis for divorce.[55] Since July 2011, both same-sex and different-sex couples have the right to marry in New York.[56]

Ohio:

In 1987, in *In re Ladrach*, an Ohio probate court denied a marriage license to a transgender applicant because "there is no authority in Ohio for the issuance of a marriage license to consummate a marriage between a post-operative male-to-female transsexual person and a male person."[57] In dicta, the court stated that "it seem[ed] obvious" that if a state allowed a transgender person to change her/his legal sex on a birth certificate, a marriage license "must issue" to that transgender person if all other statutory requirements are fulfilled.[58] However, the court asserted that Ohio's birth certificate amendment statute was "strictly a 'correction' type statute," which only allows for the correction of errors "if in fact the original entry was in error."[59] As such, the statute does not allow transgender people to change their legal sex. Having previously dismissed the transgender spouse's request to change the sex designation on her birth certificate, the probate court denied the transgender woman's application to obtain a marriage license as a female.[60]

Texas:

Texas law relating to recognition of, and access to, marriage for transgender people has been—and continues to be—shaped by both litigation and legislation. Most recently, on May 26, 2011, a Texas district court invalidated a post-transition marriage in the course of an estate dispute, holding that the decedent was not married to his transgender wife at the time of his death and that any purported marriage between them was void as a matter of law.[61] The decision has been appealed.[62]

In 2009, Texas enacted legislation amending the list of acceptable forms of proof of identification for a marriage license to include "an original or certified copy of a court order relating to the applicant's name change or sex change."[63] As a result, transgender people in Texas can apply for marriage licenses as their post-transition sex, and should thereby be able to enter into lawful post-transition marriages between different-sex spouses, the aforementioned case notwithstanding. This statute changed the common law in Texas that resulted from the Texas Court of Appeals 1999 decision in *Littleton v. Prange* holding that a transgender person's birth sex was immutable for the purpose of marriage.[64]

International:

Corbett v. Corbett, decided in 1970 by an English court and no longer good law, is the seminal case in which a post-transition marriage was nullified because the court held that the transgender spouse's birth sex was immutable for the purpose of marriage and same-sex couples were prohibited from marrying.[65] Subsequent cases invalidating post-transition marriages in the United Kingdom[66] and in American jurisdictions[67] have cited *Corbett* for this proposition.

Corbett has been reversed by case law and statute. In 2002, in *Goodwin v. United Kingdom*, the European Court of Human Rights held that refusing to allow a post-transition marriage violated the European Convention for the Protection of Human Rights and Fundamental Freedoms.[68] Moreover, the subsequent enactment of the Gender Recognition Act 2004 (GRA) changed the legal standard for authorizing transgender people's marriages in England.[69] GRA delegated authority to Gender Recognition Panels to acknowledge a transgender person's legal change of sex if the applicant is at least eighteen years of age, has or had gender dysphoria, has lived full-time in the acquired gender for the preceding two years, intends to live in the acquired gender permanently, and complies with the evidentiary requirements for the application.[70] There is no medical or surgical transition requirement.[71] After completing a legal change of sex, transgender individuals are allowed to marry a different-sex spouse.[72]

Outside of the United Kingdom, cases in Canada[73] and Singapore[74] have also invalidated post-transition marriages.

3.3.2 Defending a Client's Marriage Against a Fraud Claim

A transgender person's marriage may also be challenged on the basis of fraud. Post-transition marriages generally cannot be nullified because of fraud unless the fraud concerns something essential to the marriage, the transgender spouse knew and the allegedly defrauded spouse did not know the relevant information, and the allegedly defrauded spouse did not ratify the marriage after learning of her/his spouse's transgender identity.[75] An attorney should vigorously defend against a fraud claim by using state law that demonstrates the high bar to proving fraud, and by showing that the non-transgender spouse was aware of the transgender spouse's transgender identity at the time of the marriage or ratified the marriage after learning of her/his spouse's transgender identity. Securing a written acknowledgement from the transgender person's spouse prior to the marriage will go a long way towards inoculating against future fraud claims (see Chapter 10).

3.3.3 Draft Legal Instruments to Protect a Transgender Client Against a Possible Challenge to the Validity of Her/His Marriage

An attorney should advise a transgender client that, regardless of the attorney's assessment of the validity of the marriage, the couple should execute legal instruments to protect the transgender spouse should the marriage later be found invalid. Chapter 10 provides guidance about estate planning for transgender clients and the Appendix contains sample documents.

3.4 Federal Recognition of a Transgender Client's Marriage

As a result of the federal Defense of Marriage Act (DOMA), transgender clients' marriages may be subjected to additional scrutiny for purposes of federal recognition.[76] Social Security and immigration policies and reported decisions are the areas in which federal recognition of transgender clients' marriages are most often addressed. Other benefits and obligations that attach to federal marriage recognition may also be called into question for transgender people as long as DOMA remains in effect.

Federal recognition of a transgender client's marriage is contingent on the validity of the marriage at the state level and the strength of the argument that DOMA does not address transgender people. Assessing states' recognition of transgender clients' marriages is discussed above. The argument that DOMA is irrelevant to transgender people's marriages turns on plain language and legislative intent. The language and history of DOMA reflect that Congress did not contemplate transgender people's marriages when enacting this law; rather, its focus was on interstate and federal recognition of marriages between *same-sex* couples.[77]

Practice Tip: Because of DOMA, even if the jurisdiction where a transgender client was married recognizes marriages between same-sex individuals, the marriage will only be valid for federal purposes if the jurisdiction where the marriage was entered into considered it to be a marriage between different-sex individuals. Some transgender people are gay; if a transgender person is married to a same-sex spouse, then DOMA applies.

3.4.1 Marriage-Based Social Security Benefits and Transgender Clients

The Social Security Administration (SSA) follows the general choice of law rule for determining the validity of any marriage, including a transgender person's marriage: if the marriage was valid where it occurred (or if the claimant is eligible to inherit under state intestacy law), the marriage is considered valid elsewhere unless it violates another state's law or public policy.[78] The SSA acknowledges in its Program Operations Manual System (POMS) that states have different criteria for recognizing a gender change for the purpose of qualifying a transgender person for a lawful post-transition marriage.[79]

The SSA's guidance about federal recognition of pre-transition marriages suggests that this is an unsettled area of law, but in fact no court in the United States has ever invalidated a pre-transition marriage (see Section 3.1). The SSA's POMS states that a pre-transition marriage would "likely" continue to be valid after a spouse's transition in a state that does not recognize a legal change of gender for the purpose of marriage.[80] In a state that will recognize a legal change of gender for the purpose of marriage, the SSA's POMS suggests that it is "unclear" whether one spouse's gender change subsequent to entering into a marriage with a different-sex partner would invalidate the marriage for federal recognition purposes pursuant to DOMA Section 3 by transforming it into a marriage between same-sex spouses.[81]

3.4.2 Marriage-Based Immigration Benefits and Transgender Clients

If a transgender client or a client's transgender fiancé/ée or spouse is not a United States citizen, an attorney should determine whether the client's marriage will be considered valid for the purpose of marriage-based immigration benefits. If an attorney is unfamiliar with the practice of immigration law, s/he should consult with an attorney who specializes in immigration law and who is knowledgeable about the applicable law on marriage-based immigration and transgender individuals.[82]

A transgender person's marriage is recognized for immigration purposes if the marriage was considered a valid marriage between different-sex individuals in the state where the marriage was entered into. *In re Lovo-Lara* is a precedential Board of Immigration Appeals (BIA) decision recognizing the validity of a post-transition marriage for immigration purposes.[83] In *Lovo-Lara*, the BIA acknowledged that "[n]either the DOMA nor any other Federal law addresses the issue of how to define the sex of a postoperative transsexual or such designation's effect on a subsequent marriage of that individual."[84] The BIA concluded that DOMA restricts federal recognition of marriages only between *same-sex* couples; it does not invalidate marriages between persons of different sexes.[85] Therefore, if a marriage involving a transgender spouse is considered a valid marriage between different-sex spouses under the law of the jurisdiction where it was entered into, the marriage qualifies the couple for marriage-based immigration benefits.[86]

Subsequent to *Lovo-Lara*, in January 2009, the United States Citizenship and Immigration Services (USCIS) revised its Adjudicator's Field Manual (AFM) to include a new subsection titled "Transsexuals" within the existing section regarding "Petition for a Spouse."[87] In this subsection, the USCIS explains that "a claimed marriage between two persons of the same birth sex, one of whom has undergone sex reassignment surgery, is valid for immigration purposes if the petitioner establishes by a preponderance of the evidence that: (1) one of the claimed spouses has, in fact, undergone sex reassignment surgery; AND (2) that person has taken whatever legal steps exist and may be required to have the legal change of sex recognized for purposes of marriage under the law of the place of marriage; AND (3) the marriage is recognized under the law of the place of solemnization as a legally valid heterosexual marriage."[88] The AFM provides guidance about what is sufficient, but not necessarily required, to prove the validity of a post-transition marriage for immigration purposes.[89] Sex reassignment surgery should not be necessary for a marriage to be considered valid for federal purposes because it is not required by the BIA's decision in *Lovo-Lara*.[90]

In addition, the AFM enumerates which states do and do not "recognize transsexual marriages as valid heterosexual marriages" and treats this list as determinative of whether a marriage was valid where entered into unless the petitioner can demonstrate that a state's law has changed.[91] If the jurisdiction where the marriage was entered into does not have any precedent regarding whether it recognizes post-transition marriages, the AFM directs USCIS adjudicators to determine whether the jurisdiction's law recognizes a legal change of sex for the purpose of marriage.[92]

> **Practice Tip**: An attorney should consult the enumerated list contained in the AFM as part of an analysis of whether or not a client's marriage was recognized as valid in the state where s/he married.

3.5 Legal Protections for Transgender People in Relationships and Who Do Not Marry

Some states allow both same-sex and different-sex couples to enter into civil unions or domestic partnerships, so these alternative forms of legal relationship recognition may be available to a transgender client who cannot or chooses not to marry. If a transgender client who either cannot, or chooses not to, marry or enter into a legally recognized relationship status with her/his partner solicits advice about relational protections, an attorney should explore what options are available in the state to protect unmarried partners. For example, some states have statutes that allow individuals to confer decision-making authority (such as decisions about health care or disposition of remains) or assign benefits (such as providing insurance coverage) to a nonspousal partner.[93]

An attorney should also advise an unmarried transgender client about the options available to her/him to establish relational protections through the execution of legal planning instruments. Chapter 10 provides guidance about estate planning for transgender clients.

---

1   Organizing transgender people's marriages into these categories is admittedly

imperfect because the meaning and experience of "transition" is not universal, nor is it uniform. Transgender people may transition in a variety of ways, including some combination of medical or surgical treatment, changing their sex designation on legal documents, and/or social transition. How a transgender person who transitions from one gender to a different gender goes about doing so depends on a number of factors, including what s/he can afford. Moreover, transitioning may be an ongoing process, so it may be unclear when someone's transition is "complete." There are also transgender people who do not transition, but rather resist conforming to the gender binary. While classifying cases about transgender people's marriages based on the timing of the transgender spouse's transition does not fit the reality of all transgender people's lives, it nonetheless provides a useful structure for organizing and understanding these court decisions. For purposes of this publication, "post-transition" refers to when a person can plausibly make the argument that s/he has legally transitioned to a different sex, which does not necessarily require her/him to have undergone surgery. *See* 18 VT. STAT. ANN. tit. 104, § 5112 ("An affidavit by a licensed physician who has treated or evaluated the individual stating that the individual has undergone surgical, hormonal, or other treatment appropriate for that individual for the purpose of gender transition shall constitute sufficient evidence for the court to issue an order that sexual reassignment has been completed.").

2   As with all marriages between two people of the same sex, a transgender person's valid, pre-transition marriage to a person of the same sex may not be recognized by a state that does not recognize marriages between same-sex couples. *See* Defense of Marriage Act, Pub. L. No. 104-199, § 2, 110 Stat. 2419 (1996) (codified at 28 U.S.C. § 1738C). For further discussion, see Section 3.1. In these circumstances, the couple could try to remarry post-transition as a different-sex couple in the non-marriage equality state.

3   *See* COURTNEY G. JOSLIN & SHANNON P. MINTER, *Marriage and Custody Issues for Transsexual People, in* LESBIAN, GAY, BISEXUAL AND TRANSGENDER FAMILY LAW 492, 501–02 (2009). *But see* M. v. M., (1984) 42 R.F.L. 2d 55 (Can. P.E.I. Sup. Ct. Fam. Div.).

4   *See* Defense of Marriage Act, Pub. L. No. 104-199, § 3, 110 Stat. 2419 (1996) (codified at 1 U.S.C. § 7); *In re* Lovo-Lara, 23 I. & N. Dec. 746 (B.I.A. 2005).

5   Chapter 4 provides guidance regarding transgender parents' parental rights.

6   RESTATEMENT (SECOND) OF CONFLICT OF LAWS § 283 (1971).

7   *Id.* Even a marriage that was in violation of the requirements of the state where it was entered into may not be invalid because of the universal, compelling interest in validating existing marriages. *Id.*

8   *Id.*; *see, e.g.*, Fensterwald v. Burk, 98 A. 358, 360 (Md. 1916); State v. Hand, 126 N.W. 1002, 1002 (Neb. 1910); *In re* May's Estate, 114 N.E.2d 4, 6, 7 (N.Y. 1953); RESTATEMENT (FIRST) OF CONFLICT OF LAWS §§ 121, 132 (1934).

9   *See* RESTATEMENT (SECOND) OF CONFLICT OF LAWS § 283 cmt. k ("[A] mar-

riage has only been invalidated when it violated a strong policy of a state where at least one of the spouses was domiciled at the time of the marriage and where both made their home immediately thereafter."). The forum state applies its own principles to determine whether the policy of the state with the most significant relationship with the parties at the time of their marriage is sufficiently strong to invalidate the marriage. For examples where courts have recognized exceptions to the general rule for marriage validity see *In re Mortenson's Estate*, 316 P.2d 1106 (Ariz. 1957) (holding that marriage between first cousins who were residents of Arizona was void because Arizona law prohibits marriage between first cousins, gives the same effect to its residents' marriages solemnized in another state as if solemnized in Arizona, and prohibits its residents from evading its marriage laws by marrying in another state), and *Catalano v. Catalano*, 170 A.2d 726 (Conn. 1961) (holding that marriage by a resident of Connecticut to his niece in a foreign jurisdiction was invalid because the penalty for such incestuous marriage in Connecticut at the time was imprisonment for up to 10 years, which reflected the state's strong public policy against such marriages).

10   *See* Defense of Marriage Act § 2.

11   *See* Defense of Marriage Act, Pub. L. No. 104-199, 110 Stat. 2419 (1996); Lovo-Lara, 23 I. & N. Dec. 746. DOMA has no bearing on the validity of marriages between different-sex spouses as defined by the state. Indeed, federal law looks to state law to determine all other questions about the existence or validity of marriages. *See, e.g.*, Gill v. Office of Pers. Mgmt., 699 F.Supp.2d 374, 392, 393 (D. Mass. 2010).

12   *See* Defense of Marriage Act § 2; Lovo-Lara, 23 I. & N. Dec. 746. As of the time of publication, there are several challenges being waged against DOMA in federal court and the Massachusetts district court has already found it unconstitutional. *See, e.g.*, Gill, 699 F. Supp. 2d 374. Thus, the federal government's unequal treatment of lawfully married same-sex couples compared to lawfully married different-sex couples may soon be obsolete.

13   *See In re* Estate of Gardiner, 42 P.3d 120 (Kan. 2002).

14   In states that allow same-sex couples to marry, a transgender person can marry her/his partner, regardless of whether the state recognizes her/his legal change of sex and regardless of whether her/his partner is of the same sex or a different sex.

15   *See* Defense of Marriage Act § 2 ("No State, territory, or possession of the United States, or Indian tribe, shall be required to give effect to any public act, record, or judicial proceeding of any other State, territory, possession, or tribe respecting a relationship between persons of the same sex that is treated as a marriage under the laws of such other State, territory, possession, or tribe, or a right or claim arising from such relationship.").

16   *See* Dean Spade, *Documenting Gender*, 59 Hastings L.J. 731, 767–68 (2008); Sources of Authority to Amend Sex Designation on Birth Certificates, Lambda Legal, http://www.lambdalegal.org/publications/sources-of-authority-to-amend (last visited Nov. 22, 2011).

17   *See In re* Heilig, 816 A.2d 68, 82, 86–87 (Md. 2003) (holding that a court can issue a determination of a person's sex based on standards used for birth certificate amendments, even if the individual does not seek to alter a birth certificate).

18   *See In re* Ladrach, 513 N.E.2d 828 (Ohio Prob. Ct. 1987).

19   M.T. v. J.T., 355 A.2d 204 (N.J. Super. Ct. App. Div. 1976).

20   Corbett v. Corbett, [1971] P. 83 (Eng.), *available at* http://archive.equal-jus.eu/669; *see* Goodwin v. United Kingdom, 35 Eur. H.R. Rep. 18 (2002), *available at* http://archive.equal-jus.eu/74.

21   M.T. v. J.T., 355 A.2d 204.

22   *Id.* at 209.

23   *Id.*

24   *Id.* at 207.

25   *Id.* at 209.

26   *Id.* at 211. The court also remarked that "[s]uch recognition will promote the individual's quest for inner peace and personal happiness, while in no way disserving any societal interest, principle of public order or precept of morality." *Id.*

27   Minute Order, Vecchione v. Vecchione, No. 96D003769 (Cal. Super. Ct. Nov. 26, 1997) (on file with Gay & Lesbian Advocates & Defenders).

28   Cal. Health & Safety Code § 103425.

29   *See* Mary Coombs, *Sexual Dis-orientation: Transgendered People and Same-Sex Marriage*, 8 UCLA Women's L.J. 219, 254–56 (1998).

30   *Id.* at 256.

31   Memorandum from Michael McSweeney, City Clerk, City of New York, to All Staff (Feb. 7, 2011), *available at* http://www.transgenderlegal.org/media/uploads/doc_363.pdf.

32   *Id.*

33   *Id.*

34   N.Y. Dom. Rel. Law §§ 10-a, 13.

35   "[W]ritten legal opinions hav[e] precedential effect in adjudications and appeals involving veterans' benefits under laws administered by VA. The General Counsel's interpretations on legal matters, contained in such opinions, are conclusive as to all VA officials and employees not only in the matter at issue but also in future adjudications and appeals, in the absence of a change in controlling statute or regulation, Court decision, or a superseding written legal opinion of the General Counsel." *Welcome to Office of General Counsel*, U.S. Dep't of Veterans Affairs, http://www.va.gov/ogc (last visited Nov. 22, 2011).

36   Benefit Determinations Involving Validity of Marriage of Transsexual Veterans, Veterans Admin. Gen. Counsel, Dep't Veterans Affairs (Vet. Aff. Op. Gen.

Couns. Prec. 15-90 May 25, 1990), *available at* http://www.va.gov/ogc/docs/1990/PREC_15-90.doc.

37   In New Zealand, decisions of the High Court are binding on all inferior courts until overruled by the Court of Appeal or the Supreme Court. Because of its position in the New Zealand judicial structure, the High Court is the court to which application is made for authoritative declarations of law. *The Role and Structure of the High Court*, Courts of New Zealand, http://www.courtsofnz.govt.nz/about/high/role-structure (last visited Nov. 22, 2011).

38   *Att'y Gen. v Otahuhu Fam. Ct.* [1995] 1 NZLR 603, 608 (HC).

39   *Id.* at 618.

40   Goodwin, 35 Eur. H.R. Rep. 18.

41   *Att'y Gen. v Kevin* (2003) 172 Fam LR 300 (Austl.), *available at* http://www.austlii.edu.au/au/cases/cth/FamCA/2003/94.html.

42   *Id.*

43   *See* Phyllis Randolph Frye & Alyson Dodi Meiselman, *Same-Sex Marriages Have Existed Legally in the United States for a Long Time Now*, 64 Alb. L. Rev. 1031, 1033–34 (2001).

44   Kantaras v. Kantaras, 884 So. 2d 155, 161 (Fla. Dist. Ct. App. 2004).

45   *Id.*

46   *Id.*

47   *In re* Marriage of Simmons, 825 N.E.2d 303 (Ill. App. Ct. 2005).

48   *Id.* at 308–09.

49   *Id.* at 309–10.

50   Gardiner, 42 P.3d 120.

51   *Id.* at 122–23.

52   *Id.* at 135–36.

53   Anonymous v. Anonymous, 325 N.Y.S.2d 499, 501 (N.Y. Sup. Ct. 1971).

54   *Id.* at 500.

55   Frances B. v. Mark B., 355 N.Y.S.2d 712 (N.Y. Sup. Ct. 1974).

56   N.Y. Dom. Rel. Law §§ 10-a, 13.

57   Ladrach, 513 N.E.2d at 832. In 2003, in *In re* Nash, the Ohio Court of Appeals similarly affirmed a trial court's denial of a marriage license to a transgender man and his fiancée. *In re* Nash, Nos. 2002-T-0149, 2002-T-0179, 2003 WL 23097095 (Ohio Ct. App. 2003). The appellate court held that the trial court had given "the proper full faith and credit" to the transgender man's amended Massachusetts birth certificate because, under Massachusetts law, a birth record is only prima facie evidence of the facts recorded therein and this evidence was purport-

edly rebutted by the sex designation on his original birth certificate. *Id.* at *4–5. In addition, the court concluded that the trial court was not required to give full faith and credit to the amended birth record because doing so would violate Ohio's public policy of recognizing only marriages between different-sex spouses. *Id.* at *5, *9. Based on *Ladrach* and *Nash*, Ohio apparently does not allow transgender individuals to change the sex designation on their Ohio birth certificates and also will not recognize that an amended birth certificate from another state represents a transgender person's legal sex for the purpose of marriage.

58   Ladrach, 513 N.E.2d at 831.

59   *Id.*

60   *Id.* at 832.

61   *See In re* Estate of Araguz, No. 44575 (Tex. Dist. Ct. May 26, 2011), *available at* http://oldsite.alliancedefensefund.org/userdocs/AraguzOrder.pdf; Juan A. Lozano, *Lawyer: Transgender Widow's Marriage to be Voided*, Associated Press, May 24, 2011, *available at* http://www.huffingtonpost.com/huff-wires/20110524/us-firefighter-transgender-widow.

62   *In re* Estate of Araguz, No. 44575 (Tex. Dist. Ct. May 26, 2011), *appeal docketed*, No. 13-11-00490-CV (Tex. App. July 20, 2011), http://www.13thcoa.courts.state.tx.us/opinions/case.asp?FilingID=19940.

63   Tex. Fam. Code § 2.005(b)(8). Legislation was introduced, but did not become law, in the 2011 legislative session to excise the words "sex change" from this provision of the Texas Family Code. The text of the bill and information about its status are available at http://www.legis.state.tx.us/BillLookup/History.aspx?LegSess=82R&Bill=SB723 (last visited Nov. 18, 2011).

64   *Littleton*, 9 S.W.3d 223 (Tex. App. 1999). In *Littleton*, the Texas Court of Appeals held that a transgender woman was, as a matter of law, male, and the post-transition marriage was thus deemed invalid because Texas does not allow a man to marry a man. The evidence indicates that the court subscribed to the line of reasoning employed in *Corbett*, namely that birth sex is immutable. The transgender woman had changed her name, taken hormones, and had three surgeries resulting in "complete" sex reassignment prior to marriage; she had successfully amended her birth certificate to change her name and sex designation while the case was pending; and the court heard testimony from medical providers that she was "medically a woman" and "ha[d] the capacity to function sexually as a female." Despite the overwhelming evidence of transition, the Texas Court of Appeals did not recognize that she had legally changed her sex for the purpose of marriage. As a result of the invalidation of the marriage, the transgender woman was foreclosed from bringing a wrongful death action as her husband's surviving spouse.

65   Corbett v. Corbett, [1971] P. 83.

66   *E.g.*, Bellinger v. Bellinger, [2003] UKHL 21 (appeal taken from Eng.); Sheffield v. United Kingdom, 27 Eur. H.R. Rep. 163 (1998); Cossey v. United Kingdom, 184 Eur. Ct. H.R. (ser. A) (1990); Rees v. United Kingdom, 9 Eur. H.R.

Rep. 56 (1986).

67   Gardiner, 42 P.3d 124; Ladrach, 513 N.E.2d at 832; Littleton, 9 S.W.3d at 226.

68   Goodwin, 35 Eur. H.R. Rep. 18.

69   Gender Recognition Act, 2004, c. 7 (U.K.), *available at* http://www.legislation.gov.uk/ukpga/2004/7.

70   *Id.* §§ 1–2.

71   *See id.*

72   *See id.* § 9. Applicants are required by the GRA to declare whether they are married at the time of their application. Unmarried applicants are eligible to receive a full gender recognition certificate which is required for a transgender person to claim her/his legal change of sex by registering in the Gender Recognition Register and amending her/his birth certificate. Married applicants may only receive an interim gender recognition certificate. An interim recognition certificate makes an existing marriage voidable by either spouse for six months, after which time there are three possibilities: (1) if the marriage has been annulled, the transgender person receives a full gender recognition certificate; (2) if the marriage has been terminated by death or divorce, the transgender person may apply and receive a full gender recognition certificate; or (3) if the marriage remains valid and in effect, the transgender person cannot convert her/his interim certificate into a full recognition certificate. *Id.* §§ 4–5, sch. 2. Thus, a married transgender person is forced to choose between legal recognition of her/his change of sex and preserving her/his existing marriage.

73   *See* C.(L.) v. C.(C.) (1992), 10 O.R.3d 254 (Can. Ont. Gen. Div.) (provincial court in Ontario nullified post-transition marriage in a short, offensive opinion that described the transgender husband as "a woman who passed herself off as a man").

74   *See* Lim Ying v. Hiok Kian Ming Eric, [1991] 1 S.L.R. 184 (Sing.) (High Court, the lower level of the Supreme Court, nullified post-transition marriage). The record suggests that the petitioner may have been genuinely unaware of her transgender spouse's transgender identity at the time of their marriage. *Id.* at 186.

75   *See* Mark Strasser, *Defining Sex: On Marriage, Family, and Good Public Policy*, 17 MICH. J. GENDER & L. 57, 68–70 (2010).

76   Federal law traditionally defers to state law for establishing marriage validity, but DOMA changed the status quo so that the federal government does not recognize the validity of state-licensed marriages between same-sex couples. *See* Defense of Marriage Act, Pub. L. No. 104-199, 110 Stat. 2419 (1996). The federal district court in Massachusetts has held that DOMA is unconstitutional and this decision is currently on appeal in the First Circuit. Gill, 699 F. Supp. 2d 374. Additional litigation challenging the constitutionality of DOMA is underway in other federal courts. *E.g.*, Pedersen v. Office Pers. Mgmt., No. 3:10-cv-1750 (D. Conn. filed

Nov. 9, 2010); Windsor v. United States, No. 10 Civ. 8435 (S.D.N.Y. filed Nov. 9, 2010).

77   *See* Lovo-Lara, 23 I. & N. Dec. 746.

78   20 C.F.R. § 404.345; Social Security Online, POMS § GN 00305.005, *available at* http://policy.ssa.gov/poms.nsf/lnx/0200305005.

79   Social Security Online, POMS § GN 00305.005 (determining marital status), *available at* http://policy.ssa.gov/poms.nsf/lnx/0200305005. "The POMS is a primary source of information used by Social Security employees to process claims for Social Security benefits. The public version of POMS is identical to the version used by Social Security employees except that it does not include internal data entry and sensitive content instructions." *Program Operations Manual System Home*, SOCIAL SECURITY ONLINE, https://secure.ssa.gov/apps10 (last visited Nov. 28, 2011).

80   Social Security Online, POMS § GN 00305.005.

81   *Id.*

82   Immigration Equality is a national organization that advocates for the equality of LGBTQ and HIV-positive individuals under U.S. immigration law. Immigration Equality provides guidance and technical assistance to attorneys representing LGBTQ clients in an immigration context and maintains a database of immigration attorneys who are knowledgeable about LGBTQ people's issues. *See* IMMIGRATION EQUALITY, http://www.immigrationequality.org (last visited Nov. 28, 2011). *Immigration Law & The Transgender Client* is a publication co-authored by Immigration Equality and the Transgender Law Center and published by the American Immigration Lawyer's Association. It devotes an entire chapter to marriage-based petitions involving transgender individuals. VICTORIA NEILSON & KRISTINA WERTZ, IMMIGRATION EQUAL. & TRANSGENDER LAW CTR., IMMIGRATION LAW AND THE TRANSGENDER CLIENT (2008), *available at* http://www.immigrationequality.org/issues/law-library/trans-manual.

83   Lovo-Lara, 23 I. & N. Dec. 746. The BIA's decision in *Lovo-Lara* is consistent with *In re* Widener, an earlier unpublished decision in which the BIA also acknowledged that DOMA does not address the validity of transgender people's marriages and focused its analysis on whether the marriage at issue was considered a valid marriage between different-sex spouses in the jurisdiction where it was entered into. *See In re* Widener, 2004 WL 2375065 (B.I.A. Sept. 21, 2004). In several unpublished BIA decisions issued subsequent to *Lovo-Lara*, the BIA relied upon its reasoning in *Lovo-Lara* to either grant or deny marriage-based immigration benefits. *See, e.g., In re* Price, 2009 WL 3448162 (B.I.A. Oct. 14, 2009) (denying a petition for a marriage-based immigration visa because Florida, the state in which the marriage occurred, does not recognize post-transition marriages) (citing Kantaras v. Kantaras, 884 So. 2d 155); *In re* Ahmad, 2007 WL 3301748 (B.I.A. Sept. 26, 2007). Although unpublished, *In re* Ahmad is important because the BIA recognized the transgender beneficiary's legal change of sex—a necessary condition for her mar-

riage to be considered a valid marriage between different-sex spouses—even though Singapore, the beneficiary's country of birth, would not issue her a new birth certificate. *See id.* The BIA concluded that the fact that Singapore issued the beneficiary a new passport as a female was sufficient to demonstrate that Singapore recognized her legal change of sex. *Id.* As a result, petitioner satisfied his burden of proving the marriage was a valid marriage between different-sex spouses. *Id.*

84   Lovo-Lara, 23 I. & N. Dec. at 749.

85   *Id.* at 751.

86   *Id.* at 753.

87   U.S. Citizenship and Immigration Servs., Adjudicator's Field Manual Redacted Public Version, § 21.3(a)(2)(J), *available at* http://www.uscis.gov (follow "Laws" hyperlink; then follow "Immigration Handbooks, Manuals and Guidance" hyperlink).

88   *Id.*

89   *See id.* § 3.4 (explaining that if the AFM conflicts with another policy document, the "higher" authority controls); Cruz-Miguel v. Holder, 650 F. 3d 189, 200 (2nd Cir. 2011) (asserting that the AFM is not binding agency authority); *In re* Guzman-Gomez, 24 I. & N. Dec. 824, 829 (B.I.A. 2009) (explaining that the AFM does not have the "force and effect of law" and the BIA is not required to follow it).

90   *See* Lovo-Lara, 23 I. & N. Dec. at 753 (holding that a transgender spouse's marriage was valid and approving a visa petition based on the marriage because "[w]e have long held that the validity of a marriage is determined by the law of the State where the marriage was celebrated. The State of North Carolina considers the petitioner to be a female under the law and deems her marriage to the beneficiary to be a valid opposite-sex marriage. We find that the DOMA does not preclude our recognition of this marriage for purposes of Federal law.").

91   Adjudicator's Field Manual, *supra* note 87.

92   *Id.* The AFM is explicit that, because of *Simmons* and *Littleton*, a birth certificate amendment statute alone may not be dispositive in finding that a jurisdiction recognizes, *for purposes of marriage*, a legal change of sex. For marriages entered into in foreign jurisdictions or in states other than those enumerated and in which the law is unclear and there is no binding precedent, "a USCIS adjudicator may find that the petitioner has established the validity of the claimed marriage (or proposed marriage []) if the petitioner submits a court order or an official record or statement from an appropriate agency of the Government (such as the vital statistics registrar or similar official) indicating that the person's having undergone sex reassignment surgery has resulted in a change of the person's *legal* sex under the law of the place of marriage." *Id.*

93   *See* COLO. REV. STAT. § 15-22-101; HAW. REV. STAT. § 572C-1.

Chapter 4: Protecting Parental Rights

Shannon Price Minter and Deborah H. Wald

Introduction

A legal parent is a person the law has recognized as a child's parent. Being recognized as a legal parent is essential to ensure that a transgender parent's relationship with a child is protected. In many states, a person who is not a legal parent has no ability to seek custody or visitation with a child; make religious, medical, educational, or legal decisions for a child; or have any role in the child's life without the consent of the legal parent. Without recognition as a legal parent, a person may be cut off from any contact with a child even if the person has functioned as the child's parent in every way and has a bonded relationship with the child. In most cases, a person who is not a legal parent cannot provide health insurance or other benefits for a child. The child will not be eligible for survivor's benefits from Social Security if the person dies, and the child will not automatically inherit if the person dies without a will.

4.1 Legal Parentage

A transgender person may become a legal parent in one of two ways. In some cases, depending on the circumstances, a transgender person may qualify as a legal parent under the state's parentage statutes. In other cases, a transgender person may become a legal parent through adoption. In some states, both of these options may be available.

If a transgender person is neither a legal parent under the state's parentage statutes nor an adoptive parent, s/he may have no parental rights. However, some states recognize that a person who is not a legal parent but who has functioned as a child's parent should have at least some limited rights and responsibilities with respect to a child.[1] In some states, such a person has standing to seek custody or visitation, and may also be responsible for child support.[2] In other states, such a person may seek visitation only, and may be awarded visitation only under very limited circumstances.[3] In still other states, such a person may be considered a complete legal stranger to a child, and may have no rights or responsibilities at all.[4] In general, while having some rights and responsibilities is certainly preferable to having none, a transgender person who is parenting a child and who wishes to be protected as the child's parent should establish legal parentage through a parentage or adoption action, if doing so is possible in the state where the family lives.

To ensure that a transgender person who is not a child's biological parent is recognized as a legal parent, the only truly safe course is to get a court order saying that the person is a legal parent under state law or to obtain an adoption. It is not enough to rely on having the transgender parent's name appear on a child's birth certificate. A birth certificate is merely a record, not a legal judgment. As such, a birth certificate does not establish legal parentage and cannot be counted on to protect parental rights.[5] In addition, a birth certificate issued in one state is not necessarily entitled to full faith and credit in other states.[6] Therefore, while it is important to have a birth certificate that lists the transgender parent for many practical reasons, that alone is not sufficient to establish legal parentage or to provide protection in other states.

Similarly, a transgender parent should not rely exclusively on a presumption or legal rule that s/he is a legal parent under state law. For example, in many states, there is a presumption or rule of law that a child born to a married couple (or a couple in a civil union or registered domestic partnership) is the legal child of both parents.[7] In some states, the law may provide that a person who consents to the birth of a child through assisted reproduction with the intention of parenting the child is a legal parent.[8] Other states' laws may recognize that a person who takes a child into her/his home and holds the child out as her/his child is a presumed parent.[9] Some states may even recognize that a person who functions as a child's de facto parent for a period of time is a legal parent.[10] These presumptions and legal rules may be sufficient to protect a transgender parent *within the state*, but they generally will not protect a transgender parent if s/he moves to another state.

Even with respect to protections within a given state, if a transgender person who is not a biological parent qualifies as a legal parent under the laws of the state in which the person lives, it is still highly advisable to obtain a legal judgment declaring that the person is a legal parent. This is true for many reasons: First, having a legal judgment eliminates any ambiguity or doubt should disagreements between the parents later arise. If a court has already declared the transgender parent to be a legal parent, it will be much more difficult for the other parent (if there is one) to dispute the relevant facts establishing parentage or to challenge the transgender parent's legal status.[11] For example, if a transgender person's parentage is contingent upon the validity of the parents' marriage and the non-transgender spouse challenges the validity of the marriage, a legal judgment will be useful to help convince the court that the transgender parent retains her/his parental rights, even if the marriage is invalidated. Second, having a legal judgment provides protections against third parties such as extended family members or insurance companies who may wish to challenge the transgender person's parental rights. Third, having a legal judgment will help protect the child in the event of the parent's death by eliminating the need for an extended investigation or determination of whether a legal parent-child relationship existed.

In addition, having a legal judgment of parentage or adoption is critically important to ensuring that the transgender person's parental status and rights will be respected in other states. The federal constitution mandates that states must give full faith and credit to the judgments, records, and acts of other states.[12] In practice, however, the United States Supreme Court has held that only judgments are entitled to strict full faith and credit.[13] A state need not give full faith and credit to a record or administrative act from another state if that other state's law conflicts with a strong public policy of the forum state.[14] For example, marriages and birth certificates are considered "records" or "acts" (not "judgments"). Accordingly, the Full Faith and Credit Clause does not compel states to give full faith and credit to out-of-state marriages or birth certificates that conflict with a strong public policy of the forum state.[15]

In contrast, a state *must* give full faith and credit to a judgment from another state, even if that judgment is based on an underlying law that is repugnant to the forum state's own public policy.[16] The Supreme Court has made very clear, and reiterated a number of times, that states must honor judgments from other states, no matter how sharply the issuing state's law differs from that of the forum state.[17] As a result, a state must recognize a court order declaring that a transgender person is a child's legal or adoptive parent, even if the transgender person would not have qualified as a legal parent or been able to adopt the child in the forum state.[18] To benefit from this clearly established constitutional protection, a transgender parent should obtain a court order declaring that s/he is a legal or adoptive parent whenever possible.

There is another reason why transgender parents benefit from having a court establish that they are legal or adoptive parents; a legal parent has a recognized fundamental constitutional liberty interest in the care, custody, and control of her/his children.[19] This is a powerful constitutional protection that gives parents a great deal of autonomy to determine how to raise their children, make medical and educational decisions for their children, and generally share their own personal, religious, political, and moral values with their children. Equally important is that the state must overcome this strong constitutional protection before terminating a person's parental rights, and must show by clear and convincing evidence that a parent's conduct is causing harm to the child.[20]

4.1.1 Transgender Persons and Legal Parentage

As a general rule, the fact that a person is transgender should not affect her/his parental status or ability to become a legal parent. For example, if a person who is already recognized as a child's legal parent comes out as transgender and undergoes gender transition, that fact alone does not automatically affect the person's parental status or parental rights. In practice, however, as discussed in the next section, a few courts have taken the extreme step of terminating a transgender person's parental rights—simply because the person underwent gender transition—based on unsupported fears that being "exposed" to a transgender parent would be harmful to a child. But even in those cases, court action was required. The fact that a person legally, medically, or socially changes her/his sex does not have any direct or automatic effect on the person's status as a legal parent.

Some transgender people become parents after undergoing a gender transition. No state bars transgender people from becoming legal parents. The key question in such a case is whether the transgender person meets the legal criteria for becoming a legal parent under the relevant state parentage laws or, in the alternative, whether the transgender person meets the legal criteria for becoming an adoptive parent under the state's adoption statutes. As discussed further in Section 4.4 below, special questions and complications may arise when a transgender person gains her/his parental rights based on marriage. In those cases, it pays to take special precautions to ensure that the transgender parent's rights will be protected even if the validity of the marriage is successfully challenged.

4.1.2 Termination of Parental Rights Because of Transgender Status

Some courts have taken the extreme step of terminating a transgender parent's rights based on the erroneous belief that being exposed to a transgender person is harmful to a child. For example, in 1986, the Nevada Supreme Court terminated the parental rights of a male-to-female transgender parent who, before transitioning, had fathered a child in the context of a heterosexual marriage.[21] The court held that the transgender parent was "a selfish person whose own needs, desires and wishes were paramount and were indulged without regard to their impact on the life and psyche of the daughter."[22]

Further, in 2007, the Kentucky Court of Appeals terminated the parental rights of a male-to-female transgender parent by granting the biological mother's new husband the right to adopt the child over the objections of the transgender parent.[23] The court asserted that gender reassignment in itself is not a ground for terminating parental rights. Instead, the court claimed that it was basing its decision on the transgender parent's failure to handle the gender transition in a sensitive manner. The court found that the child was harmed by the transgender parent's actions, including, "exhibiting 'physical changes in [the transgender parent's] appearance' when the children visited in Florida, such as long fingernails, 'wearing tight shirts and short shorts (with shaved legs and arms) and breast augmentation,' without any warning to prepare [the child] or the others for those changes; sending a letter to [the child's] sister with a photograph of the appellant as a female and traveling to Kentucky from Florida dressed as a woman and demanding visitation with [the child], knowing that [the child] did not want to see the appellant."[24] The court also cited expert testimony by a psychiatrist that the child became depressed because of her father's gender reassignment and suffered suicidal ideation, problems in school, and physical symptoms of distress that "were related to the emotional injury caused by [the transgender parent's] actions."[25]

The transgender parent argued that steps less drastic than termination of her parental rights could have been used to protect the child's best interests.[26] The court acknowledged that Kentucky law required that a trial court consider less drastic measures, but held that the transgender parent had waived that argument by failing to raise it in the trial court.[27] The court also held that no less drastic measures would be sufficient "where the emotional harm to [the child] was closely related to her feeling that she was abandoned by her father and her need to have a father figure in her life."[28]

The Nevada and Kentucky cases show that transgender parents who transition after they have become parents may face harsh judicial scrutiny. In some states, transgender parents are at risk of losing their parental rights. Parents in this situation should exercise great caution in how they disclose their transgender status to their children. If possible, they should seek out the advice of a therapist with expertise in this area, and document that they are following the expert's guidance.

As explained in more detail in Section 4.4 below, a transgender person may also lose parental rights if the person's parental status is based on a marriage that is later found to be invalid.[29]

4.2 Child Biologically Related to Transgender Parent

Many people erroneously assume that biology is the main determinant of legal parentage. In fact, biology is only one factor used to determine parentage, and not every biological parent is automatically a legal parent.[30] For example, in many states, a child born to a married couple will be considered the legal child of both spouses, even if the husband is not the child's biological father.[31] In addition, a man who biologically fathers a child but makes no effort to assume responsibility for the child may be deemed to have no parental rights.[32] Further, most states provide legal mechanisms that enable individuals who use donated eggs or sperm to become legal parents, and specify that the individuals who donate the eggs or sperm are not legal parents.[33]

Nonetheless, it is also true that in many cases, a person who biologically procreates a child is considered to be a legal parent, so long as they have developed a relationship with the child and have not abused or neglected the child.[34] For example, a transgender person may become a legal parent by giving birth to a child or biologically fathering a child before undergoing a gender transition. That person will continue to be a legal parent after transitioning, based on the person's biological relationship to the child. A woman may give birth to a child and subsequently transition to male and live as a man. That person will continue to be the child's legal parent based on having given birth to the child. Similarly, a man may biologically father a child and subsequently transition to female and live as a woman. That person will continue to be the child's legal parent based on having biologically procreated the child. In these cases, because the parent's legal status is based on biology, there is less need to obtain a legal judgment of parentage than for a transgender parent who is not a biological parent, although doing so may be helpful or advisable depending on the person's circumstances.

Some transgender people become parents before they realize they are transgender. Others deliberately become parents before undergoing gender transition so that they can have the experience of biologically procreating or to ensure that they will have a legally protected relationship with their child. In a few cases, a female-to-male transgender person who had not had a hysterectomy or genital reconstructive surgery, had stopped taking testosterone for a period of time in order to permit his menstrual cycles to resume so that he could become pregnant and give birth. Such a person should be considered a legal parent based on having given birth to the child, although questions may arise as to whether the person should be designated as the child's "mother" or "father" on the birth certificate. How that issue will be resolved will depend on state law and individual state practice.

In the past, transgender people who medically transitioned

before becoming parents gave up the ability to biologically procreate. Increasingly, however, some transgender people who are in this situation are taking steps to preserve sperm or eggs so that they may have the option of biologically procreating after transition. Attorneys advising transgender clients should make their clients aware of this option.

Preserving sperm is relatively easy and inexpensive. A male-to-female transgender individual who has a female partner after transitioning may wish to use her sperm to impregnate her partner. In such a case, the transgender partner would be a legal parent to the resulting child in at least some states, based on having provided the sperm with the intention of being a parent. However, few state courts have addressed the legal parentage of children born in this situation, so attorneys advising these clients should encourage them to take every possible step to protect both partners' parental rights, including obtaining a judgment or adoption decree stating that both partners are legal parents and a written acknowledgment that the person is transgender and is providing sperm for purposes of being a parent.

A male-to-female transgender individual who has a male partner may wish to provide her sperm to be used to impregnate a surrogate, who would give birth to a child who would be raised by the transgender woman and her male partner. Depending on the laws regulating surrogacy in a particular state, the transgender partner may be a legal parent to the resulting child. Again, this is a new and uncertain area of law, so whenever possible, transgender clients in this situation should obtain a parentage judgment or adoption decree stating that both partners are legal parents, as well as a written agreement in advance that both parties intend to be parents. In addition, attorneys advising transgender clients and/or their partners should strongly encourage them to familiarize themselves with the relevant laws addressing transgender people, surrogacy, artificial insemination, and any other relevant topics in the state where they live, and where the surrogate lives, before making arrangements to have a child. Given the importance of protecting both partners' parental rights, the couple may want to consider relocating to be sure they live in a jurisdiction that will allow both partners to be legal parents.

Harvesting and preserving eggs is a more invasive and expensive procedure than preserving sperm, but one that may be important for some female-to-male transgender individuals. A female-to-male transgender person who has a female partner after transitioning may wish to use donated sperm to fertilize his eggs, which could then be implanted in his female partner. In such a case, the transgender partner would be a legal parent to the resulting child in some states, based either on having a genetic connection to the child or on having consented to the procreation of a child through assisted reproduction. It is important to note, however, that most states have not addressed how to determine the legal parentage of children born under these circumstances. To ensure that both parents' rights are protected, it is essential to obtain either a judgment of parentage or an adoption that clearly identifies both partners as the child's legal parents. It is also important to have written agreements in advance that clearly spell out both parties' intentions to be parents.

Similarly, a female-to-male transgender person who has a male partner after transitioning may wish to fertilize his eggs with his partner's sperm and then implant the fertilized egg or eggs in a gestational surrogate. Depending on the laws governing surrogacy in the couple's state, both partners may be considered the child's legal parents. However, like the other situations described above, the laws concerning surrogacy and parentage are unsettled in many state jurisdictions and thus fraught with uncertainty. Couples who are in this situation should proceed with great caution and should be sure they understand their state's laws governing transgender people and surrogacy before embarking upon the procreation of a child.

4.2.1 Medical Consents and Legal Agreements

Attorneys advising transgender clients who are using their own harvested eggs or sperm to have a child with a partner should caution both partners *not* to sign medical consents that are designed for sperm or egg donors who do not wish to acquire any parental rights for the recipient of donated sperm or eggs. A transgender person in this situation is not "donating" sperm or eggs. Similarly, the partner is not receiving "donated" sperm or eggs. A donor is a person who is *not* a legal parent, whereas the transgender person in these situations is providing her/his genetic material to a partner (or a surrogate) in order to be a legal parent. The failure to use appropriate consents and legal documents in these cases can cause serious legal problems down the road. Any medical consents or legal forms or agreements should be scrutinized carefully to be sure they accurately reflect that both the transgender person and her/his partner intend to be legal parents of the child.

4.2.2 Pre-birth Decrees, Parentage Judgments, and Adoptions

When a transgender person and her/his partner use assisted reproduction to have a child, regardless of whether the genetic material derives from the transgender person's own preserved sperm or eggs or from a third-party donor, it is critical that the couple obtains formal legal recognition that both partners are the child's legal parents. In some states, it may be possible to obtain a pre-birth order specifying who will be the child's legal parents when the child is born. In other states, it may be possible to obtain a post-birth order identifying both partners as the child's legal parents. In other states, it may be possible for one or both of the partners to obtain a second-parent adoption to secure parental rights. And in some states, none of these options exist, which means there is no way to establish that both partners are legal parents. Attorneys representing transgender clients should research the relevant state law in order to properly counsel clients about the options available for protecting both parents' rights.

As a purely legal matter, a judgment of parentage and a judgment of adoption are equally valid and equally entitled to full faith and credit. Nonetheless, some attorneys representing LGBTQ parents believe that even where a legal judgment of parentage can be obtained or has been obtained, same-sex couples and couples including a transgender person (or two transgender people) should obtain an adoption. This view is based on the belief that because adoption is more familiar to most people and judges, an adoption is less likely to be challenged and more likely to be upheld in the event that either party's parentage is challenged. Other attorneys believe the decision about whether to obtain an adoption rather than, or in addition to, a judgment of parentage can only be made by the client, after being informed of the relative risks and costs associated with each option.

The impact of Defense of Marriage Acts (DOMA) should also be considered. Many states have enacted statutes or state constitutional amendments that not only bar same-sex couples from marriage, but also purport to deny recognition of any rights based upon the marriage.[35] The federal government has also enacted such a statute for purposes of all federal benefits.[36] To date, no state or federal court has used either a state DOMA or the federal DOMA to deny recognition to a parent who gained her/his parental rights based on marriage (or civil union or domestic partnership) and at least one case has recognized the nonbirth parent's rights, notwithstanding DOMA.[37] Nonetheless, the possibility of such a denial certainly exists. To be safe, the best course is to ensure that any judgment of parentage or decree of adoption does not rely primarily or exclusively upon the marital status (or civil union or domestic partnership status) of the couple.

4.3 Child Adopted by Transgender Parent

Transgender people may wish to become parents through adoption. No state formally bars transgender people from adopting, although in practice, a transgender person may encounter informal discrimination and barriers.

One question that often arises in the adoption context is whether the transgender person should disclose her/his transgender status during the home study or to the court. Ultimately, the decision about whether to disclose one's transgender status is personal and can only be made by the individual transgender person. As a practical matter, however, it may be difficult or impossible to keep that information private if the application asks for disclosure of any prior names used, or for disclosure of any prior medical diagnoses or treatment. Fingerprint checks, required in most adoption investigations, may also reveal the prior identity. In "open" adoptions, where the birth mother is selecting the person or people who will be adopting her child, there may be an issue about the validity of her consent if she were to choose the transgender person without being aware of her/his transgender status. In addition, some social workers, adoption agency staff, or courts may consider the withholding of that information to be a negative factor. In the worst case, it is possible that someone might later challenge the adoption on the ground that the adoptive parent's transgender status was not disclosed. Attorneys representing transgender clients in this situation may also wish to advise them about the importance of answering questions on their applications and on legal documents truthfully and the potential legal consequences if they do not.

While different attorneys have different views regarding disclosure of a transgender person's status, many favor disclosure as a way to avoid any possible problems or challenges down the road. The safest course is to disclose the person's transgender status both to the social worker conducting the investigation and to the court even though disclosure may subject the transgender person to bias and discrimination within the adoption process. Some attorneys ask the court to acknowledge the person's transgender status on the record or even in the adoption judgment itself.

4.3.1 Second-Parent or Co-parent Adoption

A transgender person who is in a nonmarital relationship with another person can obtain a second-parent or co-parent adoption in any of the states that permit such adoptions. Currently, seventeen states have approved such second-parent or co-parent adoptions either by statute or appellate court decision, and second-parent adoptions are granted by some trial courts in an additional twelve states.[38] In these jurisdictions, there should be no formal legal barrier to a transgender person becoming an adoptive parent.

Transgender individuals who are married may be eligible to obtain a stepparent adoption (if they are married to someone who already has a child) or to adopt jointly with a spouse, based on statutory provisions that permit a spouse to adopt. In these cases, extra considerations must be taken into account. While many transgender people marry and live as married persons without encountering any legal difficulties or challenges, some transgender people who marry do face legal challenges to their marriage; these challenges may be brought by an angry spouse in the context of a divorce or custody dispute.[39] They may also be brought by a family member seeking to invalidate the marriage for personal gain.[40] Additionally, challenges to a transgender person's marriage may be brought by a third party who seeks to have the marriage declared invalid in order to avoid an obligation to one of the spouses.[41] See Chapter 3 for more information and guidance about accessing the validity of transgender people's marriages.

If a transgender parent gains her/his parental status based on marriage, and if the validity of the marriage is challenged, the transgender parent may lose her/his parental rights.[42] For this reason, it may be safer for transgender people who are married to forego using adoption procedures that are restricted to married people and instead use the same adoption procedures that are available for unmarried couples. The purpose of that option is to ensure that the transgender person's status as a legal, adoptive parent will be preserved, even if the underlying marriage is held to be invalid. Some transgender clients may be reluctant or unwilling to forego using the same adoption procedures available to other married people and may prefer to live with the risk of their marriages being challenged. As explained further in the next section, there are strong arguments that even if a marriage is declared invalid, that should not affect the validity of an adoption; however, there is no guarantee that such arguments will prevail. As with many other areas of family law affecting transgender parents, there are currently no certainties—only degrees of risk.

4.3.2 Agency Adoption

Transgender individuals who wish to adopt a child from a private or public adoption agency generally face greater barriers than those adopting a partner's child. These barriers do not arise from formal legal prohibitions. Rather, the barriers to agency adoption arise from pervasive bias and discrimination, which may create serious obstacles.

Every state permits unmarried individuals and married couples to adopt. In addition, many states permit unmarried couples, including unmarried same-sex couples, to adopt. Currently, Utah and Mississippi are the only states that expressly bar unmarried couples from adopting.[43] As noted above, no state currently bars a transgender person from adopting.

As of 2010, six states have laws banning discrimination based on sexual orientation in adoption proceedings: Maryland, New Jersey, New York, California, Massachusetts, and Nevada.[44] Only one state, California, bars adoption agencies from considering gender identity.[45]

Typically, child placement agencies can consider a number of factors when evaluating potential adoptive parents. In New York, for example, agencies can consider a list of factors.[46]

In practice, transgender applicants may face bias from social workers or other agency staff who are unfamiliar with transgender issues and may harbor inaccurate stereotypes about transgender people. Some of the most common false stereotypes are that transgender people are sexually deviant or mentally unstable, or that transgender people are inherently unreliable, deceptive, and pose a threat of safety to children. To increase the chances of success, an attorney should contact adoption agencies that are open to lesbian, gay, and bisexual parents, and which are more likely to be open to transgender parents as well.[47] To rebut these stereotypes, it may be necessary to have a supportive therapist or doctor who is knowledgeable about transgender issues and can be a resource for social workers, adoption agency staff, and courts who may have questions or concerns.

4.4 Child Born of a Marriage and Not Biologically Related to Transgender Parent

Many transgender people marry after they transition, and many have children in the context of marriage by using assisted reproduction. A transgender man may marry a woman and, in order to have a child, use sperm from an anonymous or known donor in an alternative insemination procedure. A transgender woman may marry a man and use donated eggs, the husband's sperm, and a gestational surrogate to have a child.

In every state, both spouses are presumed to be the legal parents of a child born of a marriage, including through alternative insemination.[48] State laws with respect to surrogacy vary much more widely, ranging from states that outlaw it altogether to states that actively facilitate and encourage the use of surrogacy.[49] A growing number of states provide that a married couple may use gestational surrogacy to have a child, and when they do, both spouses are the child's legal parents.[50]

Many transgender people who become parents after marriage gain their parental rights based on the marriage. In most cases, transgender people in this situation do not face legal problems. Many transgender people stay married and raise children with their spouses. Some transgender people divorce, but their spouses do not challenge the validity of the marriage or seek to terminate the transgender person's parental rights. In some cases, however, a spouse or former spouse will challenge the validity of the marriage in an effort to deprive the transgender person of parental rights.[51] If an attorney represents a transgender client in such a case, it is imperative to defend the validity of the marriage because invalidation of the marriage could threaten the parental rights of the transgender parent.

The best arguments for defending the validity of a marriage involving a transgender person are discussed in Chapter 3. Advocates for these clients should also be aware that, even if the marriage is found to be invalid, there are a number of other arguments that often can be used to defend a transgender person's parental rights. For example, in most states, statutes or court decisions have established that even if a marriage turns out to be void *ab initio*, the invalidity of the marriage does not affect the status of any children born to the marriage, or strip either spouse of parental rights.[52] In some states, courts have held that a stepparent adoption is not retroactively invalidated by a later finding that the marriage is invalid.[53] Estoppel protections may also apply. If the non-transgender spouse was aware that the other spouse was transgender, and agreed to an adoption or otherwise encouraged the couple's child to bond with the transgender spouse as a parent, a court may find that the spouse is estopped from challenging a stepparent adoption or otherwise seeking to undermine the parental status of the transgender spouse.

In addition, in some jurisdictions, even if the marriage is found to be invalid, courts or the legislature may provide that an unmarried person who consents to have a child through assisted reproduction will be held legally responsible as a parent.[54] Some jurisdictions also may recognize that a person who has functioned as a child's parent is entitled to full or partial recognition, based on equitable theories such as de facto parentage, in loco parentis, or parentage by estoppel.[55] Attorneys representing transgender parents in these cases must be vigilant about presenting and preserving every possible argument for protecting the person's parental rights even if the marriage is found to be invalid.

In some jurisdictions, however, courts may be so biased against transgender people that even where established alternative grounds for protecting a transgender parent exist, the courts may refuse to apply them. For example, in 2005, an intermediate appellate court in Illinois rejected multiple alternative bases for protecting the parental rights of Sterling Simmons, a transgender man who was a loving and devoted parent to his thirteen-year-old son.[56] Sterling and his wife were married for more than fifteen years.[57] They planned their child's conception together, using anonymous donor sperm.[58] The child was named after Sterling and considered Sterling to be his father.[59] When Sterling filed for divorce, his wife retaliated by seeking to invalidate the marriage in order to terminate Sterling's parental rights. The trial court found that the marriage was invalid because Sterling had not undergone enough medical treatment to legally change his sex. Because it held the marriage to be invalid, the trial court also found that Sterling "lacked parental rights or standing to seek custody."[60]

On appeal, the Illinois Court of Appeals rejected every ground on which it might have preserved the longstanding parent-child relationship between Sterling and his son. First, although Sterling and his wife had signed an artificial insemination agreement, the court held that the agreement had no effect because Sterling signed as "husband."[61] Second, the Illinois Parentage Act provides that even if a marriage is invalid, the invalidity does not affect any parental rights arising from the marriage. However, the court refused to apply that law to protect Sterling because it held that he was not a "man" within the meaning of the statute.[62] Third, although the court previously held that an unmarried man who consented to the artificial insemination of his girlfriend could be held responsible as a parent, the court refused to apply that prior ruling to protect Sterling's parental rights.[63] Fourth, the court declined to treat Sterling as a de facto parent or a person in loco parentis to the child.[64] Fifth, the court rejected the argument that the wife should be estopped from challenging Sterling's parentage because she had actively encouraged him to be a parent, had agreed in writing that he would be a parent, and had encouraged the child to love and depend upon Sterling as a parent.[65] Sixth, the court rejected the argument that the wife should be barred from challenging Sterling's parentage on the ground of laches, holding that laches did not apply because Sterling had initiated the divorce and the wife was entitled to raise any applicable defense.[66] And finally, the court rejected all arguments brought on behalf of the child by the Public Guardian's office.[67]

This Illinois case is a powerful illustration of how far some courts will go to avoid protecting a parent-child relationship involving a transgender parent, even when severing the relationship will be devastating to the child. In light of that risk, a transgender parent should take every possible precaution to protect their parent-child relationship in the event that her/his marriage is challenged by the other spouse or a third party. Such measures may include signing a prenuptial agreement (and/or in some jurisdictions, a postnuptial agreement) in which the non-transgender spouse agrees not to challenge the marriage or the transgender person's parental status; creating a will that names the child as a legatee regardless of whether there is a legal parent-child relationship; and asking the other parent to nominate the transgender spouse as the child's guardian. Most important is to *always* obtain a formal legal judgment establishing a direct legal relationship between the transgender parent and the child— such as a parentage judgment or adoption—rather than *ever* allowing the transgender parent's legal relationship with the child to depend on the legal validity of the relationship between the parents. This is the only way to truly guarantee legal security for both parent and child, regardless of what happens to the couple.

4.5 Child Born to Unmarried Parents and Not Biologically Related to Transgender Parent

A transgender person may become involved in a relationship with a person who already has a child, or may have a child in the context of a non-marital relationship. In the first case, if a child already has two legal parents, the transgender partner will not be a legal parent unless the child's second parent agrees to terminate her/his rights so that the transgender parent can adopt the child. If that is not possible, the transgender partner may have limited rights in some jurisdictions as a de facto parent. In many jurisdictions, however, the nonmarital partner of a person who has a child with a previous spouse or partner has no rights with respect to the child. This is not unique to transgender partners.

In the second case, in which a transgender person has a child with a nonmarital partner using assisted reproduction, there are a variety of legal options to protect the transgender parent's rights. In many jurisdictions, the transgender partner can obtain a second-parent adoption. Where possible, this option is highly advisable and provides the most secure protection.

In a handful of states, the transgender partner can obtain a parentage decree recognizing that s/he is a legal parent by virtue of having consented to the conception of a child through assisted reproduction. This option is also highly advisable and provides secure protection. As noted above, some attorneys believe that even where this option exists, transgender parents should obtain a second-parent adoption instead of, or in addition to, a parentage decree.

In states where neither an adoption nor a parentage decree is available, transgender parents who are in a nonmarital relationship with the child's biological or adoptive parent may have limited rights based on statute or case law recognizing doctrines such as de facto parentage, parentage by estoppel, psychological parentage, in loco parentis, or related doctrines. Transgender parents who live in these jurisdictions are vulnerable, as none of these protections are comparable to being recognized as a full legal parent. Or, the transgender parent may live in a jurisdiction in which s/he has no rights with respect to the child at all, regardless of how committed s/he is or how deeply bonded to the child.

Nonetheless, transgender parents can take steps to protect themselves and their children by entering into a parenting or co-parenting agreement stating that: (1) both partners agree that the transgender person will be a full parent to the child and have equal parental rights and obligations; (2) the biological or adoptive parent is voluntarily and knowingly agreeing to give up her/his exclusive constitutional parental rights to the child by sharing those rights with the transgender parent; (3) the biological or adoptive parent will not challenge the transgender person's parental status based on the lack of a biological or legal tie to the child; (4) in the event of a disagreement, the parties agree to mediate their dispute; and (5) the biological or adoptive parent is aware of the other person's transgender status. A sample co-parenting agreement is included in Appendix 4A. To the extent possible, these agreements should be written with the formality typical of genuine legal contracts, should make clear that both parents have had the benefit of the advice of legal counsel, and should recite valuable consideration (typically a promise to provide financial support for the child in exchange for a promise of continued, on-going access to the child). The more formal and "legal" a co-parenting agreement appears, the more likely a court is to enforce it.

Transgender parents who cannot adopt or otherwise establish legal parentage can also take additional steps to protect their parent-child relationships. These include: (1) obtaining written authorization from the biological or adoptive parent for the transgender co-parent to make decisions regarding the child's medical treatment and decisions relating to the child's education; (2) having the biological or adoptive parent nominate the transgender parent as the child's guardian in the event of the biological or adoptive parent's death or incapacity; (3) creating a will that names the child as one of the transgender co-parent's legatees in the event that both partners die simultaneously; or, (4) establishing a trust to benefit the child. To the extent possible, it is also worthwhile, under circumstances where formal legal protections are impossible to secure, to obtain the clear written support of the child's extended family for the relationship between the transgender parent and the child. In cases where a non-legal parent's relationship with a child is threatened, the response of the rest of the child's family can be critical. Providing documentation showing that the legal parent's family acknowledges and supports the parent-child relationship between the transgender parent and the child will be extremely helpful under these circumstances.

---

1   COURTNEY G. JOSLIN & SHANNON P. MINTER, *Dissolution/Separation Issues Where Only One Parent is a Legal Parent*, *in* LESBIAN, GAY, BISEXUAL AND TRANS-GENDER FAMILY LAW 422–50 (2011).

2   *Id.*; *see also, e.g.*, V.C. v. M.J.B., 748 A.2d 539 (N.J. 2000); *In re* Parentage of L.B., 122 P.3d 161 (Wash. 2005).

3   JOSLIN & MINTER, *supra* note 1. *See also, e.g.*, Thomas v. Thomas, 49 P.3d 306 (Ariz. Ct. App. 2002); Holtzman v. Knott, 533 N.W.2d 419 (Wis. 1995).

4   JOSLIN & MINTER, *supra* note 1. *See also, e.g.*, Music v. Rachford, 654 So.2d 1234 (Fla. Dist. Ct. App. 1995); *In re* Thompson, 11 S.W.3d 913 (Tenn. Ct. App. 1999).

5   *See, e.g.*, MASS. GEN. LAWS ch. 46, § 19 ("The record of the town clerk relative to a birth … shall be prima facie evidence of the facts recorded"); Dudley's Adm'r v. Fid. & Deposit Co. of Md., 240 S.W.2d 76 (Ky. Ct. App. 1951) (finding that other evidence was sufficient to overcome the prima facie evidence of paternity

provided by a birth certificate); *In re* Marriage License for Nash, Nos. 2002-T-0149, 2002-T-0179, 2003 WL 23097095 (Ohio Ct. App. Dec. 31, 2003).

6   *See In re* Estate of Gardiner, 42 P.3d 120 (Kan. 2002).

7   *See, e.g.,* D.C. CODE § 16-909; VT. STAT. ANN. tit. 15, § 1204(f).

8   *See, e.g.,* DEL. CODE ANN. tit. 13, § 8-201; MASS. GEN. LAWS ch. 46, § 4B; N.M. STAT. ANN. § 40-11A-201. *See also* Elisa B. v. Super. Ct., 117 P.3d 660 (Cal. 2005).

9   *See, e.g.,* Elisa B., 117 P.3d at 667.

10   DEL. CODE ANN. tit. 13, § 8-201; *see also* Smith v. Gordon, 968 A.2d 1, 7 (Del. 2009).

11   For example, in California, the law provides that a person who takes a child into his home and holds the child out as his own is a presumed parent. The presumption can be rebutted, but the California courts have held that evidence that a man is not a child's biological father does not automatically rebut the presumption. *In re* Nicholas H., 46 P.3d 932 (Cal. 2002); Elisa B., 117 P.3d at 666–67. If a transgender parent meets these criteria, s/he would be wise to get a court order declaring her/him to be a legal parent before any possible disputes with the child's other parent or parents arise.

12   U.S. CONST. art. IV, § 1.

13   Baker *ex rel.* Thomas v. Gen. Motors Corp., 522 U.S. 222 (1998).

14   Nevada v. Hall, 440 U.S. 410 (1979).

15   *In re* Gardiner, 42 P.3d 120.

16   Finstuen v. Crutcher, 496 F.3d 1139 (10th Cir. 2007) (holding unconstitutional an Oklahoma statute refusing to recognize valid out-of-state adoptions by same-sex couples).

17   Baker, 522 U.S. at 232–34; Estin v. Estin, 334 U.S. 541, 546 (1948) (Full Faith and Credit Clause "ordered submission by one State even to hostile policies reflected in the judgment of another State").

18   *See* Finstuen, 496 F.3d 1139 (adoption decree for same-sex couple, though against the public policy of the domicile, is still entitled to Full Faith and Credit).

19   Pierce v. Soc'y of Sisters, 268 U.S. 510 (1925); Meyer v. Nebraska, 262 U.S. 390 (1923).

20   Troxel v. Granville, 530 U.S. 57 (2000).

21   Daly v. Daly, 715 P.2d 56 (Nev. 1986).

22   *Id.* at 57. *See also In re* Darnell, 619 P.2d 1349 (Or. Ct. App. 1980) (mother's parental rights terminated in large part because of continued relationship with transgender spouse, whose parental rights had previously been terminated).

23   M.B. v. D.W., 236 S.W.3d 31 (Ky. Ct. App. 2007).

24   *Id.* at 35.

25   *Id.*

26   *Id.* at 37.

27   *Id.*

28   *Id.*

29   *See, e.g., In re* Marriage of Simmons, 825 N.E.2d 303 (Ill. App. Ct. 2005) (marriage invalidated because the court did not recognize the transgender spouse's legal sex change and Illinois does not recognize marriages between same-sex individuals; as a result of invalidation of the marriage, the transgender parent's parental rights were terminated and the transgender parent did not have standing to seek custody).

30   *See, e.g., In re* Guardianship of Palmer, 503 P.2d 464 (Wash. 1972) (holding that rights of biological parents should not be given greater weight than those of grandmother who had previously been granted custody); Solberg v. Metro. Life Ins. Co., 185 N.W.2d 319 (Wis. 1971).

31   *See, e.g.,* Cal. Fam. Code § 7540; Lohman v. Carnahan, 963 So.2d 985 (Fla. Dist. Ct. App. 2007).

32   Lehr v. Robertson, 463 U.S. 248 (1983).

33   *E.g.,* Cal. Fam. Code § 7613; Courtney G. Joslin & Shannon P. Minter, *Assisted Reproduction, Excluding Surrogacy, in* Lesbian, Gay, Bisexual and Transgender Family Law (2011); Courtney G. Joslin & Shannon P. Minter, *Surrogacy, in* Lesbian, Gay, Bisexual and Transgender Family Law (2011).

34   *See, e.g.,* Jermstad v. McNelis, 258 Cal. Rptr. 519 (Cal. Ct. App. 1989).

35   *See State Laws and Legislation on Marriage and Relationship Recognition,* Human Rights Campaign, http://www.hrc.org/laws-and-legislation/state/c/marriage (last visited Nov. 9, 2011).

36   1 U.S.C. § 7; 28 U.S.C. § 1738C.

37   Miller-Jenkins v. Miller-Jenkins, 661 S.E. 2d 822 (Va. 2008).

38   Nat'l Ctr. for Lesbian Rights, Legal Recognition of LGBT Families (2011), http://www.nclrights.org/site/DocServer/Legal_Recognition_of_LGBT_Families_04_2008.pdf?docID=2861.

39   Kantaras v. Kantaras, 884 So.2d 155 (Fla. Dist. Ct. App. 2004); *In re* Simmons, 825 N.E.2d 303.

40   *In re* Gardiner, 42 P.3d 120.

41   Littleton v. Prange, 9 S.W.3d 223 (Tex. Ct. App. 1999).

42   *See, e.g., In re* Simmons, 825 N.E.2d 303.

43   Miss. Code Ann. § 93-17-3(5); Utah Code Ann. § 78B-6-117.

44   Cal. Welf. & Inst. Code § 1601; Md. Code Regs. 07.05.03.09; 110 Mass. Code Regs. 1.09; Nev. Admin. Code § 127.351; N.J. Admin. Code §§ 10:121C-2.6, 4.1(c); N.Y. Comp. Codes R. & Regs. tit. 18, § 421.16(h).

45   Cal. Welf. & Inst. Code § 16013. Further, a bill was introduced in Congress in 2009, named the "Every Child Deserves a Family Act." The goal of the Act is "to prohibit discrimination in adoption or foster care placements based on the sexual orientation, gender identification, or marital status of any prospective adoptive or foster parent." H.R. 3827, 111th Cong. (2009).

46   N.Y. Comp. Codes R. & Regs. tit. 18, § 421.16; *see also, e.g.,* 7 Colo. Code Regs. § 2509-6.500.2.

47   *See All Children – All Families: List of Participating Agencies,* Human Rights Campaign, http://www.hrc.org/resources/entry/all-children-all-families-list-of-participating-agencies (last visited Nov. 9, 2011).

48   *See, e.g.,* Cal. Fam. Code § 7540; D.C. Code § 16-909; N.M. Stat. Ann. § 40-11A-705; Ohio Rev. Code Ann. § 3111.03.

49   D.C. Code § 16-402; Ind. Code § 31-20-1-1 (specifically prohibits all forms of surrogacy on the basis that such agreements are against public policy and therefore unenforceable); Mich. Comp. Laws § 722.855 (all forms of surrogacy agreements are prohibited); Wash. Rev. Code §§ 26.26.210 *et seq.* (statute authorizing surrogacy agreements which states that an agreement including compensation to the surrogate mother for expenses other than medical or legal is deemed unenforceable); Johnson v. Calvert, 851 P.2d 776 (Cal. 1993); Jaycee B. v. Super. Ct., 49 Cal. Rptr. 2d 694 (Cal. Ct. App. 1996).

50   *See, e.g.,* Doe v. N.Y.C. Bd. of Health, 782 N.Y.S.2d 180 (N.Y. Sup. Ct. 2004); J.F. v. D.B., 879 N.E.2d 740 (Ohio 2007).

51   *E.g., In re* Simmons, 825 N.E.2d 303.

52   *See, e.g.,* 750 Ill. Comp. Stat. 45/5; N.M. Stat. Ann. § 40-11A-204.

53   750 Ill. Comp. Stat. 5/303.

54   *See, e.g.,* K.B. v. J.R., 887 N.Y.S.2d 516 (N.Y. Sup. Ct. 2009).

55   Joslin & Minter, *supra* note 1.

56   *In re* Simmons, 825 N.E.2d 303.

57   *Id.* at 307.

58   *Id.*

59   *Id.* at 312.

60   *Id.* at 315.

61   *Id.* at 311.

62   *Id.* at 312.

63   *Id.* (holding that common law theories could only be used to impose support but not to establish parentage or standing to seek custody).

64   *Id.* at 313.

65   *Id.* at 313–14.

66   *Id.* at 314.

67   *Id.* at 314–15.

CHAPTER 5: DIVORCE AND RELATIONSHIP DISSOLUTION

Jennifer L. Levi

Introduction

Like non-transgender people, transgender people enter into marital (and marital equivalents) relationships that do not always last for the intended life-long duration. The major difference for transgender people involved in such marital relationship dissolution is that transgender people in the family court systems face systemic and widespread bias against a core element of their identity.[1] The focus of this chapter is to advise transgender clients who are interacting with the family court systems at the point of relationship dissolution. The analysis describes the ways in which social and cultural bias may enter into contested divorces and relationship dissolution and offers practice recommendations on ways to neutralize or challenge such bias. The primary focus is on cases where a transgender person enters into a legally recognized relationship (whether marriage, civil union, domestic partnership, or otherwise) prior to initiating gender transition and that relationship subsequently dissolves. Some of the guidance may also be relevant in combating discrimination transgender litigants may face in court where they have entered into a lawful marriage or marriage equivalent after transition.

Many of the practice recommendations and much of the legal guidance offered in this chapter are location-specific and may be impacted by the degree of visibility of transgender people within the community and public awareness about societal discrimination faced by transgender people. Because of that, attorneys are well-advised to consult local family law attorneys with lesbian, gay, bisexual, transgender and queer clientele, or practice sections of the state or local bar focused on issues of LGBTQ concerns, to assess the wisdom of these practice suggestions with respect to their local practice.

In addition, while the legal issues transgender clients face are different from those faced by lesbian, gay, bisexual, and queer clients in the family court systems, the biases and misunderstandings are similar and related. Thus, the experiences of lesbian, gay, bisexual, and queer litigants in a particular family court system or before specific judges is a reasonable, if not perfect, indicator of the kind of treatment transgender clients may expect. Attorneys for transgender clients are well-advised to seek counsel from attorneys with experience representing lesbian, gay, bisexual, and queer clients in the local court system.

5.1 Impact of Gender Transition on Marriage

Like any other life-altering event, the gender transition of a spouse can put a major strain on a marital relationship. Notwithstanding that strain, many marital relationships involving a transgender spouse remain intact and even thrive after a time of initial adjustment. In a forthcoming University of Houston study examining the romantic relationships of transgender men, one in two subjects in a relationship with a primary partner at the time of their transition reported that their relationship survived the transition.[2] Only one in four of the relationships that were dissolved after transition ended specifically because of the transition of one of the partners.[3] The 2011 National Transgender Discrimination Survey, conducted by the National Gay and Lesbian Task Force and the National Center for Transgender Equality, reported similar results, with 55% of the more than 6,000 transgender respondents reporting that their relationship was intact after transition.[4]

Unfortunately, when a relationship does not remain intact post-transition, the non-transgender spouse may perceive, rightly or wrongly, that the gender transition was the root cause of the marital breakdown. Even in cases where there are clearly many contributing factors to the breakdown of the relationship, the non-transgender spouse may make the gender transition the focus of the dissolution. This may be because the non-transgender spouse views her/his spouse's gender transition as the major contributing factor or because focusing on the gender transition may elicit sympathy from outsiders to the relationship and put the non-transgender spouse in a position perceived to be stronger in both family law-related negotiations and litigation. Compounding the challenges faced by the transgender spouse is the fact that there exists much bias and misunderstanding about transgender people and transsexualism in society, and this bias and misunderstanding may be shared by judges, court personnel, court officers, attorneys, and mediators.

Pervasive bias and misunderstanding about transgender people makes it more difficult negotiating divorces for transgender clients, even those divorces in which the fact of a spouse's gender transition should be irrelevant. It also increases the financial and emotional risks associated with a contested divorce.

5.2 Issues Potentially Impacted By Gender Transition

While every jurisdiction has adopted some form of no-fault divorce, the remnants of fault divorce that remain, either as grounds for pursuing divorce (in states with combined fault and no-fault rules) or as factors that may be considered in determining property distribution, spousal support, rehabilitation, or alimony (however denominated), can sometimes be exploited by the non-transgender spouse and used to gain an advantage either in negotiations or in securing a judgment in a contested case. In addition, the fact of a person's gender transition or its impact on sexual function has sometimes been used to challenge the validity of a marriage in an action for annulment.

5.2.1 Annulment

As long as the parties to the marriage met the basic requirements for eligibility to marry at the time of the inception of the marriage (that is, the spouses were each of a different sex, at least in most jurisdictions), the fact of one spouse undergoing or initiating gender transition during the marriage is not grounds for an annulment. As long as two people of different sexes otherwise satisfy all of the qualifications for marrying, there are no grounds to challenge the validity of that marriage at its dissolution simply because one of the spouses initiates or undergoes gender transition during the marriage, even if the transgender spouse knew that s/he was transgender at the marriage's inception. In a marriage of very short duration where the non-transgender spouse sought an annulment based on the transgender spouse's alleged "fraudulent concealment" of her/his transgender identity, the court still affirmed the validity of the marriage as a marriage between different-sex spouses.[5]

The case may be more complicated where a transgender person enters into a marriage after undergoing gender transition. Several reported cases reflect facts in which a non-transgender spouse challenged the validity of a marriage on the basis that it was invalid at the outset of the marriage due to the other spouse being transgender at the time of the marriage's inception.[6] Those cases raised the legal issue of whether the person had (or could have) lawfully transitioned from her/his assigned birth sex such that s/he was of a different sex than her/his intended spouse and, therefore, eligible to marry. The dominant rule, consistent with the strong public policy of affirming marriages, is that with a few notable exceptions, a marriage is lawful in a state that exclusively permits marriages between different-sex spouses if the transgender spouse can demonstrate that s/he meets the lawful standard in that state for having transitioned by the time of inception of the marriage.[7] See Chapter 3 for guidance about advising a transgender client about the validity of her/his marriage in a state that only allows marriages between different-sex couples.

Two slightly variant cases bear mention. In *Anonymous v. Anonymous*, the husband was an army officer who married his transgender wife, allegedly without ever having seen her unclothed or having had sexual relations with her (notwithstanding having "spent a short time together" at a "house of prostitution").[8] Between the date of the marriage and the date the husband sought to dissolve the marriage, the wife reportedly had surgical sex reassignment. The court held that the marriage was not lawful at its inception because the transgender spouse was "not a female at the time of the marriage ceremony."[9] Notably, the New York court commented that the case was "different from one in which a person seeks an annulment of a marriage or to declare the nullity of a void marriage because of fraud or incapacity to enter into a marriage contract or some other statutory reason. . . . [Here] the marriage ceremony was itself a nullity."[10] Accordingly, the statutory provision for securing an annulment was inapplicable.

That decision is in some tension with the later reported New York decision, *Frances B. v. Mark B.*, in which the court did not dismiss an annulment action brought by a wife against her transgender husband where the transgender husband had undergone surgical sex reassignment prior to the marriage (mastectomy and hysterectomy but not genital reconstruction).[11]

No reported decisions have sustained an annulment where a spouse married someone of a different sex and later transitioned. Notwithstanding, to the extent that the non-transgender spouse would seek an annulment or declaration of invalidity of such marriage based on alleged fraud or misrepresentation because, for example, the transgender spouse did not disclose the fact of being transgender prior to the marriage (and in many, or most cases, prior to the transgender spouse's becoming fully conscious of her/his own transgender identity), counsel should use the strategies described below for addressing the related argument of fault in challenging an action for annulment of such an otherwise lawful marriage.

Attorneys are strongly advised not to stipulate to an annulment of a marriage involving a transgender client for a number of reasons. If there are children of the marital relationship, an annulment could negatively impact the transgender spouse's parental rights including, in some jurisdictions, a stepparent's right to visitation or custody, where applicable. In addition, an annulment may impact property distribution and debt assumption. It may also be used in a later relationship dissolution or divorce as either evidence of the transgender spouse's sex or as a basis to collaterally attack the validity of a subsequent relationship.

5.2.2 Gender Transition as Grounds for Divorce and its Impact on Support and Property Distribution

Gender transition is not a statutory ground for divorce in any state. However, the non-transgender spouse may use information relating to the transgender spouse's gender identity, cross-gender behavior (such as crossdressing) or gender transition in a number of different ways (depending on local law), including as a reason for pursuing a fault-based divorce (in jurisdictions that retain fault-based divorce), or in defending against a support action in a jurisdiction where fault is a factor in that determination. Facts of a spouse's gender transition may also be raised in jurisdictions that take fault or comparable legal standards (such as dissipation of assets during the marriage) into account in property distribution and when setting spousal support orders. Several courts have been sympathetic to these arguments.

In *Steinke v. Steinke*, the Pennsylvania court considered whether the husband's gender transition constituted legal grounds for a divorce.[12] Finding that it did, the court commented, "[t]hat the appellant-wife in the present case has come to find life with her husband intolerable and burdensome does not indicate unusual sensitivity or extraordinary delicacy on her part" and that it is to be anticipated that a reasonable woman whose husband undergoes gender transition would be "shocked and repelled."[13]

Facts of a spouse's transgender identity or crossdressing may even be introduced and considered by a court in no-fault jurisdictions. In *Vicas v. Vicas*, a Connecticut Superior Court evaluated a divorce under an irretrievable breakdown standard, commenting in passing that, "[n]eedless to say the desire of the defendant [husband] to dress as a woman had a depressing effect on the marriage and the sexual relations between the parties."[14]

Facts relating to a spouse's transgender identity may also be exploited in the context of spousal support. For example, in *McKolanis v. McKolanis*, the court considered the legal question of whether the wife's departure from the home without the husband's consent was justified such that she could nonetheless seek spousal support.[15] In that case, the couple had been married for nearly ten years and had parented two children at the time that the wife left the marital home allegedly because the husband disclosed to her that he engaged in crossdressing behavior.[16] The husband, seeking to distinguish the facts of the case from *Steinke*, argued that there was no evidence of humiliating or degrading actions and that he had, in fact, informed his wife of his crossdressing conduct in order to seek counseling to strengthen their marriage.[17] Notwithstanding evidence that the wife had never been witness to the husband's crossdressing and acknowledging that it had been twenty years since *Steinke* was decided and that "acceptance of alternative lifestyles ha[d] increased over the years," the court found in favor of the wife, holding that the crossdressing conduct justified the wife's departure.[18]

The final way in which a transgender spouse's gender transition or evidence of crossdressing conduct has been used offensively (in both senses of that word) by the non-transgender spouse is in the context of property distribution. Some states, such as Massachusetts, take into account, among other factors, financial conduct of a party, including dissipation of assets during the marriage, as a factor to consider in determining the equitable distribution of assets subject to division upon divorce.[19] The same factors are also used by courts in Massachusetts when fashioning an alimony award. Anecdotally, some non-transgender spouses have argued that financial assets being used to pay for care and treatment of a spouse's transgender condition, whether for psychotherapy, hormone therapy, or other transition-related care, should constitute dissipation of assets.

Each of these approaches and the ways in which some courts have regarded or assessed the relevance of a spouse's transgender identity (including crossdressing conduct) or gender transition is unprincipled and should be redressed by counsel for the transgender spouse. It is hard to overemphasize how rampant bias and misunderstanding about transgender people is, including in the judicial system. The cases cited above are very much just the tip of the iceberg in terms of how the introduction of facts of a spouse's transgender identity and gender transition can negatively influence decision makers. More importantly, transgender spouses, forced to negotiate divorces and settlement agreements in the shadows of bias and perceived bias, often feel compelled to exchange any rights to a continued relationship with their children for property and support agreements that are far less favorable than any judgment that would be entered by a court. Counsel should work hard to overcome the bias their clients may face in contested cases, ferret out the often (though not always) unstated biases that counsel for the non-transgender spouse may be relying on during negotiations, and, should negotiations fail, urge the transgender spouse to make a careful and proper assessment of the potential influence of bias in a contested case. While all settlements in a divorce matter should balance the priorities of a client, no client should feel forced to unnecessarily barter or trade any property or support rights for rights to a relationship with a child or children.

Some practice recommendations are offered below on how best to address bias against the transgender spouse's gender identity, gender-related behavior, and gender transition, in the context of relationship dissolution. Obviously, this is an area where education (including judicial education) is ongoing, so practitioners are well-advised to consult with colleagues who have any experience representing transgender clients in the local jurisdiction. If the experience of representing gay, lesbian, and bisexual clients is any indication, it may be many years before transgender litigants in dissolution cases are treated with dignity, respect, and as equal participants in many family court systems.

5.2.3 Dissolution of Marriage Equivalents

As more and more jurisdictions permit same-sex couples to marry ("marriage equality" states), some of the questions about the validity of the marriage at the outset may disappear for transgender spouses. That is, as the sex of the persons entering into the marriage becomes irrelevant for state law purposes of determining who may lawfully marry, fewer non-transgender spouses may be able to challenge the validity of the marriage because of the spouse being transgender for any purposes (whether for reasons of property or support, or in relation to parentage, see Chapter 4). Even in marriage equality states, however, questions may remain about the validity of the marriage for federal law purposes, even though there may be no basis to challenge the legal union as a state matter, as long as the federal Defense of Marriage Act (DOMA) survives.

The legal irrelevance of the sex of the parties should also be true in states, such as New Jersey and California ("marriage equivalent" states), that do not allow same-sex couples to marry but do allow them to enter into marriage equivalents such as civil unions or domestic partnerships. Attorneys representing couples in both marriage equality states and marriage equivalent states should be able to successfully argue that there are no grounds to pursue an annulment or otherwise challenge the validity of the legal relationship simply because the union in question involves a transgender spouse. Of course, the other ways in which a non-transgender spouse may inject the fact of the transgender spouse's identity, i.e., by raising it as an issue of fault or in the context of property distribution or alimony/support, remain. For guidance in that context, practitioners should consult the practice recommendations below. In addition, practitioners should always advise clients, whether in marriage equality or marriage equivalent states, about the transferability or nontransferability of the rights the marital relationship has conferred should they move to a state that does not have the same legally recognized relationships.

5.2.4 Dissolution of Non-Marital Relationships

Marriage brings along with it well-established state protocols for distribution of property and financial obligations of spousal support.[20] Except in a minority of jurisdictions,[21] non-marital couples are not generally entitled either to equitable distribution of property or under any obligation of post-dissolution financial support for one another. Notwithstanding, many courts have struggled to ensure that persons in longstanding non-marital relationships, that look marital in every way but are not legally sanctioned, are not unfairly left without property or support after the committed relationships fail. One common approach is for courts to bring a broad and liberal view of contract (and quasi-contract) law in enforcing oral and written agreements between longstanding committed partners upon the breakup of their relationship.[22]

Another approach is for courts to liberally allow the former intimate partners to pursue equitable doctrines to obtain judicial remedies that, in some ways, approximate divorce laws' equitable distribution principles both as to property and ongoing obligations of financial support. For example, many former partners have sought and obtained equitable judgments through the use of constructive trust, unjust enrichment, and equitable liens.[23] In the case of intimate partners, courts have relied on these doctrines to look behind formalities of title of both individually and jointly owned property in order to enforce the parties' expectations about breakups and to avoid unfairness.

A detailed analysis of developed and developing common law on non-marital dissolution is beyond the scope of this chapter. However, relevant to the concern of effective representation of transgender clients in this context, it bears mention that courts that may hear these kinds of contract and equitable claims likely share the same biases, prejudice, and misunderstanding about transgender people that are reflected in the divorce cases. The same offensive and defensive strategies described below that would be relevant in the divorce context may be relevant to attorneys pursuing these kinds of claims for transgender clients dealing with dissolution issues in the non-marital context. While fault should generally not be relevant at all in the contract or equitable claims contexts, some courts may introduce it or look to it in the guise of equitable doctrines (such as "unclean hands"). While that would be problematic and unprincipled, counsel should be aware of it and use the same education (and, sometimes, avoidance of introduction of gender identity or transgender status) discussed in Section 5.3, below.

5.3 Practice Recommendations

5.3.1 Defensive and Offensive References to Transgender Identity in Divorce and Dissolution Cases

5.3.1.1 Defensive

Because the court does not typically have to find or specify how much one factor weighs over any other, it is difficult to predict how influential fault-based arguments based on the fact of a spouse's transgender identity may be, particularly where there are other facts that support fault-based grounds for the non-transgender spouse (such as infidelity, for example).

Practice recommendations for addressing the non-transgender spouse's use of her/his spouse's gender identity or gender transition fall into the defensive and offensive categories. On the defensive side, counsel is well-advised to present significant evidence, whether in the form of an expert report (or testimony) or personal testimony, to explain why neither the transgender spouse's failure to come to consciousness about her/his transgender identity nor her/his failure to transition prior to the marriage is in any way evidence of fault, maliciousness, or deception. Counsel may need to provide significant information to explain that, rather, such facts are an understandable and predictable outcome based on social and cultural biases and prejudices against transgender people.

In strategically determining what experts, if any, should testify, counsel should keep in mind the scope and limits of the client's patient-physician and patient-psychotherapist privileges and discuss the appropriateness of waiving any such privileges. One way to avoid having the client waive any of these privileges is to hire an expert solely for the purposes of litigation who has no prior relationship with the client. Counsel should remind the client that communications, if any, between the client and the expert are not confidential.

The way in which this argument may develop will differ, obviously, on a case-by-case basis and is factually specific. However, in all cases, the attorney should assemble facts to explain several basic principles to a court. First, counsel should establish that gender identity, the internalized sense of who a person is as male or female is a deep-seated core element of human identity.[24] Everyone has a gender identity. For most people, their gender identity is consistent with their assigned birth sex as well as with the expectation that society has on whether a person is male or female based on their anatomy and physiology. For transgender people, that is not the case.[25] Transgender people have a deep, internalized sense of themselves as male or female or some combination of both that is inconsistent with their assigned birth sex or anatomy and physiology.[26]

A second key fact to establish is that gender identity is established in most people by a very young age, as early as two years old.[27] Because it is so deep-seated, a person's gender identity is impervious to change and unaffected, once it is established, by external influences such as culture or society.[28] However, because there is such bias and stigma against transgender people in our society (indeed across most contemporary cultures), most young people with a cross-gender identification quickly learn to suppress or try to change their gender identity.[29] Like gay or lesbian youth who learn that being public about their sexual orientation will cause them to face bullying, ostracism, and violence, many transgender people soon learn from family members, school personnel, and peers, that expressing a gender identity that does not match others' expectations of them may subject them to scorn, ridicule, harassment, discrimination, and even violence.[30]

This message for most transgender people is so loud and so clear that many actually, for a time, become alienated from their own gender identity, often taking steps to embrace or affirm a gender identity that is not their own.[31] Some people can live functionally for a time in this way. However, because a person's gender identity cannot be changed simply by force of will or in reaction to negative cultural reinforcement, such persons typically find themselves expressing their gender identity only in private or in smaller, controlled environments where they are not denigrated or ostracized. Sometimes that means privately attending a support group, keeping that fact concealed even from a spouse or partner. Other times, it may mean secretly wearing clothes appropriate for someone of a different sex, here again concealing that information even from a spouse or partner. It is this effort on the part of transgender persons to create a safe place in which to express their cross-gender gender identity that is often used by the non-transgender spouse to attempt to demonstrate that the transgender spouse was in some way deceptive or fraudulent.[32]

Being able to put such conduct or prior history during the marital relationship into a proper framework that gives it context may be essential to many transgender clients' cases. Providing such background and information is also essential to humanize the litigant and her/his experience for a court, many of which have never had a transgender litigant before it. Counsel should assume that most judges will share the negative bias and stereotypes about transgender people that are commonly represented in the media. Expert or personal testimony that lays out the fundamental points described above may be essential to disabuse the court of unfounded assumptions as well as conscious and unconscious bias.

5.3.1.2 Offensive

On the offensive side, the fact of a soon-to-be former spouse being transgender may need to be taken into account in considering how statutory factors such as age and station in life or future financial vulnerability impact legal issues such as spousal support or equitable property distribution. Strategically, counsel may want to consider introducing the fact of her/his client being transgender before the other party has the opportunity to do so. In other cases, that choice may not be wise.

Where the transgender spouse can anticipate that the fact of her/his transgender identity or gender transition will be introduced to the court by either party, the attorney for the transgender spouse should be prepared to do a significant amount of education with the court in order to neutralize the non-transgender spouse's manipulation of the client's transgender identity or gender transition. Some of the ways to do so are described in Section 5.3.1.1, above.

The other ways in which the offensive use of a transgender client's identity can be redressed is to explain to a court the costs, financial and societal, that will likely be born by a transgender person. In most jurisdictions under an equitable distribution standard, items such as future medical costs and likelihood of employment may be taken into account in determining property distribution as well as future support or maintenance. Counsel for transgender litigants may need to introduce evidence relating to those predictable costs of medical care and societal discrimination. While facts relating to these costs may be introduced by testimony of the transgender client, they will be given more weight if introduced by an expert whether by report or testimony.

On the financial side, gender transition-related medical care can be expensive. Gender transition-related surgeries can range from several thousand dollars, to the tens of thousands, up to over a hundred thousand dollars for some people.[33] Hormone therapy, as well, is a life-long expense that, while not as expensive as surgery, can add up significantly over a lifetime.[34] In addition, for most people, such medical expenses are often paid out-of-pocket because gender transition-related medical care is not typically covered by either private or public insurance plans.[35] Gender transition-related medical care is an essential health care matter[36] which if not properly obtained can lead to serious medical consequences including self-harm or death.[37] Most courts will need careful explanation to understand that transition-related health care for a transgender person is the equivalent of, for example, the ongoing and significant medical costs for a person with Type I diabetes. To the extent that any of the standards applied by a court in the divorce or dissolution context take into account future medical expenses (whether for property or alimony/support awards), transition-related medical expenses must, of course, be considered for a transgender litigant.

Like the costs of medical care, costs of societal discrimination against transgender people may also be taken into account under equitable standards in the form of factors such as "station in life," future employment practices, and the like. Many courts will be unaware that transgender people face massive discrimination in employment, housing, and lending. A recent study by the National Gay and Lesbian Task Force and the National Center for Transgender Equality showed that transgender respondents experienced underemployment at twice the rate of the general population.[38] Ninety percent experienced harassment, mistreatment, or discrimination at the workplace, and forty-seven percent reported having an adverse job outcome, such as being fired, not hired, or denied a promotion, on account of being transgender or gender nonconforming. Nineteen percent of respondents reported having been refused a home or apartment, while eleven percent reported having been evicted because of their gender identity or expression.[39]

The reality is that for many transgender people, gender transition means that they will be either unemployed or underemployed for the duration of their lives as well as face challenges in securing housing and sometimes credit. Obviously, these facts have a very real impact on future earnings and, in many cases, should be taken into account in determining equitable property awards as well as future obligations of support, alimony, or rehabilitation.

5.3.2 Cases in Which to Avoid Any Reference to Transgender Identity

Notwithstanding the very real potential negative financial consequences gender transition may have, the fact of bias in and out of the judicial system means that it may not always be advantageous to affirmatively introduce the facts of a person's gender identity or transgender status in a divorce or dissolution case. The potential adverse impact of introducing such information must be weighed against the potential benefit and should also take into account the likelihood of such information being introduced by the non-transgender spouse.

The set of cases in which it may be better not to introduce any information relating to the spouse's transgender gender identity are those in which the marriage did not result in any children and the non-transgender spouse does not know of the fact of the transgender spouse's gender identity. In such cases, which typically only involve property distribution and/or spousal support, the likely bias against the transgender spouse will usually outweigh almost any conceivable benefit such information relating to the transgender spouse's gender identity could have in a case.

For example, consider a case involving only issues of property distribution where the non-transgender spouse does not know or is not likely to introduce facts regarding the transgender spouse's gender identity. While it is conceivable, and maybe even just and equitable, to argue that the transgender spouse will be facing future significant medical costs relating to gender transition that should be taken into account under equitable distribution of assets principles, the fact of the intended gender transition is likely to introduce so much bias into the assessment that, on balance, it should probably be avoided.

In one case, a transgender spouse was denied spousal support sought in order to have funds available for pending surgical sex reassignment, on the grounds that the litigant was at fault for the dissolution of the marriage.[40] While the court cited a pattern of misconduct on the part of the transgender spouse, including physical and emotional harassment of the non-transgender spouse, it concluded that these actions, "together with petitioner's consummation of the alteration of petitioner's sexual characteristics constituted a course of conduct 'of such character as to render the condition of any woman of *ordinary sensibility* and *delicacy of feeling* intolerable and her life burdensome.'"[41] Evidence of bias was rampant in the opinion.[42]

Similarly, even though a transgender spouse can undoubtedly anticipate facing employment discrimination that may well negatively impact earnings and earning potential, the expected bias the transgender spouse can anticipate facing in the court system by the introduction of her/his gender identity, in most cases, far outweighs any likely positive benefit from introduction of such facts.

In such cases, the transgender client is well-advised to make every effort to keep facts relating to her/his gender identity from being disclosed until final resolution of the divorce. Because orders relating to property distribution are not modifiable once final, subsequent disclosure of the transgender identity should not impact any such orders.

The exception to such guidance is the set of cases in which there are child custody, visitation, and child support issues involved at the outset. In such cases, because the fact of the parent's (or stepparent's) gender identity or gender transition will become apparent at some point in the future, regardless, and could be grounds for changed circumstances and thereby the basis for attempted modifications to a parenting plan, such facts are better disclosed sooner rather than later. Obviously, counsel will have to make an assessment on a case-by-case basis as to the wisdom of such guidance.

---

1   Because many divorces involving transgender clients risk the exposure of personal, private, and sometimes medical information about a party, counsel is urged to consider mechanisms to protect against public access to such information. Such mechanisms include motions to seal, impound, or proceed with case names using initials or pseudonyms. Facts to support such requests may include data regarding risks of discrimination and violence that transgender people face.

2   Stacey "Colt" Meier et al., Can a Romantic Relationship Survive a Gender Transition?: Examining the Romantic Relationships of Female to Male (FTM) Trans Men, Presentation at the Ass'n of Behav. & Cognitive Therapies Annual Convention (Nov. 2010) (poster on file with Gay & Lesbian Advocates & Defenders).

3   *Id.*

4   Jaime M. Grant et al., Nat'l Ctr. for Transgender Equal. & Nat'l Gay & Lesbian Task Force, Injustice at Every Turn: A Report of the National Transgender Discrimination Survey 95 (2011), *available at* http://www.thetaskforce.org/downloads/reports/reports/ntds_full.pdf.

5   *See* Morin v. Morin, No. 2006-418, 2007 WL 5313306 (Vt. May 2007).

6   *See, e.g.,* Kantaras v. Kantaras, 884 So.2d 155 (Fla. Dist. Ct. App. 2004); *In re* Marriage of Simmons, 825 N.E.2d 303 (Ill. App. Ct. 2005); M.T. v. J.T., 355 A.2d 204 (N.J. Super. Ct. App. Div. 1976).

7   *See, e.g., In re* Marriage of Joy & John R., No. E039132, 2007 WL 2319143 (Cal. Ct. App. Aug. 15, 2007) (court granted jointly-stipulated request for annulment because petitioner, at inception of marriage, did not meet local rule for gender transition and the marriage was thus not a valid one at the outset).

8   Anonymous v. Anonymous, 325 N.Y.S.2d 499 (N.Y. Sup. Ct. 1971).

9   *Id.* at 501.

10 *Id.*

11 Frances B. v. Mark B., 355 N.Y.S.2d 712 (N.Y. Sup. Ct.1974).

12 Steinke v. Steinke, 357 A.2d 674 (Pa. Super. Ct. 1975).

13 *Id.* at 676.

14 Vicas v. Vicas, No. FA 980076120S, 1999 WL 512673, at *1 (Conn. Super. Ct. July 8, 1999).

15 McKolanis v. McKolanis, 644 A.2d 1256 (Pa. Super. Ct. 1994).

16 *Id.* at 1257.

17 *Id.* at 1259.

18 *Id.*

19 *See* Mass. Gen. Laws ch. 208, § 34. *See also* Colo. Rev. Stat. § 14-10-113; Conn. Gen. Stat. § 46b-81; Del. Code Ann. tit. 13, § 1513; 750 Ill. Comp. Stat. 5/503; Md. Code Ann., Fam. Law § 8-205; Nev. Rev. Stat. § 125.150; N.H. Rev. Stat. Ann. § 458:16-a; N.Y. Dom. Rel. Law § 236; N.C. Gen. Stat. § 50-20; Ohio Rev. Code Ann. § 3105.171; 23 Pa. Cons. Stat. § 3502; R.I. Gen. Laws § 15-5-16.1; Tenn. Code Ann. § 36-4-121; Vt. Stat. Ann. tit. 15, § 751; Va. Code Ann. § 20-107.3.

20 The reference to marriage in this sentence includes lawfully recognized civil marriage and marriage equivalents such as civil unions or domestic partnerships and includes both formal (statutory) and informal (common law marriage).

21 *See In re* Marriage of Lindsey, 678 P.2d 328, 331 (Wash. 1984) ("[W]e adopt the rule that courts must 'examine the [meretricious] relationship and the property accumulations and make a just and equitable disposition of the property.'") (quoting Latham v. Hennessey, 554 P.2d 1057, 1059 (Wash. 1976)).

22 *See* Marvin v. Marvin, 557 P.2d 106 (Cal. 1976).

23 *See, e.g.*, Hanselman v. Shepardson, No. 94 Civ. 4132, 1996 WL 99377 (S.D.N.Y. Mar. 7, 1996); Bramlett v. Selman, 597 S.W.2d 80 (Ark. 1980); Seward v. Mentrup, 622 N.E.2d 756 (Ohio Ct. App. 1993); Doe v. Burkland, 808 A.2d 1090 (R.I. 2002); Doe v. Roe, 475 S.E.2d 783 (S.C. Ct. App. 1996); Zaremba v. Cliburn, 949 S.W.2d 822 (Tex. Ct. App. 1997).

24 *See, e.g.*, Suzanne J. Kessler & Wendy McKenna, Gender: An Ethnomethodological Approach 8–11 (1978); John Money, *Gender Role, Gender Identity, Core Gender Identity: Usage and Definition of Terms*, 1 J. Am. Acad. Psychoanalysis 397 (1973).

25 *See, e.g.*, C.M. Cole et al., *Treatment of Gender Dysphoria*, 90 Tex. Med. 68 (1994).

26 *See, e.g., In re* Heilig, 816 A.2d 68, 76 (Md. 2003) ("The medical community's experience with patients born with ambiguous genitalia has led many researchers to believe that the brain 'differentiates' *in utero* to one gender or the other and

that, once the child's brain has differentiated, that child cannot be made into a person of the other gender simply through surgical alterations."). *See generally* STEPHANIE BRILL & RACHEL PEPPER, THE TRANSGENDER CHILD: A HANDBOOK FOR FAMILIES AND PROFESSIONALS 12–15 (2008).

27   *See, e.g.,* M.T. v. J.T., 355 A.2d at 205 (in which expert testified that there was "'very little disagreement' on the fact that gender identity generally is established 'very, very firmly, almost immediately, by the age of 3 to 4 years'"); Doe v. McConn, 489 F. Supp. 76, 78 (S.D. Tex. 1980) (finding that the general consensus among experts is that gender identity is established "very early, before the child is capable of elective choice in the matter"). *See also* BRILL & PEPPER, *supra* note 26, at 61–71.

28   *See, e.g.,* Heilig, 816 A.2d at 78 (noting that "transsexualism is universally recognized as inherent, rather than chosen"); BRILL & PEPPER, *supra* note 26, at 4; Gerald P. Mallon, *Practice with Transgendered Children, in* SOCIAL SERVICES WITH TRANSGENDERED YOUTH 49, 55–58 (Gerald P. Mallon ed., 1999); Robert J. Stoller, *The Sense of Maleness*, 34 Psychoanalytic Q. 207 (1965).

29   *See, e.g.,* BRILL & PEPPER, *supra* note 26, at 63–65.

30   *See, e.g.,* GIANNA E. ISRAEL & DONALD E. TARVER II, TRANSGENDER CARE: RECOMMENDED GUIDELINES, PRACTICAL INFORMATION, AND PERSONAL ACCOUNTS 37 (1998); JOSEPH G. KOSCIW ET AL., GAY, LESBIAN & STRAIGHT EDUC. NETWORK, THE 2007 NATIONAL SCHOOL CLIMATE SURVEY: THE EXPERIENCES OF LESBIAN, GAY, BISEXUAL AND TRANSGENDER YOUTH IN OUR NATION'S SCHOOLS 25–26, 29–32 (2008), *available at* http://www.glsen.org/binary-data/GLSEN_ATTACH-MENTS/file/000/001/1290-1.pdf; Barbara Fedders, *Coming Out for Kids: Recognizing, Respecting, and Representing LGBTQ Youth*, 6 NEV. L.J. 774, 787–99 (2006).

31   *See, e.g.,* RANDI ETTNER, GENDER LOVING CARE: A GUIDE TO COUNSELING GENDER-VARIANT CLIENTS 101–06 (1999).

32   *See id.*

33   *See* Jody Marksamer & Dylan Vade, *Recommendations for Transgender Healthcare,* TRANSGENDER LAW CENTER, http://www.transgenderlaw.org/resources/tlchealth.htm (last visited Sept. 26, 2011) ("Hormones cost approximately $100 per month. Therapy is about $100 per session. Surgeries typically cost between $7,000 and $50,000; some phalloplasties can cost upward of $100,000.").

34   *See id.*

35   *See, e.g.,* Medicare Program, General Notice of National Coverage Decisions, 54 Fed. Reg. 34555, 34572 (Aug. 21, 1989); 130 MASS. CODE REGS. 405.418 ("MassHealth does not pay a CHC for performing, administering, or dispensing experimental, unproven, or otherwise medically unnecessary procedures or treatments, specifically including, but not limited to, sex-reassignment surgery, thyroid cartilage reduction and any other related surgeries and treatments including pre- and post-sex-reassignment surgery hormone therapy."); Dean Spade, *Documenting Gender,* 59 HASTINGS L.J. 731, 755 (2008) ("Finally, genital surgeries are more expensive pro-

cedures than other options, and are still not covered by a majority of private insurance or Medicaid programs in the United States."). The American Medical Association recently denounced such unprincipled insurance exclusions and some private insurance companies, such as Aetna and Cigna, have begun to introduce inclusive plans. *See* Am. Med. Ass'n House of Delegates, Resolution 122: Removing Financial Barriers to Care for Transgender Patients (2008), *available at* https://ssl3.ama-assn.org/apps/ecomm/PolicyFinderForm.pl?site=www.ama-assn.org&uri=%2fresources%2fdoc%2fPolicyFinder%2fpolicyfiles%2fHnE%2fH-185.950.HTM *and on file with author.* Some major companies, including Coca Cola and Morgan Stanley, have also recently announced that they will cover transition-related care. *See* Lisa Leef, *Transgender Surgery Covered by Growing Number of U.S. Companies*, Associated Press, Feb. 21, 2011, *available at* http://www.huffingtonpost.com/2011/02/22/transgender-surgery-cover_n_826385.html.

36   *See* The Harry Benjamin Int'l Gender Dysphoria Ass'n, Standards of Care for Gender Identity Disorders (7th ed. 2011), *available at* http://www.wpath.org/documents/Standards%20of%20Care%20V7%20-%202011%20WPATH.pdf; Clarification on Medical Necessity of Treatment, Sex Reassignment, and Insurance Coverage for Transgender and Transsexual People Worldwide, World Prof'l Ass'n for Transgender Health (June 17, 2008), *available at* http://www.wpath.org/medical_necessity_statement.cfm.

37   *See, e.g.*, De'Lonta v. Angelone, 330 F.3d 630, 634–35 (4th Cir. 2003) (in which inmate needed protection against compulsive self-mutilation following cessation of her hormone therapy for GID); Sundstrom v. Frank, No. 06-C-112, 2007 WL 3046240, at *3 n.4 (E.D. Wis. Oct.15, 2007) ("Some ... individuals suffer so profoundly without effective GID treatment that they mutilate their own genitals"). *See also* George R. Brown, *Transvestism and Gender Identity Disorder in Adults, in* Gabbard's Treatments of Psychiatric Disorders 2007 (Glen O. Gabbard ed., Am. Psychiatric Publishing 4th ed. 2007).

38   Jaime M. Grant et al., Nat'l Ctr. for Transgender Equal. & Nat'l Gay & Lesbian Task Force, Injustice at Every Turn: A Report of the National Transgender Discrimination Survey 3 (2011), *available at* http://www.thetaskforce.org/downloads/reports/reports/ntds_full.pdf.

39   *Id.* at 4.

40   *See* Phillips v. Plotkin, 12 Pa. D. & C.3d 54 (Pa. Com. Pl. 1979).

41   *Id.* at 64 (quoting Commonwealth *ex rel.* Whitney v. Whitney, 50 A. 2d 732, 734 (Pa. Super. Ct. 1947)).

42   *See, e.g., id.* at 60 ("'Every so often a judge finds his legal sense overwhelmed by common sense.' So in the case before us, our *common sense* immediately declared the result: petition denied.") (quoting Steinke v. Steinke, 357 A. 2d 674, 678 (Pa. Super. Ct. 1975)); *id.* at 62 ("Did not petitioner fraudulently represent himself to be a normal heterosexual male at the time he induced respondent to enter into the marriage contract?").

Chapter 6: Parental Rights After Relationship Dissolution

Patience Crozier

Introduction

Disputes about parental rights and responsibilities involving a transgender parent require sensitivity and careful advocacy. Although the legal standards should be the same for transgender clients as for all other clients, the reality is that transgender parents often face discrimination from their former partners and/or from the legal system, and family law attorneys must be prepared to address these challenges. This chapter provides practical guidance for family law attorneys who are helping transgender clients with parenting plans and rights after relationship dissolution. The chapter first explains legal parentage, because the client's parental status is key to her/his rights and obligations regarding custody, visitation, and support. Next, the chapter discusses the best interests of the child standard as it relates to transgender parents, including research on transgender parents and a discussion of the discrimination transgender parents frequently encounter in child custody disputes. Finally, the chapter describes some methods of responding to and challenging the discrimination in the legal system.

6.1 Parental Status

In most circumstances, creating a parenting plan for a child following parental separation is a straightforward determination of the child's best interests. Unfortunately, the analysis often starts elsewhere when one parent is transgender, frequently focusing first on the transgender person's legal parental status. An attorney must assess whether the client has a legal relationship to the child or whether the client will have to resort to equitable claims to assert parental rights. A checklist of facts potentially relevant to determining the client's legal relationship with the child and the status of the other parent or parents is essential so that the attorney can gather the facts needed to appropriately advise the client.[1]

Legal parentage provides the most secure and privileged status in regard to parental rights and responsibilities. A legal parent has a fundamental constitutional right to the care and custody of her/his child.[2] Given that constitutional right, when facing claims from a party who is not a legal parent, a legal parent's rights and wishes will generally prevail, unless the party seeking access to the child proves that the legal parent is unfit to parent that particular child[3] or that special circumstances, including harm to the child, warrant protecting her/his relationship with someone who is a parent-in-fact.[4] As discussed in greater detail in Chapter 4, legal parentage can be established in various ways, depending on the law of the state.

First, biology or genetics is usually a basis for legal parentage, though not in every circumstance.[5] Second, legal parentage can also be established through court orders like adoption or pre-birth orders.[6] Third, presumptions of parentage may apply for children born into a legal spousal relationship such as a marriage, civil union, or registered domestic partnership. These presumptions vary and may be rebutted by biology or genetics in some instances. Fourth, in some states, receiving a child into one's home and holding the child out as a "natural" child establishes parentage.[7] Legal parentage is determined by state law, and every state differs as to how legal parentage is established. As such, it is critical to review closely the particular state statutes and cases as they relate to presumptions of parentage, paternity, maternity, and adoption to determine whether a client is a legal parent.

Transgender parents who have a child to whom they are related by blood or adoption should have an unchallengeable legal parental relationship to those children. Transgender parents who have had children born during their legal spousal relationship to whom they are not biologically related or whom they have not adopted may face challenges to their parental status by hostile former spouses disavowing the lawfulness of the spousal relationship. Those challenges should fail in states that have removed sex as an eligibility requirement for a spousal relationship[8] but may be more complicated elsewhere. If a parent's relationship with the child is contingent on recognition of a spousal relationship, the practitioner should assess whether the state will recognize the validity of that relationship.[9]

Even if a client is not a legal parent, that client may still have an equitable claim for parentage.[10] Equitable parentage claims arise because a client has developed a parent-child relationship, with the consent of the legal parent, such that it is in the child's best interests to continue having a relationship with the equitable parent.[11] In states where equitable parentage is recognized,[12] it exists to avoid harm to a child that may come from severing the child's ties with a person who has acted as a parent to that child.[13] It is the protection of that significant relationship and the legal parent's role in consenting to and supporting its formation that allow a claim for equitable parentage to overcome the legal parent's right to control who may have custody of or visitation with the child.[14] The law governing these claims, the standard for demonstrating the existence of the equitable parent-child relationship, and the scope of parental rights and responsibilities available to an equitable parent are state specific.

In some states, these equitable claims are governed by statute, while others rely on the general equity powers of the courts to protect children.[15] In addition, beyond the existence of the parent-child bond and the role of the legal parent in supporting its development, what a party must show to have standing to bring an equitable claim for parentage varies but often requires the party to have provided substantial direct parental caretaking for the child for a significant period of time.[16] In terms of scope of remedy once equitable parentage is established, some states limit equitable parents to visitation; other states consider equitable parents equally eligible for both custody and support obligations.[17]

If a client will be relying on equitable arguments, an attorney must conduct a detailed intake to understand the client's day-to-day involvement in caretaking and decision making for the child. Detailed background is critical to prepare the pleadings so that the client demonstrates standing as an equitable parent and can survive a legal parent's motion to dismiss any claim for custody or visitation. Often with equitable claims, a parent must make a preliminary showing of fact beyond the general notice pleading standard.[18] A client asserting equitable claims must be counseled early on that such litigation is often hotly contested and, therefore, expensive, intrusive, and stressful. Clients will need to access all available support—emotional, financial, and logistical—to see the litigation through to the end.

Establishing the parental status of both the client and any other adults claiming parental rights is critical to determining next steps and the analysis that is relevant to the claim. Allocations of parental rights and responsibilities between legal parents are assessed under a best interests of the child standard to determine an appropriate parenting plan for the child and what amount of child support, if any, is due to be paid. For an equitable parent, the assessment will be two-tiered and will be, first, whether the parent can establish herself/himself as an equitable parent, and, second, what allocation of parental rights and responsibilities will serve the child's best interests. In either circumstance, once everyone's legal status is clear, best interests of the child controls.

6.2 Best Interests of the Child Standard

If legal parents cannot agree on a legal and physical custody and visitation arrangement, then the "best interests of the child" standard is the guiding principle for resolving the conflict. The "best interests of the child" standard is fact-intensive and subjective.[19] The standard is a "twentieth century legal construct intended as a gender-neutral standard for determining child custody" and is the prevalent test utilized by courts today.[20]

When one parent seeks to modify a parenting plan or custody judgment or order, the standard differs and is somewhat more stringent. To succeed in a modification action, the parent seeking the modification must show there has been a material and substantial change in circumstances and that a modification is necessary to serve the child's best interests. Although the best interests test remains central, the modification standard is two-pronged, and the modification often fails on the first prong which requires proof of a material and substantial change in circumstances.[21] Some courts, in practice, conflate these two steps into one—a kind of heightened best interests review.

Whether in an initial allocation of parental rights and responsibilities or in a complaint for modification, for a factor to be relevant to the best interests analysis, it should relate to someone's ability to parent. A parent's gender identity, transgender status, or other identity characteristic does not relate to parenting ability.[22] The American Law Institute's *Principles of Family Law Dissolution* states explicitly that courts should be prohibited from considering certain factors in creating a parenting plan; one of those factors is the sex of a parent.[23] In addition, personal characteristics or conduct having no relation to the ability to care for the child should not be considered.[24]

Therefore, whether a parent is transgender or has a nonconforming gender identity or expression has no legitimate place in a best interests of the child analysis.[25] This conclusion is supported by the reported empirical research, which, though scant, consistently demonstrates that there is no nexus between transgender identity and the ability to parent.[26] Children of transgender parents "can and do accept their parents' transgender identities and thrive in their family relationships."[27] Richard Green conducted research on children of transgender parents in 1978 and again in 1998. He acknowledged that social opposition to transgender parents continuing in a parenting role during or after gender transition was strong, particularly at the time of his first study. He theorized that such opposition had three bases: (1) concerns that children will become confused in their own gender identity; (2) concern that children will be teased and ostracized; and (3) feelings of betrayal and hostility of the non-transgender parent. In the 1978 study, which followed sixteen children being raised by transgender parents, he concluded that "[a]vailable evidence does not support concerns that a parent's transsexualism directly adversely impacts" their children.[28] In 1998, he updated his study by interviewing eighteen children of transgender parents. He concluded that none of the children had gender identity disorder and that they reported no clinically significant cross-gender behavior. He determined that teasing was no more a problem for these children than the teasing that children generally experience. "Available evidence does not support concerns that a parent's transsexualism directly adversely impacts on the children."[29] In fact, "transsexual parents can remain effective parents and . . . children can understand and empathize with their transsexual parent."[30]

Thus, it is important for a transgender parent's advocate to understand and, if necessary, to convince the court that transgender parents are not flawed parents and do not harm their children by virtue of their transgender identity.[31] Transgender parents may, like all other parents, have shortcomings, but their transgender status is not a relevant factor for a best interests analysis. In families where a parent transitions after marriage, divorce sometimes ensues, and it may seem difficult to parse the effects of separation and divorce from the effects, if any, of the parent's transition.[32] It is the advocate's job to help the court make this necessary distinction. Research shows that it is harmful for children to be subjected to a high-conflict divorce or relationship dissolution and that children are healthier when there is a positive relationship between their two parents.[33] This research suggests that it is important to ensure continuing ties between a transgender parent and child and to stop antagonistic, alienating behavior by the other parent as soon as possible. Most courts will need to be educated to understand that the non-transgender spouse's hostility toward the transgender spouse's gender transition heightens parental conflict thereby negatively impacting the child. Regardless of how negatively the non-transgender spouse (or judicial system, for that matter) may regard gender transition or transgender people, the reality is that the child has a transgender parent. As a result, a key to ensuring the mental health and positive adjustment of the child—factors central to the best interests inquiry—is to create an environment supportive of the child's acceptance of the parent's transgender status.

6.3 Confronting Discrimination Against Transgender Parents in Custody/Visitation Determinations

Transgender parents frequently face discrimination from their former partners and the court system when their parental rights are in dispute.[34] Discrimination in custody determinations is particularly common for transgender parents of color.[35] According to the recently published National Transgender Discrimination Survey, thirty-eight percent of the more than 6,000 transgender respondents identified as parents.[36] Twenty-nine percent of the respondents with children experienced a former partner limiting their contact with their children.[37] Thirteen percent of respondents with children reported that courts limited or stopped their relationships with their children, and Black, Asian, and multiracial respondents experienced the highest rates of such court interference.[38] This data comports with the published case law as well, with some courts appropriately refusing to discriminate against transgender parents and others actively doing so.

6.3.1 Good Case Law: Examples of Courts' Appropriate Treatment of a Parent's Transgender Status

There are cases wherein courts reject the discriminatory bait. For instance, in *Summers-Horton v. Horton*, a trial court awarded primary custody of children to a father who "had a history of cross dressing as a woman to achieve sexual gratification."[39] The mother tried to argue that the father's crossdressing meant she should have primary custody, but the appellate court affirmed the trial court's judgment.[40]

The case of *Christian v. Randall* demonstrates an appellate court stepping in to correct a grievous misapplication of the best interests of the child and modification standards.[41] In this case, a non-transgender parent sought to modify a custody order to gain primary custody of his four daughters following his former wife's transition and subsequent marriage to a woman. The trial court heard evidence that the children had a close and warm relationship with their transgender parent, that they were well cared for and provided with the necessities of life, that they were "happy, healthy, well-adjusted children who were doing well in school and who were active in community activities,"[42] and that they wanted to remain in their transgender parent's care.[43] The trial court, however, transferred custody to the non-transgender parent, basing its conclusion that a change of custody was in the best interests of the children because of the custodial parent's gender transition.[44] The appeals court reversed and denied the non-transgender parent's request for a transfer of custody, noting that there was no evidence to support the transfer of custody and that it is improper for a court to consider the conduct of a custodian that does not affect her/his relationship with the child.[45] The trial court had abused its discretion, and the modification was vacated. While it was vindication for the transgender parent, such vindication came at an extremely high price in terms of legal fees and stress given the trial court's initial ruling.

In *Pierre v. Pierre*, an appellate court again corrected the improper termination of a transgender parent's parental rights.[46] The children's father transitioned prior to his marriage, and he and his wife had two children together using alternative insemination.[47] The parents divorced after eight years of marriage and agreed to joint custody of their children.[48] Subsequently, the non-transgender parent sought a modification, requesting that the transgender parent's parental rights be terminated and that he have no contact with their children.[49] The trial court terminated the transgender parent's rights but determined that continued visitation with the transgender parent was in the children's best interests.[50] The non-transgender parent appealed, arguing that the trial court could not order visitation when it terminated the transgender parent's parental rights.[51] The appellate court vacated the termination of the transgender parent's parental rights, finding that the court lacked jurisdiction under the circumstances to terminate parental rights and further noting that even if a marriage is a nullity it does not follow that there is authority to terminate parental rights.[52] The appellate court, constrained by the posture of the case, affirmed the visitation order but noted that there had been no material and substantial change in circumstances and that the transgender parent should have maintained joint custody.[53] This case is a sad demonstration of the great lengths a parent went to in order to eliminate a transgender parent from the children's lives. It also demonstrates the importance of having a competent advocate at every step of the process to avoid unnecessary constraints on parenting rights.

6.3.2 Bad Case Law: Examples of Discrimination Against a Transgender Parent

Despite the positive case law, an attorney needs to always be vigilant of potential bias as shown by cases, published and unpublished, that illustrate discrimination against transgender parents. In *M.B. v. D.W.* an appeals court affirmed an adoption of a child by a stepparent over the objection of the child's transgender parent and concurrently terminated the transgender parent's parental rights.[54] The transgender parent transitioned after a divorce that awarded her joint custody of the parties' two minor children. But when the other parent and her new spouse sought for the spouse to adopt the children—a proceeding that would effectively terminate the transgender parent's rights—the court granted the adoption.[55] The trial court found that the children suffered "emotional harm" due to the parent's transition and due to not being told about the transition prior to a visit with the transgender parent.[56] As a result, the trial court found there was adequate evidence to terminate the transgender parent's parental rights.[57] The appeals court affirmed. Despite the appellate court's efforts to reject a discriminatory motive as the basis for the decision, the transgender parent's rights appear to have been terminated based on improper factors and more could have been done to educate and support the children rather than to irreversibly terminate the parent's rights. This opinion underscores why it is advisable for a transgender parent to have expert therapeutic support guiding her/his decisions on how best to inform child(ren) post-divorce of a gender transition.

Some hostile courts have emphasized the adult burden transgender parents are allegedly placing on their children. In *B. v. B.*, a New York appellate court affirmed a denial of a father's request to expand his visitation to include overnights, siding with the mother who was concerned that father was not a good role model because of his "history of cross dressing."[58] In the terse opinion, the appeals court affirmed the trial court's determination not to expand visitation between the father and his "impressionable child."[59] In an unpublished Connecticut case, a trial court kept custody of two children with their transgender parent but repeatedly mentioned the "heavy burden" that the children would face due to the transgender parent's "adult choice."[60] The trial court ordered the children to continue in counseling, suggesting that the counseling was necessary to ensure their appropriate adjustment to puberty.[61]

Other courts have relied on baseless assertions of harm to a child from interacting with transgender parents. In *Cisek v. Cisek*, an appellate court substituted its judgment for the judgment of the trial court, forcing a modification to end the visitation of a transgender parent.[62] In that case, the parties divorced and agreed at the time of divorce that the mother would have primary custody and that the father would have visitation.[63] Following divorce, the father transitioned.[64] The non-transgender parent continued to allow visitation for a time but then refused any visitation for the transgender parent.[65] After numerous hearings at the trial court, the court denied the non-transgender parent's attempts to terminate visitation, and the non-transgender parent appealed.[66] On appeal, the court reversed. The appellate court noted some testimony by the non-transgender parent that the children had been "confused."[67] The appellate court further relied on testimony from a doctor saying that it was "his opinion that the transsexualism of the appellee would have a sociopathic effect on the child" and that "physical contact should be stopped."[68] The appellate court articulated that it was "bothered by these negative medical opinions" and that there was evidence that there "might be mental harm [to the child]. Common sense dictates that there can be social harm [to the child]."[69] The appellate court faulted the transgender parent for presenting no evidence of the reason for the gender transition and asked whether "his sex change [was] simply an indulgence of some fantasy?"[70] Finding that there had been a substantial change in circumstances, the appellate court terminated the transgender parent's visitation.[71] This opinion highlights the importance of presenting expert testimony to educate the court and the reality that courts sometimes do make judgments based on assumptions about societal discrimination and status rather than on factors that actually impact the children's best interests.

6.3.3 Combating Restrictive Orders and Requirements Regarding Parenting

Even when a transgender or gender nonconforming parent succeeds in gaining custody or visitation of her/his children, some courts have required that a parent hide or deny their identity or status. For example, in a Minnesota case, an appellate court affirmed a trial court transfer of custody to a father who was a "transvestite."[72] The trial court transferred custody of a child to a father after a mother lost custody of the child to the state foster care system and was found to have physically and sexually abused the child.[73] After changing custody to the father, there was "a dramatic [positive] change in the child's well-being."[74] Despite the child's marked improvement in the father's care, the court apparently believed it had to justify affirming the custody order despite the father being transgender because it noted the father's efforts to hide his gender nonconformity from the child.[75] With approval, the court noted that the father ensured the daughter did not see him dressed as a woman, did not receive or keep "transvestite literature" in the home, and planned to tell her about his transgender identity with a therapist when she was old enough to be told.[76] This dicta suggests that the father's gender nonconformity was, in the court's view, comparable to the mother's proven unfitness and abusiveness, an unfounded and unprincipled view. That the father was a "transvestite" should not have factored into either court's custody analysis.

If a client faces such restrictions by the other parent or by the court, it is important to act swiftly to challenge them.[77] If another parent imposes improper restrictions and is not open to changing course or seeking professional advice to mediate the concerns of the transgender parent, then the transgender parent should seek court intervention as soon as possible so that the harmful restrictions do not become the default status quo. If it appears that a court is likely to impose restrictions[78] on a client's gender identity or expression, the attorney should consider requesting an evidentiary hearing in advance and should secure an expert to testify about transgender identity and the lack of nexus with parenting ability. The attorney should also prepare to offer witnesses who will discuss the status of the particular children in the case and dispel arguments that the children are being harmed by the parent's gender expression or identity. As explained in greater detail in Section 6.4, an attorney should also ensure that her/his transgender client has therapeutic support or parenting coaching to ensure that s/he is getting developmentally appropriate parenting advice. Attorneys should also research and prepare arguments about the client's constitutional rights to freedom of association and expression, rights to privacy and autonomy in personal matters, and rights to the care and custody of her/his children.[79]

6.3.4 Analogous Arguments: HIV/AIDS Status, Sexual Orientation, and Best Interests of the Child

In arguing for a transgender client to receive parental rights and responsibilities without unreasonable restrictions, it may be helpful for an attorney to refer to the analogous bodies of law regarding HIV/AIDS status or sexual orientation and parenting. During the height of the HIV/AIDS epidemic, opposing counsel utilized discriminatory and uninformed arguments to insist that HIV positive parents should not have custody of or parenting time with their children.[80] One court eloquently wrote: "Perhaps at no other time in recent history has there been an issue capable of causing such anxiety and fear. The potential for abuse in these instances is almost unlimited. Unfounded or cavalier accusations in this regard can cause the most severe and hostile consequences."[81]

Over time, however, the legal system recognized the impropriety of using a parent's HIV/AIDS status as a bar to parenting. For example, the American Bar Association's general policy, adopted in 1989 and 1990, recommends that evidence of HIV status is generally not admissible in a family law proceeding.[82] Pursuant to the ABA guidelines, evidence of HIV status may be considered in only limited circumstances and requires a preliminary showing that the evidence is relevant and probative of the issue in question. HIV status should be considered only in the same manner as other medical conditions to determine whether a parent is able to care for a particular child.[83] HIV/AIDS status is now well-established as irrelevant to determining the care and custody of children.[84] The case law relating to HIV/AIDS and parenting demonstrates the importance of resisting societal discrimination and insisting that a court focus on parenting ability rather than a parent's status or non-child-related conduct. Case law relating to lesbian, gay and bisexual parents highlights the same point.[85]

6.4 Practice Recommendations for Countering Discrimination Against a Transgender Parent Client

An attorney must be prepared to effectively challenge discrimination against transgender parents in the court system. At a minimum, an attorney should ensure that her/his transgender client is getting developmentally appropriate and child-centered parenting advice particularly around issues such as when and how to tell a child about a parent's gender transition. An attorney can request that the court appoint a guardian ad litem to investigate, evaluate, and report to the court on the children's best interests and appropriate parenting plans.[86] An attorney should be vigilant and proactive in discovery and evidentiary hearings to focus the case on the relevant issues and to protect her/his client from harassment because of the client's gender identity. Finally, if possible, an attorney should attempt to avoid court by supporting a client through alternative dispute resolution techniques like mediation. Each approach will be discussed in turn.

6.4.1 Parenting Advice

The end of a relationship is stressful, and the stress can be compounded by fear and concerns about parenting and parenting plans. Any parent in the process of a relationship dissolution would benefit from advice about how to best handle dissolution vis-à-vis her/his children. Transgender parents—particularly those who may transition following dissolution—should be encouraged to access developmentally appropriate parenting advice. Advice from a therapist who works with children and who has experience with transgender issues can be very helpful to advise a client about the best way to discuss change—including the relationship dissolution, separation, and/or a gender transition—with a child. Not only will this advice be helpful to the client in supporting a child, but the advice will also demonstrate to the court and to the other parent that the client is proactive about meeting the child's needs and will help rebut possible claims of harm to the child. It may also be helpful in countering any possible perception by the court or the other parent that the transgender parent is acting selfishly or putting her/his own needs ahead of those of the child relative to transitioning or telling the child about her/his transgender identity or status. In addition, courts often issue guidelines for parents in separation and require parenting classes. These resources are usually low-cost and should be accessed immediately upon separation.

6.4.2 Guardian Ad Litem

If there are competing claims for custody, an inability to resolve the claims by agreement, and a sense that the other parent is trying to make gender identity a central part of the custody dispute, it is wise to seek the appointment of a guardian ad litem (GAL) to investigate and report on what parenting plan is in the child's best interests.[87] In general, the investment in a reputable evaluative GAL will reap many rewards. A

GAL is able to examine the child's circumstances and needs in much greater depth than either of the parties or the court.

In selecting a GAL, it is critical to research potential GALs' experience in working with families involving a transgender parent and to make a specific recommendation to the court or agree with the other party on who should be appointed. One should never utilize a randomly selected GAL from a court list. No GAL is better than an unqualified GAL, and an excellent GAL is ideal. The key factors to research are affordability, proximity, availability, and sensitivity to transgender issues and familiarity with the reality of transgender people's lives. Once an attorney has collected a list of names, s/he should call each potential GAL and ask them a series of standard questions to assess whether they are knowledgeable about transgender issues.[88] Additionally, the attorney should assess whether the potential GAL is aware of and follows the appropriate standards, which are generally issued by each state court system.[89]

Establishing a good working relationship with the GAL is also critical given that her/his evaluative or investigatory process and ultimate recommendations will be centrally important to the resolution of the case. At the outset of the appointment, if transgender issues have been raised by the other side, it is advisable to include educational resources for the GAL and opposing counsel regarding transgender parents and gender issues to ensure that they have appropriate resources.[90] Although it may not be standard for an attorney to attend client interviews with a GAL, with a transgender client it is wise for the attorney to attend the first interview to ensure the process gets off to a child-centered start and to gauge the appropriateness of the GAL at the outset. In the GAL investigation process, the attorney should provide guidance about how a transgender client should talk to the GAL about her/his gender identity, transition, etc. (or if they should not talk about this, how they should respond if the GAL asks).

If the GAL's process begins to feel flawed or discriminatory, an attorney has some options. For example, an attorney can bring a motion to remove the GAL and to appoint another instead. An attorney could also hire an independent expert to review the report and recommendations of the GAL in an attempt to undermine or further elucidate them. Vigilance in the GAL investigation is of paramount importance to any custody investigation, particularly one involving a transgender parent. The GAL report will hopefully present the court with detailed facts about the client's actual parenting so that the focus is parenting ability rather than the client's transgender identity.

6.4.3 Vigilance in Discovery and Fact Finding

In addition to providing the court with relevant data about the client's parenting ability and the children's best interests via a GAL investigation, an attorney must also be vigilant about protecting the record from being tainted by irrelevant and discriminatory facts and arguments. To do so, an attorney must be proactive and vigilant in discovery and in preparation for evidentiary hearings and trials. Rarely, if ever, would discovery requests seeking detailed information about a client's medical history, transition, or birth documentation be appropriate to elucidating custody issues. An attorney who receives such requests should, utilizing the appropriate state rules, refuse to answer the discovery requests and, if necessary, seek a protective order from the court to ensure that the client is protected from inappropriate requests.

The case of *In re Custody of T.J.* demonstrates the power of the protective order.[91] In that case, an appellate court affirmed a protective order issued by the trial court precluding one parent from getting discovery about the other parent's gender support group or from being able to depose its members. Both courts stopped the harassing discovery, protecting the transgender client and focusing instead on the central issues in the matter.

If the opposing counsel or other parent is inappropriately raising the client's transgender identity, an attorney should also consider a proactive motion in limine prior to an evidentiary hearing or trial to preclude the opponent from questioning a client about discriminatory or irrelevant topics or from presenting expert testimony that may be harmful and irrelevant.

6.4.4 Alternative Dispute Resolution

Another approach to avoiding discrimination in the court system is to suggest the client seek alternative dispute resolution (ADR) outside of that system. In cases involving child custody or visitation, the method of

ADR usually utilized is mediation.[92] In addition to the general benefits of mediation of a custody or visitation dispute, for a transgender client, mediation provides a more private forum for addressing the parties' dispute. It avoids the potential for judicial bias and can involve a clinician to help guide the parties in creating a developmentally appropriate parenting plan. If mediation becomes the chosen path, the attorney can help ensure that her/his client gets referrals for reputable and effective mediators,[93] and can assist in educating the mediator and opposing counsel about transgender issues if transgender issues are relevant to the case.

6.5 Conclusion

History and case law demonstrate that transgender parents often face discrimination and draconian results in litigation following dissolution of adult relationships. Attorneys must be detail-oriented and proactive from the outset of the representation so that the attorney and client are prepared to educate the other party, attorneys, neutrals, and the court, and to neutralize and challenge discriminatory tactics. For transgender parent clients, it is critical to consult with an attorney early on in dissolution. Even if hiring an attorney throughout the case may be cost prohibitive, an early consultation or early intervention can help steer a custody dispute onto a more appropriate and child-centered path and can help educate the client to understand the legal standards and potential pitfalls so that self-representation is smoother. Attorneys generally should avoid discriminatory arguments and tactics to ensure that zealous advocacy is informed and educated.

---

1   See Appendix 6A.

2   *See* M.L.B. v. S.L.J., 519 U.S. 102, 117–18 (1996) ("[A] parent's desire for and right to the companionship, care, custody, and management of his or her children is an important interest, one that undeniably warrants deference and, absent a powerful countervailing interest, protection") (internal citations omitted).

3   *See, e.g.,* Troxel v. Granville, 530 US 57, 68–69 (2000) ("[S]o long as a parent adequately cares for his or her children (*i.e.,* is fit), there will normally be no reason for the State to inject itself into the private realm of the family to further question the ability of that parent to make the best decisions concerning the rearing of that

parent's children"); McDermott v. Dougherty, 869 A.2d 751, 754 (Md. 2005) ("We hold that in disputed custody cases where private third parties are attempting to gain custody of children from their natural parents, the trial court must first find that both natural parents are unfit to have custody of their children or that extraordinary circumstances exist which are significantly detrimental to the child remaining in the custody of the parent or parents, before a trial court should consider the 'best interests of the child' standard as a means of deciding the dispute."); D.M. v. D.R., 62 So.3d. 920, 924 (Miss. 2011) ("In a custody case involving a natural parent and third party, the court must first determine whether through abandonment, desertion, or other acts demonstrating unfitness to raise a child, as shown by clear and convincing evidence, the natural parent has relinquished his right to claim the benefit of the natural-parent presumption.") (internal quotation omitted); Bennett v. Jeffreys, 356 N.E.2d 277, 282 (N.Y. 1976) ("[N]either decisional rule nor statute can displace a fit parent because someone else could do a 'better job' of raising the child in the view of the court (or the Legislature), so long as the parent or parents have not forfeited their 'rights' by surrender, abandonment, unfitness, persisting neglect or other extraordinary circumstance").

4   *See, e.g., In re* E.L.M.C., 100 P.3d 546, 561–62 (Colo. App. 2004) ("[E] motional harm to a young child … intrinsic in the termination or significant curtailment of the child's relationship with a psychological parent" sufficient to overcome legal parent's objections); A.H. v. M.P., 857 N.E.2d 1061, 1070 (Mass. 2006) ("[D]isruption of a child's preexisting relationship with a nonbiological parent can be potentially harmful to the child, thus warranting State intrusion into the private realm of the family") (internal quotation omitted); T.B. v. L.R.M., 786 A.2d 913, 917 (Pa. 2001) ("[W]here the child has established strong psychological bonds with a person who, although not a biological parent, has lived with the child and provided care, nurture, and affection, assuming in the child's eye a stature like that of a parent … the child's best interest requires that the third party be granted standing so as to have the opportunity to litigate fully the issue of whether that relationship should be maintained even over a natural parent's objections"); *In re* Parentage of L.B., 122 P.3d 161, 179 (Wash. 2005) (role of legal parent in consenting to and fostering de facto parent-child relationship means "that the rights and responsibilities which we recognize as attaching to *de facto* parents do not infringe on the fundamental liberty interests of the other legal parent in the family unit").

5   Biology is not always determinative of parentage. *See, e.g.,* Michael H. v. Gerald D., 491 U.S. 110 (1989).

6   In some states, prebirth orders may be sought to confirm the parentage of a child born through assisted reproductive technology like gestational surrogacy before the child's birth. *See* Raftopol v. Ramey, 12 A.3d 783 (Conn. 2011); Culliton v. Beth Israel Deaconess Med. Ctr., 756 N.E.2d 1133 (Mass. 2001).

7   States such as California have adopted the Uniform Parentage Act ("UPA"). The California case *Elisa B. v. Super. Ct.,* 117 P.3d 660, 667 (Cal. 2005), is an example of application of the UPA to establish legal parentage in a nonbiological

parent.

8   *See* Miller-Jenkins v. Miller-Jenkins, 912 A.2d 951 (Vt. 2006).

9   See Chapter 3.

10   Different states use different terms for parents-in-fact who seek parental rights and responsibilities under equity, including de facto parents and psychological parents. *See, e.g.*, E.N.O. v. L.M.M., 711 N.E.2d 886, 891 (Mass. 1999) ("de facto parent"); Latham v. Schwerdtfeger, 802 N.W.2d 66 (Neb. 2011) ("in loco parentis"); V.C. v. M.J.B., 748 A.2d 539, 549 (N.J. 2000) ("psychological parent").

11   *See* Principles of the Law of Family Dissolution: Analysis and Recommendations § 2.03 (2003).

12   Not every state allows equitable parentage claims. *See, e.g.*, *In re* C.B.L., 723 N.E.2d 316 (Ill. App. Ct. 1999) (enactment of Illinois Marriage and Dissolution of Marriage Act foreclosed standing as a common law de facto parent or as an individual in loco parentis to seek visitation); Debra H. v. Janice R., 930 N.E.2d 184, 194 (N.Y. 2010) (refusing to recognize de facto parentage absent legislative authorization); Jones v. Barlow, 154 P.3d 808, 815–18 (Utah 2007) (refusing to recognize equitable parentage).

13   *See* Principles of the Law of Family Dissolution, *supra* note 11, § 2.18.

14   *See, e.g.*, Mullins v. Picklesimer, 317 S.W.3d 569, 579 (Ky. 2010) (legal parent "waived … her right to be the sole decision-maker regarding her child and the right to sole physical possession of the child" by co-parenting with ex-partner and recognition of that waiver "is legally justified as well as necessary 'in order to prevent the harm that inevitably results from the destruction of the bond that develops' between the child and the nonparent who has raised the child as his or her own") (internal citation omitted); E.N.O. v. L.M.M., 711 N.E.2d at 893 ("The child's interest in maintaining his filial ties with the plaintiff counters the defendant's custodial interests."); V.C. v. M.J.B., 748 A.2d 539 at 554 (when "the legal parent has created a family with the third party and the child, and has invited the third party into the otherwise inviolable realm of family privacy…, the legal parent's expectation of autonomous privacy in her relationship with her child is necessarily reduced from that which would have been the case had she never invited the third party into their lives. Most important, where that invitation and its consequences have altered her child's life by essentially giving him or her another parent, the legal parent's options are constrained"); Mason v. Dwinnell, 660 S.E.2d 58, 69 (N.C. App. Ct. 2008) (when legal parent "voluntarily chose to invite [her partner] into that relationship and function as a parent from birth on, thereby materially altering her child's life[, s]he gave up her right to unilaterally exclude [the partner] (or unilaterally limit contact with [the partner]) by choosing to cede to [the partner] a sufficiently significant amount of parental responsibility and decision-making authority to create a permanent parent-like relationship with her child"); T.B. v. L.R.M., 786 A.2d at 919 ("[A] biological parent's rights do not extend to erasing a relationship between her partner and her child which she voluntarily created and

actively fostered simply because after the parties' separation she regretted having done so") (quotation omitted); Rubano v. DiCenzo, 759 A.2d 959, 973 (R.I. 2000) ("[T]he rights of a child's biological parent do not always outweigh those of other parties asserting parental rights, let alone do they trump the child's best interests").

Some states have recognized equitable parents to stand on equal constitutional footing with legal parents. *See, e.g.*, Smith v. Guest, 16 A.3d 920, 931 (Del. 2011) (de facto parent has "a co-equal 'fundamental parental interest' in raising" her child) (internal citation omitted); Parentage of L.B., 122 P.3d at 178 (de facto parents stand in parity with biological and adoptive parents; thus, "[t]he State is not interfering on behalf of a third party in an insular family unit but is enforcing the rights and obligations of parenthood that attach to *de facto* parents").

15   *Compare, e.g.*, Egan v. Fridlund-Horne, 211 P.3d 1213 (Ariz. Ct. App. 2009) (claims for visitation and custody by de facto parent governed by Arizona statute), *and In re* E.L.M.C., 100 P.3d 546 (Colorado statute governs parental rights and responsibilities for psychological parent), *and* Smith v. Guest, 16 A.3d 920 (Delaware Code governs claims of de facto parentage), *with* E.N.O. v. L.M.M., 711 N.E.2d 886 (trial court had equity authority to order visitation with de facto parent), *and* Latham v. Schwerdtfeger, 802 N.W.2d 66 (standing under common law doctrine of in loco parentis to seek custody and visitation), *and In re* Custody of H.S.H.-K., 533 N.W.2d 419, 435 (Wis. 1995) (circuit court has equitable power to hear visitation claim by de facto parent).

16   *See, e.g.*, A.H. v. M.P., 857 N.E.2d at 1072 ("[O]ne who is not a legal parent and who invokes the equity powers of the court to establish herself as a de facto parent [must] demonstrate a history of substantial direct, loving, appropriate involvement in the child's supervision and care"); Latham v. Schwerdtfeger, 802 N.W.2d at 74 ("The primary determination in an in loco parentis analysis is whether the person seeking in loco parentis status assumed the obligations incident to a parental relationship."); *In re* H.S.H.-K., 533 N.W.2d at 435–36 ("To demonstrate the existence of the petitioner's parent-like relationship with the child, the petitioner must prove four elements: (1) that the biological or adoptive parent consented to, and fostered, the petitioner's formation and establishment of a parent-like relationship with the child; (2) that the petitioner and the child lived together in the same household; (3) that the petitioner assumed obligations of parenthood by taking significant responsibility for the child's care, education and development, including contributing towards the child's support, without expectation of financial compensation; and (4) that the petitioner has been in a parental role for a length of time sufficient to have established with the child a bonded, dependent relationship parental in nature.").

17   *Compare* C.E.W. v. D.E.W., 845 A.2d 1146, 1151–52 (Me. 2004) (when an individual's status as a de facto parent has been established, "the court may consider an award of parental rights and responsibilities to that individual as a parent … based upon a determination of the child's best interest"), *and* L.S.K. v. H.A.N., 813 A.2d 872, 877–78 (Pa. Super. Ct. 2002) (de facto parent liable for

child support), *and* Parentage of L.B., 122 P.3d at 171 ("[R]ecognition of a person as a child's *de facto* parent necessarily 'authorizes [a] court to consider an award of parental rights and responsibilities ... based on its determination of the best interest of the child'") (internal citations omitted), *and* Randy A.J. v. Norma I.J., 655 N.W.2d 195, 201 (Wis. Ct. App. 2002) ("Once a court determines that a party is an equitable parent, there is no distinction between the equitable parent and any other parent; each is endowed with the same rights and responsibilities of parenthood."), *with* Chatterjee v. King, 253 P.3d 915 (N.M. Ct. App. 2010) (de facto parent may seek visitation under equity, but statute forecloses seeking custody as remedy in equity). The variations in protections attendant to equitable parentage depend in part on whether a statute governs.

18   Troxel v. Granville, 530 U.S. 57. *See* Chatterjee, 253 P.3d 915 (partially reversing a dismissal based on insufficient pleading).

19   *See* Seymour v. Seymour, 433 A.2d 1005 (Conn. 1980); Bordelon v. Bordelon, 390 So.2d 1325 (La. 1980); El Chaar v. Chehab, 941 N.E.2d 75, 80 (Mass. App. Ct. 2010); Ellis v. Carucci, 161 P.3d 239 (Nev. 2007). For a multi-state overview of statutory factors and links to each state statute, see CHILD WELFARE INFO. GATEWAY, ADMIN. ON CHILDREN, YOUTH & FAMILIES, U.S. DEP'T OF HEALTH & HUMAN SERVS., DETERMINING THE BEST INTERESTS OF THE CHILD: SUMMARY OF STATE LAWS (2010), *available at* http://www.childwelfare.gov/systemwide/laws_policies/statutes/best_interest.pdf.

20   Helen Chang, *My Father is a Woman, Oh No!: The Failure of the Courts to Uphold Individual Substantive Due Process Rights for Transgender Parents under the Guise of the Best Interest of the Child*, 43 SANTA CLARA L. REV. 649, 656, 657–658 (2003).

21   *See, e.g., In re* Marriage of Burgess, 913 P.2d 473 (Cal. 1996); *In re* Marriage of Frederici, 338 N.W.2d 156 (Iowa 1983); Adams v. Adams, 464 P.2d 458 (Nev. 1970) (custody award reversed and remanded for analysis of second prong); Kendrick v. Shoemake, 90 S.W.3d 566 (Tenn. 2002) (holding that father's petition for change in custody failed to show material change in circumstances).

22   Palmore v. Sidoti, 466 U.S. 429 (1984).

23   PRINCIPLES OF THE LAW OF FAMILY DISSOLUTION, *supra* note 11, § 2.12.

24   *Id.*

25   *See, e.g.,* Christian v. Randall, 516 P.2d. 132, 134 (Colo. App. 1973).

26   Richard Green, *Transsexuals' Children*, 2 INT'L J. TRANSGENDERISM 4 (1998), *available at* http://www.wpath.org/journal/www.iiav.nl/ezines/web/IJT/97-03/numbers/symposion/ijtc0601.htm; Tonya White & Randi Ettner, *Disclosure, Risks and Protective Factors for Children Whose Parents Are Undergoing a Gender Transition*, 8 J. GAY & LESBIAN PSYCHOTHERAPY 129, 131 (2004), *available at* http://www.glad.org/uploads/docs/publications/i._ii_._WhiteEttner_Disclosure,_Risks,_and_Protective_Factors_for_Children_Whose_Parents_are_Undergoing_a_Gender_Transition_.pdf.

27   Timothy F. Murphy, *The Ethics of Helping Transgender Men and Women Have Children*, 53 Persp. Biology & Med. 46, 56 (2010), *available at* http://muse.jhu. edu/journals/perspectives_in_biology_and_medicine/v053/53.1.murphy.pdf.

28   Richard Green, *Sexual Identity of 37 Children Raised by Homosexual or Transsexual Parents*, 135 Am. J. Psychiatry 692, 697 (1978).

29   *See* Green, *Transsexuals' Children*, *supra* note 26.

30   *Id.*

31   White & Ettner, *supra* note 26.

32   *Id.* at 132.

33   Tonya White & Randi Ettner, *Adaptation and Adjustment in Children of Transsexual Parents*, 16 Eur. Child & Adolescent Psychiatry 215, 219 (2007). This study covered children who had witnessed their parent's gender transition and focused mainly on male to female transgender parents. *See also* White & Ettner, *supra* note 26.

34   *See* Jaime M. Grant et al., Nat'l Ctr. for Transgender Equal. & Nat'l Gay & Lesbian Task Force, Injustice at Every Turn: A Report of the National Transgender Discrimination Survey (2011), *available at* http:// www.thetaskforce.org/downloads/reports/reports/ntds_full.pdf.

35   *See id.*

36   *See id.*

37   *Id.* at 88.

38   *See id.*

39   Summers-Horton v. Horton, No. 88AP-622, 1989 WL 29421, at *2 (Ohio Ct. App. 1989).

40   *Id.*

41   Christian v. Randall, 516 P.2d. 132.

42   *Id.* at 133.

43   *Id.*

44   *Id.* at 134.

45   *Id.*

46   Pierre v. Pierre, 898 So.2d 419 (La. Ct. App. 2004).

47   *Id.* at 421.

48   *Id.* at 420–21.

49   *Id.* at 422.

50   *Id.* at 423.

51   *See id.* at 424. Father did not appeal; he just responded to mother's appeal.

This case is an example of the need for competent legal counsel to ensure that substantive parental rights are protected.

52   *Id.* at 424–25.

53   *Id.* at 426. The appellate court wrote that "[e]ven though Pierre is not the biological parent of the children, there was an award of joint custody by consent between the parties, and there was no showing of a change in circumstances impacting the children between the time that the award was made and the time of the hearing." *Id.*

54   M.B. v. D.W., 236 S.W.3d 31 (Ky. Ct. App. 2007).

55   *Id.* at 33–34.

56   *Id.* at 35.

57   The trial court in *Daly v. Daly* also terminated a transgender parent's parental rights, and the Nevada Supreme Court affirmed the termination. 715 P.2d 56 (Nev. 1986). The strong dissent remarked that the motivation in the termination petition was transgender status alone and determined that there was no clear and convincing evidence demonstrating a need to terminate parental rights. *Id.* at 60. The dissent called out the ignorance and bias of the court as follows: "[W]e are being unnecessarily and impermissibly punitive to the exercise of a medical option we personally find offensive, thereby depriving a child of a legal relationship which might well be to the child's advantage in the future." *Id.* at 64.

58   B. (Anonymous) v. B. (Anonymous), 585 N.Y.S.2d 65 (N.Y. App. Div. 1992).

59   *Id.*

60   M. v. M., Nos. FA 940064700, FA 890050074, 1996 WL 434302, at *21, *23 (Conn. Super. Ct. 1996).

61   *Id.* at *23.

62   Cisek v. Cisek, No. 80 C.A. 113, 1982 WL 6161 (Ohip Ct. App. 1982).

63   *Id.* at *1.

64   *Id.*

65   *Id.*

66   *Id.*

67   *Id.*

68   *Id.*

69   *Id.* at *2.

70   *Id.*

71   *Id.*

72   *See generally In re* Welfare of V.H., 412 N.W.2d 389 (Minn. Ct. App. 1987).

73   *Id.*

74   *Id.* at 392.

75   *Id.* at 390, 393.

76   *Id.*

77   It is also critical to object on the record, in a timely manner and using all available arguments, to evidence or arguments that improperly address the gender identity or expression of a parent. *See* M.R. v. Super. Ct., Nos. A122117, A122281, 2008 WL 4650440, at *11 (Cal. Ct. App. 2008). It is also critical to assess a social worker's directives and, if appropriate, address them as soon as possible to ensure the directives are clinically appropriate and child-centered rather than simply based on bias.

78   See, for example, the case of *J.L.S. v. D.K.S.*, 943 S.W.2d 766, 775 (Mo. Ct. App. 1997), where the appellate court upheld an order requiring a father not to "cohabit with other transsexuals or sleep with another female." The father argued that the order violated his constitutional rights and bore no relationship to the best interests of the children. *Id.* The appellate court determined that the father did not adequately support his arguments, and that the trial court can consider conduct of parents, particularly, "the effect which the conduct of a parent may have on a child's moral development." *Id.* As the dissent noted, the findings showed that the father was a loving parent and that credible expert testimony supported that it was imperative for the children to be reunited with the father. *See id.* at 776. The trial court's holdings, affirmed by the appellate court, were, in effect, focused primarily on the parent's transgender status and identity, and demonstrate extreme discrimination despite careful advocacy. *See id.*

79   *See, e.g.*, Lawrence v. Texas, 539 U.S. 558 (2003); Troxel v. Granville, 530 U.S. 57; Boy Scouts of Am. v. Dale, 530 U.S. 640 (2000); Roberts v. U.S. Jaycees, 468 U.S. 609 (1984); Palmore v. Sidoti, 466 U.S. 429; Moore v. City of E. Cleveland, 431 U.S. 494 (1977); Stanley v. Illinois, 405 U.S. 645 (1972); Eisenstadt v. Baird, 405 U.S. 438, 453 (1972); Griswold v. Conn., 381 U.S. 479 (1965); Prince v. Mass., 321 U.S. 158, 166 (1944); Pierce v. Soc'y of Sisters, 268 U.S. 510, 534–35 (1925).

80   Stewart v. Stewart, 521 N.E.2d 956, 965 (Ind. Ct. App. 1988) (trial court had terminated father's visitation rights, stating, "[w]hat you have proved is that Mr. Stewart has AIDS, and, even if, even if there's a one percent chance that this child is going to contract it from him, I'm not going to expose her to it," and appellate court reversed).

81   Anne D. v. Raymond, D., 528 N.Y.S.2d 775 (N.Y. Sup. Ct. 1988).

82   *AIDS Coordinating Committee Policy*, AM. BAR ASS'N, http://www.american-bar.org/groups/individual_rights/projects/aids_coordinating_project/policy.html (last visited Nov. 21, 2011).

83   North v. North, 648 A.2d 1025, 1030 n.2 (Md. Ct. Spec. App. 1994) (holding that "a child's visitation with a non-custodial HIV-positive parent cannot be restricted on the basis of that parent's HIV status unless the court finds that visita-

tion without that restriction might endanger the child's physical health or impair his or her emotional development").

84   Stewart v. Stewart, 521 N.E.2d at 965 (reversing trial court's termination of father's visitation with his daughter because he had AIDS; noting that the medical evidence at trial showed that HIV was not transmitted through everyday household contact, appellate court criticized the trial court's termination of visitation as being "an extreme and unwarranted action" and cautioned the trial court to ensure that any action alleging protecting a child "corresponds to the danger presented"; *id.* (many parents suffer from varying degrees of disabilities and illnesses, and a court cannot deprive parents of all visitation just because some danger exists); Newton v. Riley, 899 S.W.2d 509, 510 (Ky. Ct. App. 1995) (affirming the denial of a father's attempt to modify custody when mother remarried a man with HIV, noting that "[o]ther jurisdictions . . . have addressed the issue at bar, and perhaps without exception have found that proof of HIV infection in a parent does not pose a direct threat to the child's health and cannot serve as the sole ground for modifying custody"); Jane W. v. John W., 519 N.Y.S.2d 603 (N.Y. Sup. Ct. 1987) (although mother curtailed father's visitation with their child based on her purported concern that the fact that he had AIDS affected his ability to care for the child, the court concluded that there was no evidence requiring limited visitation or supporting the notion that unsupervised visitation would be contrary to the child's best interests and that the father was "entirely capable of caring for the child"). *But see* H.J.B. v. P.W., 628 So.2d 753 (Ala. Civ. App. 1993) (appellate court upholding transfer of custody from an HIV-positive father to the child's mother largely it seems because there was "ample evidence in the record regarding the father's admitted homosexuality and his medical problem of being HIV positive," despite there being no nexus between the father's conduct, HIV status, and parenting).

85   In *S.N.E. v. R.L.B.*, 699 P.2d 875 (Alaska 1985), the Alaska Supreme Court reversed a trial court decision flipping custody to a father based on the mother's lesbianism. The high court concluded that "there is no suggestion that [her lesbianism] is likely to affect the child adversely . . . . Simply put, it is impermissible to rely on any real or imagined social stigma attaching to Mother's status as a lesbian." *Id.* at 879. "Consideration of a parent's conduct is appropriate only when the evidence supports a finding that a parent's conduct has or reasonably will have an adverse impact on the child and his best interests." *Id. See also* Bezio v. Patenaude, 410 N.E.2d 1207, 1216 (Mass. 1980) ("In the total absence of evidence suggesting a correlation between the mother's homosexuality and her fitness as a parent, we believe the judge's finding that a lesbian household would adversely affect the children to be without basis in the record.").

86   Obviously, just as there is potential for bias and discrimination among the bench and the bar, there is potential for discrimination among GALs. Attorneys are well-advised to seek as much information as possible in order to increase the likelihood of securing a GAL who is impartial and does not share the bias or discrimination being fostered by the non-transgender parent.

87   Guardian ad litem investigations can be extremely costly. It is important to assess cost as much as possible at the outset. A clinician may charge $200 per hour and perform 20 to 30 hours of work doing interviews and writing the report.

88   See Appendix 6B.

89   The Association of Family and Conciliation Courts ("AFCC") has model standards for custody evaluations. MODEL STANDARDS OF PRACTICE FOR CHILD CUSTODY EVALUATION (Ass'n of Family & Conciliation Cts. 2006), available at http://www.afccnet.org/Portals/0/PublicDocuments/Guidelines/ModelStdsChild CustodyEvalSept2006.pdf. AFCC is a national organization comprised of lawyers, clinicians, and court personnel aimed at improving the lives of children through resolving family conflict. *See What is AFCC?*, Ass'n of FAM. & CONCILIATION CTS., http://www.afccnet.org/about/index.asp (last visited Dec. 7, 2011).

90   *See* Green, *supra* notes 26, 28; White & Ettner, *supra* notes 26, 33. Some additional helpful resources may include policies and guidelines of the American Medical Association ("AMA"), the American Psychological Association ("APA"), and the National Association of Social Workers ("NASW"). The AMA, a powerful group representing the medical establishment, has a clear policy prohibiting discrimination with regard to gender identity. *See AMA Policy Regarding Sexual Orientation*, AM. MED. ASS'N, http://www.ama-assn.org/ama/pub/about-ama/our-people/member-groups-sections/glbt-advisory-committee/ama-policy-regarding-sexual-orientation.page (last visited Nov. 21, 2011). Another AMA policy notes, "[o]ur AMA continues (1) to support the dignity of the individual, human rights and the sanctity of human life, and (2) to oppose any discrimination based on an individual's sex, sexual orientation, gender identity, race, religion, disability, ethnic origin or age and any other such reprehensible policies." *Id.*

The policy of the APA is to oppose "all public and private discrimination on the basis of actual and perceived gender identity and expression and urges the repeal of discriminatory laws and policies." *APA Policy Statement: Transgender, Gender Identity, & Gender Expression Non-Discrimination*, AM. PSYCHOL. ASS'N (2008), http://www.apa.org/about/governance/council/policy/transgender.aspx (last visited Nov. 21, 2011). The APA further supports "access to civil marriage and all its attendant benefits, rights, privileges and responsibilities, regardless of gender identity or expression." *Id.* Those rights, of course, include presumptions of parentage and laws governing the care and custody of children.

The NASW also has a policy statement that affirms the dignity of transgender people and condemns discrimination against them. "NASW recognizes the considerable diversity in gender expression and identity among our population. NASW believes that people of diverse gender—including all those who are included under the transgender umbrella—should be afforded the same respect and rights as that for any other people. NASW asserts that discrimination and prejudice directed against any individuals on the basis of gender identity or gender expression, whether real or perceived, are damaging to the social, emotional, psychological, physical, and economic well-being of the affected individuals, as well as society as a whole[.]" Nat'l Ass'n of Soc. Workers, *Transgender and Gender Identity Issues*, *in* Social Work Speaks (8th ed. 2009).

91   *In re* Custody of T.J., No. C2-87-1786, 1988 WL 8302 (Minn. Ct. App. 1988). This case also affirmed a trial court order granting custody to a transgender parent, noting, among other things, that "respondent's condition does not automatically disqualify him from having a relationship with his child." *Id.* at *3.

92   Another method—collaborative law—is gaining momentum. Arbitration, however, is disfavored for children's issues for fear of usurping the court's parens patrie role as the ultimate arbiter of a child's best interests.

93   One source for mediator referrals are national licensing and educational groups such as the Association for Conflict Resolution, a national organization with local chapters, and local groups such as the Massachusetts Council on Family Mediation and the Connecticut Council for Divorce Mediation and Collaborative Practice. *See* Ass'n for Conflict Resol., http://www.acrnet.org (last visited Nov. 21, 2011); Mass. Council on Fam. Mediation, http://www.mcfm.org (last visited Nov. 21, 2011); Conn. Council for Divorce Mediation & Collaborative Prac., http://www.ctmediators.org (last visited Nov. 21, 2011).

Chapter 7: Custody Disputes Involving Transgender Children

Shannon Price Minter and Deborah H. Wald

Introduction

Our society is undergoing an important change in the way it treats transgender people. In the past, a transgender person typically had to repress her/his gender identity during childhood and youth and did not go through the process of gender transition until adulthood—often after many painful years of struggling to live in her/his birth sex. The psychological cost of waiting to express one's true identity is high, and the difficulties faced by individuals who transition in mid-life are often severe. By middle age, a person may have married or otherwise committed to a long-term relationship, had children, and established a career. Going through a gender transition at that point is often very difficult. Many transgender adults in this situation lose their relationships and, far too often, their careers. In addition, the physical treatments and medical interventions that many transgender people wish to undergo are often significantly less effective when undertaken later in a person's life.

In the not-so-distant past, a transgender child who could not hide or suppress her/his identity was frequently subjected to brutal rejection and damaging efforts to force the child to be "normal." In some cases, children as young as five were sent to psychiatric facilities, simply for insisting that they were "really" a girl or a boy, when their gender identity did not match their birth sex. Even today, there is a shrinking minority of therapists who purport to be able to "cure" transgender children and youth.

Today, this picture is starting to change. Due to the increased visibility and acceptance of transgender people, transgender children and youth are increasingly coming out to their parents and other family members rather than hiding their gender identity from them. More parents with transgender children are reaching out to peer support groups, medical providers, and legal organizations. And unlike in the past, when parents primarily wanted to change their children, today more parents are supportive and accepting of their transgender children.[1]

As a result, for the first time in contemporary Western culture, there is a generation of transgender children and youth who have a chance to grow up with parental and familial nurturance and support, and to live their entire lives authentically—without suffering the debilitating pain and trauma of suppressing their gender identity for years. This is a watershed moment, and one that will make a huge difference in the quality of life for many transgender people. Rather than having to overcome the damage inflicted by parental rejection or suppressing their true selves, many members of this generation of transgender children and youth will enter their adult years with the strength and self-confidence that comes from having a solid foundation of family love and support.

Medically, doctors and other providers now recognize that transgender youth can be spared the trauma of going through the "wrong" puberty by being prescribed hormone blockers.[2] Hormone blockers suppress puberty to give the young person a chance to reach an age at which s/he can make an informed decision about whether to begin hormone therapy. This prevents a female-to-male transgender youth from experiencing the trauma of growing breasts, starting to menstruate, and developing typically female patterns of fat distribution around the hips and thighs. It prevents a male-to-female transgender youth from experiencing the trauma of developing unwanted facial and body hair, roughening of skin texture, increasing muscle mass, and other unwanted secondary sex characteristics. The relief provided by this intervention can be enormous and provides a transgender youth the opportunity to develop a strong, positive sense of self.

7.1 A Note on the Diversity of Transgender Identities

It is important to note at the outset that there is a wide range of transgender identities, and medical interventions such as hormone blockers may not be appropriate for all transgender-identified youth. For example, some children and youth may be gender nonconforming, but may be comfortable with their bodies. This would include some traditionally "butch" girls and "feminine" boys, who may be happy living their lives as gender nonconforming youths. Other youth may not identify exclusively as either a boy or a girl, or may identify as some combination of the two. They may or may not experience distress about their bodies. In every case, it is important to give children the space to discover and determine who they are and to respect their emerging identities. No child should be prematurely labeled or pushed into one category or another. At the same time, children who strongly identify as a gender different than the one stereotypically associated with their birth sex should be respected and supported.

7.2 Standards for Parental Fitness and Best Interests of the Child

7.2.1 When Parents Agree on How to Deal with a Transgender Child

The United States legal system generally gives parents a great deal of authority over how to raise their children. In fact, parents have a constitutionally protected fundamental right to the custody, care, and raising of their children.[3] This includes the right to make medical decisions for a child without interference from the government.[4] As a general rule, the state can only intervene in a parent's decision about how to raise a child if the child is being abused or neglected, or if the child's health and well-being are threatened.[5]

In practice, however, the state is more likely to intervene in the family lives of poor people, which has a disproportionate impact on people of color. This is true, in part, because poor families are more likely to interact with various state agencies and to receive their healthcare from public sources. As a result, they are more vulnerable to government scrutiny. The higher level of state scrutiny and intervention also reflects deep-seated prejudice against, and stereotypes regarding, poor parents.

If a transgender child's parents agree on any medical treatment, such as hormone blockers, there should be no reason for the state to intervene. The same is true if a child has only a single parent or guardian. So long as the parent or parents are basing their decisions on accepted medical standards for dealing with transgender children, they have a constitutionally protected right to make their own decisions about how to raise their child.

Despite this legal standard, however, there are several unreported cases in which child welfare workers have removed a child from a parent's home, or investigated the home, because the parent is permitting a child to live consistently with the child's gender identity rather than the child's birth sex. These cases reflect the reality that many people still lack basic information about transgender issues—particularly those affecting children. For uninformed child welfare workers, the idea that a parent would treat a child who is "really" a girl as a boy, and vice-versa, may seem shocking and upsetting.

The removal of a child from a supportive home is traumatic and damaging for both the child and the family. The fear that the state may intervene and remove a transgender child is a source of great anxiety and stress for many parents with transgender children. In most cases where a child has been removed from the home, the child was returned to the family after the social worker or court was educated about contemporary medical standards for dealing with transgender children. For practical tips on how parents can insulate themselves from having a child removed from their custody, see Section 7.3 below.

7.2.2 When Parents Do Not Agree on How to Deal with a Transgender Child

7.2.2.1 Custody Disputes

Courts are most likely to become involved in family law cases involving transgender children when divorced, separated, or otherwise estranged parents disagree about whether their child is transgender or about how to handle the child's gender issues. Typically, these cases arise when the custodial parent comes to understand and accept the child's transgender identity, but cannot persuade the other parent to do so. Over time, the gap between the two parents' understanding of the situation and perspective on what is best for their child may widen. As the custodial parent learns more about transgender issues and becomes more accepting of the child, the other parent may become entrenched in her/his resistance to believing the child is transgender—and often increasingly convinced that the custodial parent is causing the problem or "pushing" the child to embrace a cross-gender identity.

Conflict over how to deal with the child's gender issues may escalate when the custodial parent decides, usually in conjunction with a therapist, that the child's continued healthy development and well-being require supporting the child's desire to be called by a different name, to change pronouns, and/or to dress in clothing consistent with the child's gender identity rather than birth sex. Taking these steps is often referred to as "social transition," meaning that the child starts to live in the social role consistent with the child's gender identity.

Once this threshold is crossed, the nonsupportive parent may rush to court seeking emergency custody. If the custodial parent is not well prepared (or in some cases, even if s/he is), a family court judge may be so shocked by the novelty of the situation or so uninformed about transgender issues that the court may grant the petition and remove the child from the custodial parent. As a result, the child may be abruptly removed from a supportive parent who understands and accepts the child's gender identity and placed instead with a parent who may punish the child for being transgender or try to change the child's identity.

After placement with the former noncustodial parent, that parent will typically seek to suppress the child's transgender identity by forcing the child to live consistently with the child's birth sex. The nonsupportive parent may search for therapists who believe they can "cure" the child or prevent the child from growing up to be transgender. The nonsupportive therapist may encourage the child to renounce the other parent and search for evidence that the other parent is causing or encouraging the child's behavior.

For example, in the Ohio case, *Smith v. Smith*, following dissolution of the marriage, a mother had been designated, by separation agreement, as the custodial parent of her two sons.[6] The older boy had shown strong cross-gender identification since he was a small child. As the child grew older, he began to confide in his mother that he felt that he was a girl and wanted to live a normal life as a girl. The mother was initially resistant, but eventually learned more about transgender issues and sought out expert advice. She had the child assessed by two experts who confirmed that the child likely had gender identity disorder and advised her to let the child try living and going to school as a girl. The mother attempted to discuss these issues with the noncustodial parent, the child's father, but he was resistant and refused to meet with the therapists or discuss the matter with the mother. When the father learned that the mother intended to enroll the child in school as a girl, he filed a petition for emergency custody, which was granted.

At trial, the mother presented testimony from the two experts who had evaluated the child, but the judge chose to believe the father's testimony that the mother was causing and encouraging the child's behavior. The judge also credited one of the father's experts who did not evaluate the child, but who testified that he did not believe the child was transgender and that the child would benefit from spending more time with his father in order to develop a stronger male identity. The judge awarded custody to the father, despite testimony from the court-appointed evaluator that being separated from the mother would be damaging to the child. The judge ordered that all parties refer to the child by his male name and by male pronouns, and even ordered that he must wear male underwear.

Cases like this underline the importance of having legal, medical, and psychological support available prior to embarking on a custody battle involving a transgender child, and of being prepared if a custody challenge seems likely. Attorneys should always assume that the court will be unfamiliar with transgender issues—and particularly with issues affecting transgender youth—and should put court education high on their agenda. (See Section 7.3.6 for more guidance on this point). The importance of alternative dispute resolution in these cases also cannot be over-emphasized. If the parents can be brought into mediation with a skilled mediator who has the training and experience necessary to address the complex custody issues raised by these cases, the chance of a result that benefits the child increases dramatically.

7.2.2.2 Legal Standards Regarding a Child's Medical Care

Most states have established law about the standards that courts must apply when a child's parents disagree about the appropriate course of medical care for their child.[7] In most states, if the custodial parent has been given sole or primary authority to make medical decisions, a court is not permitted to intervene unless the other parent can show that the custodial parent's decisions are harming the child.[8] The mere fact that the parents disagree is not enough to trigger court intervention. In practice, however, courts presented with a petition to change custody by a parent who objects to the custodial parent's support of a transgender child may disregard this standard and change custody merely because the court agrees with the noncustodial parent. Or, a court may simply presume—without requiring any evidence—that supporting the child's transgender identity is harmful and wrong.

In some cases, the parents may have joint legal custody over medical decision making. Joint legal custody typically requires the parents to keep one another informed about the child's medical issues and to agree on significant medical decisions. When the parents cannot agree, a court may have to decide either to give one parent legal control over medical decision making or to make a judicial determination about what is in the best interests of the child.

7.3 Practice Recommendations

7.3.1 Determine the Scope of the Parent's Authority over Medical Decision Making

When representing the parent of a transgender child in a dispute between parents, it is important to examine the initial custody order to determine the scope of the custodial parent's authority over medical decision making. A parent who has sole legal custody, and therefore sole authority to make medical decisions, is on stronger ground than a parent who has to share this authority with the other parent. Even in a joint custody case, it may be possible to carve out medical decision-making power from the general decision-making powers shared by joint custodial parents. In other words, parents can still share joint custody in decision making regarding education, religion, and so forth, while one parent has sole custody over medical decision making. Courts may be more likely to accept narrowly tailored requests for sole custodial rights than to strip a fit parent of all custodial authority over her/his child. And in some cases, it may be the noncustodial parent who supports the child's transgender identity and may wish to petition for joint or sole legal custody for that reason.

7.3.2 Encourage the Supportive Parent to Obtain and Document Professional Medical Guidance

Obtaining professional medical guidance about how to deal with a transgender child is essential to protect the supportive parent in the event of a dispute with the nonsupportive parent. Whenever possible, a parent should seek advice from a child welfare professional with expertise in gender identity issues, and should carefully follow and document that person's advice. A parent with a transgender child should also seek advice from a pediatrician who is willing to consult with a knowledgeable mental health professional. Every step that the supportive parent takes should be carefully documented. If the parent's actions are later scrutinized closely by a court, it is important to be able to show that the parent was not acting alone and without basis, but rather was carefully seeking out and following expert medical advice.

In some cases, courts have reacted negatively to parents who researched gender identity issues on the Internet, who relied heavily on peer support groups, or who became involved in transgender advocacy groups. This is extremely unfortunate and unfair, as such groups can provide valuable information and support, and research has shown that transgender children benefit greatly when parents become strong advocates for their children.[9] Nonetheless, a parent who is in a contested custody dispute may wish to exercise some degree of caution about these activities and rely on medical experts instead of, or in addition to, these resources.

7.3.3 Encourage Communication Between Custodial and Noncustodial Parents

As noted above, many custodial parents initially try to involve the noncustodial parent in learning more about the child's gender issues. Over time, however, if the other parent is not receptive, the custodial parent may give up on communicating with the noncustodial parent about this issue and simply focus on supporting the transgender child. The problem with this approach is that as the noncustodial parent has less information about the child's transgender identity, that parent may be extremely upset by the custodial parent's decision to permit the child to start dressing and living consistently with the child's gender identity, rather than the child's birth sex. The noncustodial parent may respond by rushing to court to seek a custody modification, which then puts the supportive parent in a vulnerable, defensive legal situation.

The best advice to a supportive parent is to keep the other parent in the loop about the child's gender issues to the maximum extent possible, especially if the parents have joint legal authority over medical decision making. Ideally, the other parent will eventually gain some increased insight and acceptance. If nothing else, it will be helpful to be able to document efforts to keep the other parent informed in the event of a subsequent custody dispute.

7.3.4 Encourage the Supportive Parent to Slowly Accommodate the Child's Gender Identity

Where the noncustodial parent is resistant to the child's transgender identity, a supportive parent should be strongly encouraged to go as slowly as possible with respect to accommodating the child's transgender identity and expression, consistent with protecting the child from harm. For example, in some cases, a transgender child might benefit by moving more quickly toward social transition. However, it is important to consider that doing so may result in the nonsupportive parent seeking and winning custody, in which case the net result for the child could be disastrous.

In assessing how best to protect and support a transgender child, the supportive parent must consider the very real danger that a court may not understand issues surrounding transgender children and youth and may give custody to the nonsupportive parent. Therefore, if the supportive parent anticipates a custody challenge, s/he should make decisions about how to best support her/his transgender child with this real threat in mind. In many cases, a transgender child may gain sufficient relief in the short-term by having a safe space at home, or with a few close trusted friends, to explore and express her/his transgender identity. While being able to live openly and consistently with the child's gender identity at school and in the community may be ideal, the most important thing is to avoid having the child placed with a nonsupportive parent, where the child may suffer lasting and very real harm.

7.3.5 Consider the Age of the Child

The urgency of addressing custody issues involving a transgender child can depend on the child's age when the custody dispute comes to a head. Young children can often get away with wearing gender-nonconforming clothes and playing with gender nonconforming toys. It is not atypical for young girls and boys to have sleepovers together, and be invited to each other's birthday parties. As such, a more casual approach to a child's gender identity is often possible throughout elementary school.

However, once a child reaches middle school, things often change. As adolescence approaches, children tend to become more rigid in their approach to gender, and nonconformity becomes more obvious—and, as a result, more socially and physically dangerous. A transgender child may need to be moved to a new school where her/his birth sex is unknown to peers. This is also the stage at which parents have to think about medical interventions, including whether to suppress the onset of puberty in a transgender child for whom such interventions are appropriate.

If a child involved in a custody dispute is close to the age of puberty, the attorney may face the issue of getting the court's approval for administration of hormone blockers. If puberty is still years away, there is time to educate, negotiate, and mediate; but if adolescence is starting, there will be a far greater urgency to get custody issues addressed immediately. A pediatrician can assess where a child is in puberty, and give a sense of timing for the onset of secondary sexual characteristics in a process called "Tanner Staging."[10] This information may be critical in developing the best strategy for moving forward.

7.3.6 Prepare to Present Expert Testimony

Most judges hearing custody disputes involving a transgender child have never heard such a case before and know little or nothing about transgender issues. In fact, most judges are likely to have the same misinformation and hold the same false stereotypes about transgender people as any other member of the public. Thus, it is essential that an attorney representing the parent of a transgender child be extremely proactive, strategic, and thoughtful about educating the court about transgender children. At the earliest opportunity, the attorney should present expert testimony from a psychologist who has experience dealing with transgender children.[11] The expert will need to educate the court on the importance of being sensitive to, and supportive of, a child's fundamental gender identity, while not pushing the child to make permanent, life-changing decisions before the child is mature enough to do so (which will almost certainly be one of the court's concerns). The expert will need to explain to the court why gender nonconforming behavior is not a product of the parenting style of the custodial parent, or of the custody dispute itself. And finally, the expert should be familiar with, and explain, the research showing that children are severely harmed by parental rejection and by attempts to change their gender identity, so the court can understand the critical nature of the decisions it is making.[12]

7.3.7 Insist that Any Court-Appointed Evaluator Has Expertise in Dealing with Transgender Children

It is critical that any court-appointed evaluation of the child be conducted by a mental health professional with expertise in dealing with transgender children. While this is a highly specialized area, there are a growing number of mental health providers with significant experience and knowledge in this area. If an experienced evaluator is not available, counsel for the supportive parent will have to go to extra lengths to provide the court-appointed evaluator with appropriate resources—including experts, as well as written materials—to assure that the evaluator takes the child's gender identity seriously and fully assesses it in her/his report. See Chapter 6 for guidance about how to find a supportive guardian ad litem and how to educate a guardian ad litem.

7.3.8 Be Prepared to Rebut Religious Arguments

The nonsupportive parent may be, or may become, involved in a religious faith that views being transgender as sinful and wrong. The nonsupportive parent may invoke her/his religious beliefs to bolster opposition to the other parent's support of the child or medical decisions regarding the child. For example, a court may order that the child be taken to a supportive therapist, but the nonsupportive parent may attempt to evade that order by arguing that s/he has a constitutionally protected right to expose the child to her/his religious beliefs and therefore must be permitted to take the child to a religious counselor or teacher.

It is true that parents generally have a protected right to share their religious beliefs with their children.[13] However, there is a well-established exception to that rule: a parent may not expose a child to religious teachings or beliefs when doing so will harm the child.[14] When confronted with a religious argument against supporting the child's gender identity, it is essential that the supportive parent present the court with research showing that exposing children to counseling intended to change their core identity dramatically increases the risk of suicide, as does exposing children to religion-based messages of rejection.[15] Presented with this evidence, a court can order that the nonsupportive parent refrain from exposing the child to damaging counseling or teachings that will put the child at risk of serious psychological harm.

7.3.9 Look to Other Professionals and Witnesses in the Child's Life

Especially in custody disputes over transgender children, it will be essential to show the court that the child's gender identity issues are not (a) being fabricated by the custodial parent or (b) the result of the custody battle itself. Family courts are used to seeing a variety of "acting out" behavior from children whose parents are unable to co-parent effectively, and one important challenge for the attorney representing a supportive parent and a transgender child will be to distinguish their case from other types of cases where the child's "acting out" behavior is not supported or encouraged by the court.

Transgender children, when raised by supportive and loving parents, are not typically "angry" or "troubled"—they are often happy, healthy children whose gender does not conform to their birth sex. People who spend time with transgender children will experience them as happy, well-adjusted children. Conveying this to the court can be absolutely critical to success in a dispute between parents.

From a very young age, children are in contact with a variety of adults other than their parents, and these adults can be critical witnesses to the truth of the child's identity. Teachers, pediatricians, and the parents of playmates can all provide "objective" verification of the child's gender identity that will take the issue outside the context of the parents' custody battle. For example, teachers and other parents may be able to verify that the child's interests and self-identification were manifest at an early age and have been consistent over time. This external verification can be critical to winning the court's support for handling the child's gender identification as a legitimate, important aspect of the child's fundamental identity and not as an indication of overall distress at the family situation.

7.3.10 Keep the Focus on the Best Interests of the Child

Cases involving transgender children call for humility on the part of all concerned, including the attorney representing the supportive parent. The best way to present the case to a court is not to presume that either the attorney or the parent knows what is best for the child, but rather that the court should look carefully at the evaluations and recommendations of the experts in the case. Any responsible judge will recognize that protecting these vulnerable children is of the utmost importance, and will appreciate being presented with credible, expert guidance as to the best interests of the transgender child.

---

1   *See, e.g.*, Diane Ehrensaft, Gender Born, Gender Made: Raising Healthy Gender Non-Conforming Children (2011).

2   The Harry Benjamin International Gender Dysphoria Association, Standards Of Care For Gender Identity Disorders 8–11 (7th ed. 2011),

available at http://www.wpath.org/documents/Standards%20of%20Care%20 V7%20-%202011%20WPATH.pdf.

3   Troxel v. Granville, 530 U.S. 57, 65 (2000); Prince v. Massachusetts, 321 U.S. 158, 166 (1944); Pierce v. Soc'y of Sisters, 268 U.S. 510, 534–35 (1925); Meyer v. Nebraska, 262 U.S. 390, 399–401 (1923). *But see* C.N. v. Ridgewood Bd. of Educ., 430 F.3d 159, 182 (3d Cir. 2005) (asserting that parental rights are not absolute).

4   Parham v. J.R., 442 U.S. 584, 602–05 (1979).

5   Croft v. Westmoreland County Children & Youth Servs., 103 F.3d 1123, 1125–26 (3d Cir. 1997) ("[The court] must balance the fundamental liberty interests of the family unit with the compelling interests of the state in protecting children from abuse.").

6   Smith v. Smith, No. 05 JE 42, 2007 WL 901599 (Ohio Ct. App. Mar. 23, 2007).

7   *See, e.g., In re* Baby K., 832 F. Supp. 1022, 1030 (E.D. Va. 1993); *In re* Doe, 418 S.E.2d 3, 7 (Ga. 1992).

8   *In re* K.I., 735 A.2d 448 (D.C. 1999).

9   Caitlyn Ryan et al., *Family Acceptance in Adolescence and the Health of LGBT Young Adults*, 23 J. Child & Adolescent Psychiatric Nursing 205 (2010), *available at* http://familyproject.sfsu.edu/files/FAP_Family%20Acceptance_ JCAPN.pdf.

10   Stephanie Brill & Rachel Pepper, The Transgender Child: A Handbook for Families and Professionals 206 (2008).

11   If a client cannot afford to retain an expert, the transgender child's supportive healthcare providers (mental health provider and pediatrician) may be willing to testify or submit affidavits that can be used to educate the court.

12   Ryan, *supra* note 9; Jaime M. Grant et al., Nat'l Ctr. for Transgender Equal. & Nat'l Gay & Lesbian Task Force, Injustice at Every Turn: A Report of the National Transgender Discrimination Survey 101–02 (2011), http://www.thetaskforce.org/downloads/reports/reports/ntds_full.pdf.

13   *See* Wisconsin v. Yoder, 406 U.S. 205 (1972); Pierce v. Soc'y of Sisters, 268 U.S. 510 (1925).

14   Prince v. Massachusetts, 321 U.S. 158 (1944); *see, e.g., In re* McCauley, 565 N.E.2d 411 (Mass. 1991) (upholding a hospital's decision to administer blood transfusion to child despite parents' religious beliefs).

15   *See* Caitlin Ryan, Family Acceptance Project, San Francisco State University, Supportive Families, Healthy Children: Helping Families with Lesbian, Gay, Bisexual & Transgender Children 6, 8 (2009), *available at* http://familyproject.sfsu.edu/files/English_Final_Print_Version_Last.pdf; Caitlin Ryan et al., *Family Rejection as a Predictor of Negative Health Outcomes in White*

*and Latino Lesbian, Gay, and Bisexual Young Adults,*123 Pediatrics 346 (2009), *available at* http://pediatrics.aappublications.org/content/123/1/346.full.pdf.

Chapter 8: Legal Protections for Transgender Youth

Zack M. Paakkonen

Introduction

Representing transgender youth in the legal system involves unique challenges and carries high stakes. Misperceptions and misunderstandings regarding transgender people, and transgender youth in particular, abound. Therefore, attorneys advocating for transgender youth must be prepared to educate parents, medical providers, other attorneys, various youth-related facilities including schools and out-of-home placements, and even courts[1] about the special needs and concerns of transgender youth. In addition, legal representation of youth, transgender or otherwise, invariably also raises age, consent, and capacity concerns. Law regarding transgender youth spans much of the same variety of law that is handled in a general practice, from family to criminal to education law and beyond.[2] Because the legal consequences flowing from the representation of youth may have life-long impacts on a client, any attorney taking on this challenge must pay particular attention to evolving law.

This chapter is intended to address many of the issues that practitioners who work with transgender youth will face. Those issues include transition-related matters such as name changes and privacy in schools, and also more general youth-related issues that relate to situations that all youth sometimes encounter but that have special impact on transgender youth, such as juvenile incarceration and out-of-home care.

8.1. Identifying the Client

Because an attorney's ethical duties run directly to the client, it is essential to be able to determine who that is at the outset of the representation. In working with youth, some attorneys initiate their representation because of a court appointment, others because parents, caretakers, or guardians find the attorney, and for some, the youth herself/himself directly contacts the attorney. Each of these situations may have different implications for determining who is the client. When representing a youth's parents, caretakers, or legal guardians, the attorney's ethical duties are to the parents, caretakers, or legal guardians, whose interests could be adverse to the youth. Alternatively, when representing the youth, the attorney's ethical duties run to that youth, whose interests may not always align with those of the parents, caretakers, or legal guardians.

There are practical matters that differentiate representation of youth from representation of adults. For example, while an adult with capacity can enter into a representation agreement with an attorney, a young minor client is analogous in some ways to an adult without capacity and thus may not be able to contract for services.[3] Older minors, still below age eighteen, may be able to enter into a valid contract. If the youth is not mature enough or is otherwise not capable of contracting for services, in some cases, an attorney will enter a representation contract with a client's parents. In such cases, it may be best to draft the agreement in such a way that states clearly that although the contract is with the parent or parents, the client is the youth and the attorney represents the youth, not the parents. In most states, there is no bright line rule as to what age a minor has to be to enter into a valid contract, so an attorney will have to perform an inquiry into the minor's ability to understand the rights and obligations that s/he is entering into before having a minor execute a services agreement.

The sometimes divergent interests of caretakers and youth can have severe effects on the child and family dynamic. For example, if a youth wants to medically transition and is approaching puberty, the timing of initiating medical treatment may have a significant impact on the outcome of gender transition. Hormone blockers, which are medications given to some youth to suppress the onset of puberty, are sometimes available and appropriate to suppress the development of secondary sex characteristics associated with the child's birth sex. However, once the physical changes that come with puberty begin, the effect of hormone blockers is diminished. As a result, if one or both parents oppose such treatment where a child desires it and where it is medically indicated, the consequences of delay can have life-long and irreversible consequences.[4]

If an attorney is representing the youth, and not the youth's parents, although the ethical duties are the same as they would be with any other client, the attorney should also be aware that the client does not necessarily have the emotional maturity of an adult. An attorney must develop trust with the youth. Transgender or gender nonconforming youth in particular need to know that their attorney understands them and is advocating for them. At the same time, an attorney also needs to be aware of special issues regarding consent, capacity, and authorization. Generally speaking, unless representing a youth who has an adverse position to her/his parents, an attorney will require the permission of the youth's parents in order to represent the youth because parents have certain fundamental parenting rights, including the right to control the upbringing of their children.[5] In some cases, such as emancipation cases or child protection cases in states that appoint attorneys for the child, the attorney may be initially representing the youth without a parents' knowledge; however, the parents will become aware of the representation.

An attorney should also be cautious about how much information regarding the client's gender identity to provide to others in the course of representation. An attorney must be careful not to disclose the youth's gender identity if it is not warranted or if s/he does not want her/his gender identity to be disclosed. As with any client, when representing a youth, an attorney has an ethical duty to protect the client's confidences. Even if the attorney feels that it is in the best interest of the youth to disclose confidential information about her/his gender identity, ethics rules require the attorney to honor the client's wishes. Concerns may be discussed with the client, but the decision is ultimately the client's to make. A list of resources for practitioners representing transgender youth is included in Appendix 8A.

8.1.1 Practice Suggestions for Working with Youth (If Youth Is the Client)

- Always address mail to the client if that client is a youth who has the capacity to understand the substance of the correspondence.

- Hold meetings with clients who are older youth without including the parents, provided that the client has sufficient capacity to understand what is being discussed and the decisions s/he is making. Remember privilege issues and always respect the client's privacy. If representing the youth, and not the parents, do not tell the parents anything that the client requests be kept confidential unless disclosure is mandated by ethics rules.

- Consider the audience in all of the attorney's interactions with the client—in person, by phone, and in writing. Use language appropriate to the age and maturity of the client. Consider dressing more casually for a meeting with youth than would be typical for a meeting with the youth's parents, caregiver, or legal guardian.

- Be attuned to the client's wishes, but make sure to fully explain the consequences of all choices in a way that the client comprehends so that the client may make a fully informed decision.

8.2 Social Transition

The term "transition," when referring to transgender youth, often encompasses several different stages. Not all stages apply to youth of all ages. For example, it is highly unlikely that very young transgender youth would undergo surgery or hormone treatment. Rather, very young and prepubescent transgender children will generally transition without this kind of medical intervention, an experience called "social transition." They will often require legal services related to schools, protection of records relating to birth sex, or assistance with a legal name change. Transgender children who are close to reaching puberty may transition socially and may also commence medical transition by beginning hormone blockers. When they become slightly older, they may begin taking hormones appropriate to their desired gender. Not all transgender children begin the transition process at the same age; for example, an attorney may encounter a youth who wants to begin transition in her/his late teenage years or a child under age five who has already socially transitioned and is beginning school. To advocate effectively for a transgender youth, an attorney must first understand that youth's needs; an attorney should know that not all transgender youth have the same needs and that transgender youth may transition in different ways and at different ages.

If a youth wants to transition in any way, it may be easier if her/his parents consent. Without parental consent, although there may be some options for a youth, those options are limited. Where the youth's parents consent, the widest range of options will be available to help the youth.

8.2.1 Name Change

Securing recognition of a transgender youth's name change is often a key component of successful social transition. Often, the youth has a first name that is a name typical of her/his birth sex, but the youth prefers to be called by a name that is consistent with the gender with which s/he identifies. Just as with adults, it is important to obtain official documentation of a youth's name change so that the youth's name can be changed on relevant identity documents and records.[6]

Name change procedure is governed by statute in most states. If a state has a statute governing name change procedures, an attorney should follow the procedures laid out in the statute. If a state does not have a statute or procedure set out in court rules, there may be variations in procedure or requirements in different jurisdictions. While there is a significant body of reported case law regarding surname changes for minors, there is very little reported case law about changes of minors' first names.[7] This is likely because court actions to change a minor's first name are relatively rare, and also because many states allow sealing of the record in cases involving minors.[8] Courts generally will rely on cases relating to change of minor's surnames for guidance in considering a first name change.[9]

Courts have held that a name choice made by parents is presumptively in the child's best interests.[10] However, this presumption may be rebutted by evidence that a different name would better serve the child's best interests.[11] Factors used to determine the child's best interests include: the preference of the child; the child's ability to make a meaningful choice; the effect that the name change will have on the relationship with each parent; the length of time the child has had a given name; the problems the child may have with either the current or the new name; and the occurrence of any parental misconduct or neglect.[12] Such factors may easily be satisfied for a transgender youth. For example, the child's preference for a gender-typical name will be relevant to the best interests analysis. Similarly, a court would likely consider relevant that the child will experience extreme embarrassment, harassment, or bullying if s/he must live with a name associated with the child's birth sex while living in the post-transition gender.

However, just because a name change is presumptively in the child's best interests does not mean that a court will automatically grant a name change for a transgender child if both parents file a signed consent. Parental testimony of some sort may be critical to the court's determination. Courts also often find medical providers to be helpful sources of information. Finally, most courts will want some input from the child. In some jurisdictions, a court may appoint an attorney or a guardian ad litem for the child to protect her/his interests. If the court seeks direct input from the child, an attorney can advocate for the child to meet with the judge in chambers.

The issues related to a name change for a transgender youth are different than the issues regarding name changes for non-transgender youth or name changes for adults in several ways. The first and most important difference is that minor name changes in most states are governed by a "best interests of the child" standard, while adult name changes are not.[13] Thus, courts may conduct a fact-specific inquiry as to whether or not the name change will be in the best interests of the child. It is important to remember that courts, including court staff, court marshals, and the judiciary, are not always educated regarding transgender adults, and are usually even less so regarding transgender youth. An attorney may have to educate and provide relevant documentation to a court to allow it to decide that the name change is in the child's best interests, including having a child's medical providers testify, or even producing expert witnesses.

8.2.1.1 When Both Parents Consent to the Name Change

Naming a child is generally considered to be a right and a privilege belonging to the child's parents.[14] A name change for a minor child, when both parents consent, should largely be straightforward. Name changes in most states involve filing a petition in a family court, probate court, or other court that deals with issues relating to family and children. The form of the petition varies, but generally, both parents must receive notice of the proposed name change or must sign a consent form agreeing to the name change. If both parents consent, they may still need to convince a court that the name change is in the best interests of the child depending on the age of the child, the familiarity of the judge with transgender issues, and the requirements of the state's name change statute or procedure.

Once a name change is complete, the state's and federal government's procedures for changing the youth's identity documents must still be followed. At a minimum, the youth's Social Security record, birth certificate, and passport should be changed to reflect the new name. The attorney should tell the client that it is necessary to present the name change order to every institution where the child has a record, including schools and doctors' offices. The attorney must also ensure that the youth's parents understand that the name change will not change gender markers on Social Security records, birth certificates, or on other documents and in other databases.

8.2.1.2 When Only One Parent Consents to the Name Change

Where parents have different opinions with respect to decisions regarding a transgender youth, including name changes, a practical suggestion is to either seek a court order that allocates decision making to the more supportive parent regarding the transgender youth's care and treatment, or to seek the appointment of a transgender-friendly and knowledgeable guardian ad litem to represent the child, or investigate the child's best interests.

If only one parent consents to a minor's proposed name change and the other parent objects, the attorney will almost certainly have to litigate whether or not the name change is in the best interests of the child, instead of handling the case in a more informal way. A legal parent not in favor of the name change has standing to object, and if s/he objects, the parent who consents to the name change will have to prove to the court that the name change is in the best interests of the child. In these circumstances, an attorney should expect to have a hearing on the issue, and should prepare fully to put on a case demonstrating why the name change meets the state's best interests of the child test or alternatively meets the limited factors that may be relevant to a name change in the state. A court will consider the interests of both of the parents as well as the interests of the child.[15]

8.2.1.3 When Neither Parent Consents to the Name Change

If the client is a minor who wants to change her/his name without parental consent, an attorney should research state statutes to determine if there is a specific statutory procedure permitting a minor to change her/his own name. Further, some courts have held that even absent a provision in a name change statute that has a specific procedure for changing a minor's name, a minor may file a name change petition on her/his own behalf.[16] Even though parental consent may be unnecessary, a custodian, guardian, or other individual responsible for the minor may still need to file such a petition, and the court might still make an inquiry into the best interests of the child. In these cases, the court may appoint a guardian ad litem for the child in states where that option is available.

8.2.2 Sealing Records and Protecting the Client's Privacy

In some states, name change records, even of minors, are public. In such a circumstance, an attorney should consider filing a "Motion to Seal" or similar motion as permitted in the jurisdiction. Some states have statutes that permit individuals to seal name change records if the petitioner can make a showing that an open record may risk their safety.[17] It is often possible to use these statutes to seal a minor's record by convincing a judge that exposing a child as transgender, by means of publicly available court records, would risk the youth's safety.

Nonetheless, at the outset of representation, an attorney should make sure that the parents and the youth understand that these records may be public or may become public, and if the youth's gender identity is listed as a reason for the name change, that reason may be on record and publicly available forever. To protect the client's privacy, the attorney might also want to consider filing the case under a pseudonym or under initials. The attorney should also be prepared to explain to the court the risks to the child's safety and privacy caused by allowing the court record to remain public. Finally, in some jurisdictions, it may be possible to file a motion to close the courtroom to the public if minor name change proceedings are generally public.

8.3 Medical Transition

Parents have a fundamental right to control the upbringing of their children, including control of their medical treatment.[18] In *Parham v. J.R.,* decided by the United States Supreme Court in 1977, the Court held that a Georgia procedure for voluntary commitment of children met due process requirements where the parents consented to institutionalization of the children, and where there was an observation period to determine whether the children exhibited evidence of mental illness prior to admission.[19] The Court held that although a child has a substantial liberty interest in not being confined unnecessarily for medical treatment, and although minors have some rights that exceed their parents' rights to make choices when their physical or mental health is jeopardized, parents generally have the authority to decide what is best for their child.[20] Thus, if a client wants to begin medical transition but the client's parents are opposed, an attorney will have a very difficult battle that may involve litigation in order for the client to begin the medical transition process against her/his parents' wishes.

Indeed, with some exceptions, minors do not have the right to consent to their own medical treatment until they attain the age of majority, typically eighteen.[21] Exceptions to this rule include a minor's right to consent to emergency treatment,[22] a minor's right to consent to other special types of treatment,[23] and when a minor has been emancipated or can demonstrate sufficient maturity according to a court's evaluation.[24] In some states, minors are statutorily permitted to consent to medical treatment without first being deemed emancipated and may even keep their records private.[25] Of these exceptions, the situation of the emancipated minor is most applicable to transgender youth. In the event that a minor's parents are opposed to transition-related medical treatment, the attorney may have to help the minor emancipate, or seek a court order appointing a guardian ad litem for the child. Without parental consent, the unemancipated minor often cannot obtain treatment.

In practice, however, in most situations a minor will not be able to medically transition without parental support even when emancipated due to financial constraints.[26] Because of the cost of medical services required for transition, unless the minor has insurance coverage of her/his own that covers such treatment, s/he may not be able to fund transition. However, emancipated youth may, in some states, qualify for public insurance that may or may not cover some transition-related treatment.

8.3.1 Payment for Medical Transition

Once parents determine that it is medically appropriate and in their child's best interests to medically transition, a critical issue for many families is how to pay for such treatment. Although some families can afford to pay out-of-pocket for medication and even surgery, most cannot. In the instances where a family cannot afford to incur costs associated with age-appropriate transition-related medical treatment, an attorney may be able to provide advice regarding how to get insurance companies, or even public assistance programs, to pay for treatment, or alternatively, advice on what to do if coverage is denied.[27]

8.3.1.1 Private Insurance Coverage

Parents of a transgender or gender nonconforming youth may need help obtaining insurance coverage for transition-related treatment for their child. Most insurance policies specifically exclude any transition-related treatment; however, the exact language of the insurance contract will determine what is and is not covered. Often, parents will not have the entire insurance policy, and an attorney may have to help them obtain a copy from their employer or from the company directly.

Generally, when a parent is facing an insurance coverage issue, it is most commonly because their child has been denied coverage for some transition-related treatment, such as hormone blockers. Because insurance coverage is governed by contract law, if the language of the contract allows the provider to deny coverage for transition-related treatment, although there may be some legal steps available, the parents' options are limited.[28] The scope of health insurance coverage is generally a matter of state law.[29] In the event that a claim is denied, insurance plans generally have an appeal process for denial of claims, and an attorney should review the client's plan to determine the time deadlines and process for appeal. There may be different levels of appeal. The appeals process often involves an internal review and, in many states, an external appeal to a state board or to an outside agency. A sample insurance appeal letter is included in Appendix 8B.

Insurance coverage for most conditions is based upon the diagnosis or the diagnostic code.[30] Parents should be aware that insurance coverage may be available for certain transition-related treatment for their minor child even if the insurance contract has a transition-related treatment (such as hormones) or sexual reassignment surgery exclusion, if the treatment, although possibly also related to transition, is medically indicated for a medical condition that is covered. For example, parents of transgender youth are sometimes able to obtain insurance coverage for hormone blocking medication if a doctor prescribes the medication to treat another presenting condition that is not excluded, such as "precocious puberty." Hormone blockers may also be necessary to alleviate disabling anxiety. An attorney should strongly caution parents who are obtaining treatment coverage in this way for transition-related costs of potential risks; the insurance company could eventually deny a claim, seek reimbursement for past paid benefits, or seek other remedies or penalties if they believe that claims were paid for excluded diagnoses based on false or misleading information.[31]

8.4 Emancipation

If an attorney has a client who is a minor child who wants to begin the process of medical transition but her/his parents do not consent, the attorney may help the client file a petition for emancipation. State requirements for emancipation vary. Some states have procedural statutes for emancipation of a minor under eighteen years of age, and some states do not.[32] If a state has a statute, the attorney should review that statute and the court rules for the relevant requirements and procedure.

At common law in the United States, a minor could become emancipated if s/he was able to support herself/himself and was not living with parents,[33] if the minor became married,[34] or if the minor was serving in the military or had graduated from high school.[35] In states that do not have statutory processes for emancipation, an attorney should ensure that the transgender minor client has the means to support herself/himself and the ability to find safe and adequate housing apart from parents or family to create the best possible case for emancipation. However, the attorney should also be mindful of state runaway, truancy, and parental abuse/neglect laws that permit the State to take custody of a child who has left home without parental consent.[36]

8.5 Transgender Youth in the Custody of the State

8.5.1 Foster Care

Youth generally enter foster care when they have been removed from their homes by their state's child protective service due to abuse or neglect by their parents. State statutes as to what constitutes child abuse and neglect vary, but generally include physical abuse, sexual abuse, neglect and abandonment. Federal law defines abuse and neglect as, "at a minimum, any recent act or failure to act on the part of a parent or caretaker, which results in death, serious physical or emotional harm, sexual abuse or exploitation, or an act or failure to act which presents an imminent risk of serious harm."[37] Most states include emotional injury to a child or abandonment in the definition of abuse and neglect. Some states include failure to provide education to a child.[38] Some states provide certain exemptions to their statutory definition of child abuse and neglect for religious beliefs,[39] corporal punishment,[40] or poverty.[41] Other states exempt no special conditions from their definition of abuse or neglect. Transgender youth are involved in the foster system for the same reasons as non-transgender youth; however, transgender youth also sometimes become involved in the foster system because of real or perceived parental neglect or abandonment that is specifically related to the child's gender identity.[42]

Youth in foster care have rights, including the right to be safe from physical, emotional, and sexual harm and abuse. Some states have codified the rights of youth in foster care.[43] Specific rights of youth vary from state to state, but generally, youth have the right to be placed in the least restrictive placement available that meets their needs, the right to an education, the right to practice their own religion, and the right to access appropriate medical care. An attorney should advocate for a transgender minor client to continue treatment with any medical providers who were treating her/him for transition-related services prior to her/him entering state care.

A particular concern with transgender youth in foster care is the reunification and permanency planning process. In general, when a child is removed from her/his parents' care by the State, the State has an obligation to begin a process for the parents to reunify with the child. But many transgender children come into state care because their families are not supportive of their gender identity or transition. It may not always be in a transgender child's best interests to reunify with her/his birth family if the parents continue to be unsupportive of the child's identity. When advocating for a transgender youth, if her/his parents are not supportive of the client's gender identity or transition, an attorney should seek out potential family placements with family members who are. If an attorney is the guardian ad litem for the youth, s/he may have to educate the parents and their attorney(s) about the importance of them supporting their child.[44] If the youth is going to be placed back with her/his parents, an attorney should also work to ensure that the youth's parents obtain appropriate services that will hopefully make it safe for the youth to return home, and that there is a concurrent permanency plan in place that would provide for a safe and supportive home for the youth in the event that reunification fails.

An attorney may face child protective workers or group home workers who try to convince a transgender youth to dress in accordance with her/his birth sex in order to fit in at a foster home or other residential placements. It is often difficult to find an appropriate placement for any youth in foster care, let alone a transgender youth, and foster care workers may be motivated to preserve a placement rather than to support a youth's gender identity. If an attorney is faced with this situation, s/he should advocate for relevant workers to support the youth's gender identity. This may require substantial education of the workers as to why it is not appropriate and not in the youth's best interest to force her/him to dress in a manner to make others comfortable. An attorney may have to invoke antidiscrimination policies or laws, or even disability law.

Some courts have held that transgender children in state custody have a right to dress in accordance with their gender identity. In *Doe v. Bell*, the Supreme Court of New York County in New York held that the New York City Administration for Children's Services could not prevent a seventeen-year-old transgender minor from wearing skirts and dresses in accordance with her gender identity.[45] In making this ruling, the court held that the minor's diagnosis of gender identity disorder was a disability under New York's Human Rights Law and thus Children's Services was required to provide her with a reasonable accommodation to permit her to wear female clothing. This case is an example of how an attorney can use state antidiscrimination and disability statutes (where gender identity is not specifically excepted from disability definitions) to obtain a favorable result for a transgender client, even possibly in states whose statutes do not provide specific protections based on gender identity.[46]

A youth in foster care has the right to access medical and mental health care.[47] That care should be appropriate to a youth's needs, which may include transition-related care. The right to adequate medical care includes a right to be free from certain types of therapy, such as reparative therapy, which attempts to persuade the youth to identify with her/his birth sex, and may be harmful to a transgender youth.[48] Youth in foster care also have rights regarding religious freedom in foster care,[49] including the right to be free from proselytizing or unwanted religious services.[50]

To effectively advocate for a client who is in foster care, an attorney may need to spend substantial time educating state child protective workers, case managers, attorneys, parents, and foster parents. Some foster programs provide training and education for foster parents about LGBTQ youth. Casey Family Programs, a multi-state organization that provides foster licensing and foster-care services, including reunification programs in many states, offers some publications and training related to LGBTQ youth.[51] The national Court Appointed Special Advocate (CASA) program also offers some training regarding LGBTQ youth.[52] The Child Welfare League of America has several publications about LGBTQ youth in foster care, including some that focus on transgender youth.[53] In addition, the American Bar Association's Opening Doors Project[54] and National Center for Lesbian Rights' (NCLR) Youth Project[55] both provide resources to help attorneys effectively represent LGBTQ youth in out-of-home placements, including publications specifically about representing transgender youth.

An attorney may also need to intercede for a transgender youth client for her/him to receive appropriate treatment by child protective workers or staff.[56] An attorney should ensure that a transgender client in foster care is given safe and appropriate placement if s/he is placed in a group home, especially if it is sex segregated. An attorney should also ensure that staff refers to a transgender client using the youth's preferred name and preferred gender pronouns. A client should be treated respectfully at all times by staff, and by other residents of the placement. An attorney can and should advocate for a change in placement if a transgender client is being discriminated against or harassed based upon gender identity.

8.5.2 The Juvenile Justice System

A large national survey found that fifteen percent of youth in the juvenile justice system are lesbian, gay, bisexual, transgender, or queer.[57] LGBTQ youth in the juvenile justice system have experienced high rates of child abuse, conflict with parents, home removal, out-of-home placement, and homelessness, experiences which are often linked to their involvement with the juvenile justice system.[58]

Juveniles who are involved in the juvenile justice or "delinquency" system have a constitutional right to counsel.[59] Attorneys who work with youth should familiarize themselves with the specific issues affecting transgender youth, including the possible bias, ignorance, and/or discriminatory practices of judges, court personnel, probation officers, and/or detention facility staff.[60]

Key issues transgender youth face once they become involved

with the juvenile justice system is where they will reside and who will be responsible for their care. Courts will address these questions for youth during the pretrial phase as well as upon final adjudication of a matter. Because many transgender youth do not have family support, it is important for an attorney to ascertain the relative safety of a placement, whether that placement is release to her/his parents, to a temporary alternative home placement, or in an institutional setting. The decision about whether or not to detain a youth may be based, in part, on risk-screening instruments that measure factors such as school attendance and history of running away from home. Judges and court counselors should be informed that in the case of many transgender youth these "risk factors" might reflect harassment and abuse suffered by the youth, rather than delinquency.[61] Often, transgender youth are inappropriately at risk of prolonged detention because of challenges in finding a placement that can safely and competently meet their needs. An attorney should be proactive in challenging any prolonged detention simply because of a youth's transgender status. Furthermore, an attorney working with a transgender youth should advocate for her/him to be placed in a setting that will permit her/him to use her/his preferred name and pronoun, to wear clothing appropriate to her/his gender identity, and to feel safe,[62] and should be prepared to defend against a transgender youth's gender nonconforming behavior being erroneously categorized as "acting out."[63] Also, an attorney should be prepared to advocate against any inappropriate sex offender treatment or reparative therapy based on the youth's gender identity.

Zealous advocacy for youth in juvenile justice systems includes educating the court about the dangers of detention for transgender youth. Concerns about health and safety are paramount. Transgender youth, particularly male-to-female transgender youth, face a high risk of sexual assault in a group incarceration setting where housing classifications are often made based on assigned birth sex.[64] Unless a residential institutional placement has policies and practices to ensure the safety of transgender youth, an attorney should consider advocating against a transgender youth's placement at a residential facility.

When a youth is detained, s/he has a constitutionally protected interest in reasonably safe conditions of confinement; however, it is often up to the attorney to make sure the juvenile is afforded these rights.[65] Youth in custody also have a right to adequate medical care.[66] For transgender youth, this may mean access to therapy with a gender specialist, hormone blockers, hormone treatment, or even basic medical checkups with a doctor who understands transgender issues.[67] An attorney should be careful about which medical reports s/he and the client provide to the court as this information will be accessible to probation officers, the judge, and potentially district attorneys, and can not only be used against the client but also often remains a permanent part of the client's file.

8.6 Transgender Youth in Shelters

Studies indicate that twenty percent of the homeless youth population is lesbian, gay, bisexual, transgender, or queer,[68] and transgender individuals are disproportionately overrepresented in the homeless population.[69] Homeless transgender youth have often experienced economic discrimination, and are at risk of violence, sexual exploitation, disease, and substance abuse.[70] Youth who reside in homeless shelters face similar issues to those that youth face in foster care, although they do not have some of the rights associated with being in state custody. Shelters are often unsafe and hostile environments for transgender youth, in large part because such facilities are typically sex-segregated.[71] Male-to-female transgender youth face particular risks if they are housed with boys or men and must share sleeping and showering facilities with them. For in-depth information and a model policy for making shelters safer for transgender youth, see *Transitioning Our Shelters: A Guide for Making Homeless Shelters Safe for Transgender People*, by Lisa Mottet and John M. Ohle.[72]

8.7 Transgender and Gender Nonconforming Youth in Schools

8.7.1 Change of Name and Gender Marker in Student Records

The Federal Educational Rights and Privacy Act (FERPA) allows individuals to control their personal information held by educational institutions.[73] Transgender youth generally face FERPA issues when attempting to change their name and gender marker in their school records. Only parents or students who have reached eighteen years of age or who are attending postsecondary schools are able to amend records under FERPA, thus not permitting minor transgender youth to amend their record without parental consent.[74] A parent or adult student may request an amendment to her/his educational record under FERPA if s/he believes the record is "inaccurate, misleading, or in violation of the student's rights of privacy."[75] A student may wish to amend her/his educational record to reflect her/his change of name and/or change of sex. The educational institution will either amend the record or will notify the parent or student of her/his right to a due process hearing.[76] Some states also have statutes that mandate accurate state records, and an attorney may also be able to use such a statute, if available, to make a school system change a student's name or gender marker in her/his records.[77]

If a school that receives some federal funding refuses to amend a transgender youth's name or gender maker in her/his school records upon written request, an advocate may request a hearing.[78] School departments have discretion about how they conduct administrative hearings, and although FERPA provides some requirements, the requirements are minimal.[79] So long as the hearing is conducted by a noninterested individual and presents a full and fair opportunity to present evidence relevant to the issues, it will probably satisfy due process requirements. An advocate may have to present medical or other expert testimony regarding the youth's gender identity in order to prevail.

If a school still refuses to change the student's record after a hearing, in addition to further remedies through the court process, a student or parent has the right to place a statement in the record regarding the disputed information.[80] That statement will be kept for as long as the record is kept, however, and will be disclosed to anyone to whom the record is disclosed in the future.[81] This could result in a student's transgender identity being disclosed to future employers, educational facilities, or licensing boards, whereas a simple nonmatching gender marker, absent further explanation, may not draw attention or may be dismissed as simply a mistake or clerical error.

FERPA also mandates that before a school may disclose personally identifiable information from a student's educational record, with some exceptions, the student or student's parent must provide written consent.[82] Among other exceptions, disclosure of educational information is generally allowed without consent if it is for an institutional or educational purpose.[83] In addition, "directory information," defined as including the student's name (but not the student's gender), may be disclosed without a student's written consent in some circumstances.[84] For violations of the disclosure regulations, an aggrieved student or student's parent can make a complaint with the Department of Education, and the Department may initiate an investigation.[85]

8.7.2 Nondiscrimination Laws

When a transgender youth is being treated differently in school than non-transgender students because of her/his gender identity, an attorney should research the state's antidiscrimination statute to determine if it applies to the school in question and if it covers discrimination based upon gender identity. Gender-identity discrimination is sometimes covered under the definition of sexual orientation.[86] Other states include gender-identity discrimination as an additional type of unlawful discrimination separate from sexual orientation.[87] Even where nondiscrimination laws do not explicitly prohibit discrimination on the basis of gender identity, laws that prohibit sex and sometimes disability discrimination in education may be used to advocate for a transgender student.

Some states explicitly provide that their antidiscrimination statutes apply to public schools. If a state statute does not, but it prohibits discrimination in public accommodations, public-accommodation discrimination law may serve as the basis for a transgender student's discrimination claim.[88]

An attorney may have a variety of available forums in which to pursue a client's discrimination claim, such as an administrative board that hears discrimination cases.[89] Sometimes, state remedies or court temperament may make state courts a more attractive venue for a discrimination case based upon gender identity. In other cases or locations, a transgender youth may fare better in federal court. An attorney should also consider the remedies available. Some state and federal courts have found gender-identity discrimination to be a form of sex discrimination under federal law.[90] Some state courts, in contrast, have rejected this argument.[91] A transgender student may have other claims than discrimination claims, including constitutional claims.[92]

Specific areas in which transgender youth often face disparate treatment and discrimination at school include access to bathrooms and locker rooms and participation on sports teams. Some school departments solve the "problem" of which bathroom a transgender youth should use by requiring the youth to use a gender-neutral bathroom, an option which may only serve to stigmatize the student and compromise her/his educational environment. There is currently litigation pending in Maine regarding whether forcing a transgender youth to use a gender-neutral bathroom violates state antidiscrimination laws.[93] Similarly, transgender students are often required to participate on sports teams according to their birth sex rather than their gender identity, or may be denied access to the appropriate locker room.[94]

Although an attorney can initiate litigation based on antidiscrimination statutes, it is often advisable to try a nonlitigation approach if possible. With litigation, an attorney should be aware of the consequences of publicity to transgender youth and their families. An attorney should also be aware of possible remedies. Does the transgender youth want to change the school or school department's policy or does s/he want compensation for damages or an injunction?

8.7.3 Dress Codes

Some school systems have gender-defined dress code policies that require students of a particular sex to dress in clothing stereotypically associated with that sex. Transgender children, like transgender adults, often feel uncomfortable in clothing associated with their birth sex. As in the foster care context, courts have sometimes construed gender identity as a disability that requires school departments to provide reasonable accommodations to permit a child to dress in accordance with her/his gender identity.

In *Doe v. Yunits*, a transgender student filed suit, claiming that she had been constructively expelled from the school district because of her school's requirement that she come to school wearing boy's clothing.[95] The school had prevented her from wearing clothing that was consistent with her female gender identity, citing purported fear of disruption or distraction although Plaintiff alleged no such disruption or distraction had occurred.[96] The Massachusetts Superior Court, ruling on a motion to dismiss by the Defendants, held that gender identity disorder, by means of its inclusion in the *Diagnostic and Statistical Manual of Disorders* (4th ed.), may be a physical or mental impairment that would permit the Plaintiff to pursue a claim that she had been discriminated against on the basis of disability.[97] The court further held there was evidence that coming to school in boy's clothing would endanger the Plaintiff's health, and thus she was not able to meet the school's requirements to return to school and could pursue a claim that she had been constructively expelled without due process.[98]

8.7.4 Special Education Laws

The Individuals with Disabilities Education Act (IDEA) provides protections for students with disabilities and may be a useful vehicle for ensuring that a transgender youth's educational needs are met.[99] IDEA mandates that schools with special education programs, that receive federal funding, create an Individualized Education Plan (IEP) to meet the unique educational needs of each child with a disability to enable the child to participate fully and make progress in the general education curriculum.[100] Supportive parents of transgender children may seek to have their child diagnosed as having a disability in order to permit their child to be eligible for an IEP that can, in some cases, provide a reasonable accommodation allowing a child to use a bathroom consistent with her/his gender identity, allowing the child to dress in clothing appropriate to her/his gender identity, and allowing the child to be enrolled in school under her/his preferred name.

Policy advocates and practitioners debate the pros and cons of using disability law as a means to leverage transgender rights. The approach should be carefully considered in each student's case, as the parent or caregiver may not wish to have their child labeled as disabled, or may not view the youth's transgender status as a disability. Further, the disability label may follow the youth through their educational career and possibly even later in life. In the school context, however, parents and advocates for children often find the disability label to be an attractive option that permits transgender children to attend school in a way that is consistent with their gender identity through a "reasonable accommodation." Cases such as *Doe v. Bell* and *Doe v. Yunits*, referenced above, show the utility of using disability laws to require school departments to provide reasonable accommodations that support a student's gender identity.

8.7.5 Bullying

Many states have laws to protect students from school bullying, sometimes called "Safe Schools Laws." Many of these statutes simply require schools to develop and implement antibullying policies.[101] Other states provide for a cause of action related to school harassment or bullying.[102] Many states include sexual orientation in their antibullying statutes, and some also include gender identity.[103]

Some courts have also held that severe harassment, when not prevented by a school system, may lead to an unlawful deprivation of educational opportunity. In *Shore Regional High School Board of Education v. P.S.*, the Third Circuit Court of Appeals held that a school system failed to provide a student with a free appropriate public education through an IEP when the student sought to attend a different school because of severe bullying based upon perceptions of the Plaintiff's gender nonconforming behavior.[104] An attorney should be aware of the state's antibullying statute, if any, and should also be aware that school systems that fail to prevent bullying or harassment may be liable for failing to mitigate such harassment.

Federal law provides a cause of action for students who suffer from gender-based harassment.[105] Title IX provides that harassment or bullying based on the victim's gender may be considered to be unlawful sex discrimination. Title IX applies even to bullying based on perceived gender or gender stereotyping, although it does not specifically prohibit discrimination based on gender identity.

In addition, if an attorney can argue that gender identity is an impairment needing accommodations, s/he may be able to make a disability claim under the Federal Rehabilitation Act of 1973 (FRA).[106] FRA bars discrimination in programs affiliated with the federal government,[107] and bars discrimination on the basis of disability for programs, including school programs, that receive federal assistance.[108] This provision of law is referred to as Section 504, which requires equal access to education for students with disabilities. Although the FRA was amended in 1992 to exclude gender identity disorders "not resulting from physical impairments" from the protections of the statute,[109] a student's IEP may nevertheless provide a basis for a claim under Section 504.[110] A letter from the United States Department of Education Office of Civil Rights addressing federal antidiscrimination statutes in the education context is included in the list of resources in Appendix 8C.

8.8 General Practice Recommendations for Working with Transgender Youth

- Be prepared to educate judges, school administrators, and even parents and service providers on transgender issues.

- Advocate for training programs to make foster and adoptive parents, child protective workers, group home workers, workers in the court system, school employees, providers, etc. aware of the unique needs of transgender youth, including the importance of respecting names, pronouns, and clothing choices.

- Advocate for state antidiscrimination laws and policies that include gender identity.

- Advocate for codes of judicial conduct that explicitly prohibit bias based on gender identity.

- When filing cases, consider filing with pseudonyms or initials.

- Be aware of the impact of potential media coverage on a youth's privacy and future. A very public case that exposes a child as transgender will live on forever on the Internet.

- Be aware of privacy concerns. Inform a transgender youth of the consequences of information contained in their school record.

- Ask courts to refer to litigants with their preferred pronoun, and cite cases where courts have done so as precedent the court can follow.

- Consider having court records relating to youth sealed.

- Be aware of the client's financial situation. Retaining an expert witness is not affordable for many clients. Consider trying to use your client's medical providers to provide testimony or supportive affidavits.

- Be aware of the client's goals.

- Be aware that litigation is not always the answer. Sometimes, an attorney can reach the client's desired result through education instead of litigation.

- Reach out to national and local resources for information, support, and guidance.[111]

---

1   Most states have judicial canons that include provisions requiring judges to be unbiased regarding sexual orientation. *See, e.g.*, Mass.Sup. Jud. Ct. R. 3:09 Canon 3. Some states also have anti-bias provisions regarding gender identity in their rules of professional conduct for attorneys. *See* Ariz. Rules of Prof'l Conduct ER. 8.4 cmt. 3 (2003).

2   This chapter uses the term "transgender youth," or sometimes "gender nonconforming youth." Some youth who fall within these terms may identify as "genderqueer" and occupy a space between genders, or inclusive of multiple genders, rather than medically transitioning from one gender to another.

3   In many jurisdictions, contracts entered into by minors are voidable, although not void, and may be enforceable under some circumstances.

4   Attorneys should also be wary of importing their own attitudes of what steps a transgender or gender non-conforming youth should take regarding transition. Transition decisions are personal for everyone, including youth, and not all youth want or need to take steps to medically transition.

5   *See, e.g.*, Parham v. J.R., 442 U.S. 584 (1979); Wisconsin v. Yoder, 406 U.S. 205 (1972); Prince v. Massachusetts, 321 U.S. 158 (1944); Pierce v. Soc'y of Sisters, 268 U.S. 510 (1925); Meyer v. Nebraska, 262 U.S. 390 (1923).

6   See Chapter 2 for information about adult name changes and changes to identity documents.

7   *See, e.g., In re* Marriage of Nguyen, 684 P.2d 258 (Colo. App. 1983) (court allowed a name change of the first name of the minor where there was an attorney appointed to protect the best interests of the child as part of the underlying divorce action, where that attorney supported the change, and where the name change would not undermine the relationship between the father, who opposed the change, and the child, or lead to estrangement, noting that the only objection to the name change was due to "inconvenience" with paperwork).

8 There are cases of sealed minor name changes for transgender youth in some jurisdictions.

9 *See, e.g.*, Poindexter v. Poindexter, 203 S.W.3d 84 (Ark. 2005).

10 Gubernat v. Deremer, 657 A.2d 856, 858 (N.J. 1995). As with most of the case law related to minor name changes, this case addresses a change of a minor's surname.

11 *Id.* at 869.

12 *See, e.g., id.*; *Poindexter*, 203 S.W.3d 84.

13 *See, e.g.*, Chamberlin v. Miller, 47 So. 3d 381 (Fla. Dist. Ct. App. 2010); 57 Am. Jur. 2d *Name* § 46 (noting requirement that change be in child's best interests, with footnotes to several cases); 65 C.J.S. *Names* § 23 (same).

14 D'Ambrosio v. Rizzo, 425 N.E.2d 369, 369 (Mass. App. Ct. 1981); O'Brien v. Tilson, 523 F.Supp. 494 (E.D.N.C. 1981) (holding that a North Carolina statute that required that children born of married parents be given their father's surname failed even a rational basis test).

15 *See In re* Morehead, 706 P.2d 480, 483 (Kan. Ct. App. 1985).

16 *See, e.g., id.* at 481–82 (noting that a minor could sue or be sued through a "next friend," and so, therefore, a minor could also file a petition for change of name through a similar process).

17 Maine, for example, permits limiting notice and sealing records if the petitioner is a victim of abuse and is currently in reasonable fear of her/his safety. Me. Rev. Stat. Ann. tit. 18-A, § 1-701(b)–(c).

18 *See, e.g.*, Parham v. J.R., 442 U.S. 584 (1979); Wisconsin v. Yoder, 406 U.S. 205 (1972); Prince v. Massachusetts, 321 U.S. 158 (1944); Pierce v. Soc'y of Sisters, 268 U.S. 510 (1925); Meyer v. Nebraska, 262 U.S. 390 (1923).

19 *Parham*, 442 U.S. 584.

20 *Id.*

21 *See, e.g.*, Am. Acad. of Pediatrics v. Lungren, 940 P.2d 797, 800–01 (Cal. 1997); *In re* Hudson, 126 P.2d 765, 782–83 (Wash. 1942).

22 For example, section 2504 of New York's Public Health Code, like similar statutes in other states, permits a minor to consent to emergency medical treatment. N.Y. Pub. Health Law § 2504(4).

23 Pregnancy and abortion, treatment for sexually transmitted diseases, mental health treatment and counseling services, and drug or alcohol abuse are areas in which many states permit minors of certain ages to consent to treatment. *See, e.g.*, David M. Vukadinovich, *Minors' Rights to Consent to Treatment: Navigating the Complexity of State Laws*, 37 J. Health L. 667, 677–90 (2004).

24 *See id.* at 677–81.

25 For example, Maine permits any minor who has been living separately from

her/his parents or legal guardians for at least sixty days and who is independent of parental support to give consent for any medical, mental, dental, and other health counseling and services without a requirement that s/he first be judicially emancipated. Me. Rev. Stat. Ann. tit. 22, § 1503(1). In Maine, a minor who is able to consent is also able to protect medical records from disclosure. Me. Rev. Stat. Ann. tit. 22, § 1711-C(12).

26   Youth in situations where they have no financial parental support for transition and no insurance coverage sometimes seek medical treatment, in particular, hormones, without a prescription, from friends, or off the street. *See, e.g.*, Maureen Carroll, *Transgender Youth, Adolescent Decisionmaking, and* Roper v. Simmons, 56 UCLA L. Rev. 725, 735 (2009). If an attorney represents such a client, the client should be advised regarding the potential dangers and potential criminal liability of obtaining hormones illegally.

27   Federal Medicare coverage generally does not cover youth, with some exceptions. One exception is for a disabled youth who has been receiving Social Security disability benefits for twenty-five months or more. 42 C.F.R. § 406.5. Medicaid, in contrast, is intended for low-income individuals and generally does cover dependent youth. *See* U.S. Dep't of Health & Human Servs., Medicaid Eligibility: Are You Eligible?, Ctrs. for Medicare & Medicaid Servs., http://www.cms.gov/med icaideligibility/02_areyoueligible_.asp (last visited March 12, 2012). There is no express exclusion of transition-related health care from federal Medicaid coverage, but state statutes, regulations, and practices vary and often exclude such treatment. As a practical matter, it is likely easier, as with private health insurance, to obtain Medicaid coverage for hormone blockers or hormones by means of a prescription related to a non-GID diagnosis than it is to obtain coverage for surgery.

28   What treatment is excluded from the policy might be a matter of interpretation and thus may be able to be negotiated with the insurance company.

29   While the scope of health care coverage is generally a matter of state law, Patient Protection and Affordable Care Act, Pub. L. No. 111-148, 124 Stat. 119 (enacted Mar. 23, 2010), *amended by* Health Care and Education Reconciliation Act of 2010, Pub. L. No. 111-152, 124 Stat. 1029 (signed Mar. 30), is a significant exception. This statute is currently the subject of litigation and repeal efforts. In addition, not all types of plans are governed by state law (for example, some states have "self-insured" insurance plans). An attorney should review the relevant insurance statutes for her/his jurisdiction.

30   The diagnostic code for Gender Identity Disorder in children is 302.6, and in adolescents, it is 302.85. Am. Psychiatric Ass'n, Diagnostic and Statistical Manual of Mental Disorders (rev. 4th ed. 2000). As used in the Manual, ICD refers to the International Statistical Classification of Diseases and Related Health Problems, published by the World Health Organization. World Health Org., International Statistical Classification of Diseases and Related Health Problems, Clinical Modification (9th ed. 2010), *available at* http://www.icd9data.com/. The ICD-9-CM Diagnosis Code for Gender Identity Disor-

der is 302.85 (adolescents and adults) or 302.6 (children). *Id.* Note that there are separate codes for transsexualism (302.5) and "transvestic fetishism" (302.3). *See id.*

31   In most states, it is a crime to provide false or misleading information to an insurance company in a claim or in order to obtain coverage. Even in states where it is not explicitly a crime, the client could be subjected to civil or other criminal liability for providing false or misleading information to an insurance company to obtain services.

32   New York and Massachusetts have no statutes governing emancipation procedure. *Contra* CAL. FAM. CODE § 7120–7123.

33   *See, e.g.,* Buxton v. Bishop, 37 S.E.2d 755 (Va. 1946).

34   *See, e.g.,* Lawson v. Brown, 349 F. Supp. 203, 207–08 (W.D. Va. 1972).

35   *See, e.g.,* He v. Zeng, No. 2009-CA-00060, 2010 WL 1918797, at *4 (Ohio Ct. App. May 11, 2010) ("The common law duty imposed on parents to support their minor child terminates when the child becomes emancipated, either reaching the age of majority or graduating from high school, [whichever comes later]."); Baker v. Baker, 41 Vt. 55 (1868) (parental consent of child's enlistment emancipated the child).

36   *See, e.g.,* ME. REV. STAT. ANN. tit. 15, § 3501-1(b) (permitting law enforcement officer to take custody of juvenile and inform state child welfare service when the officer has a reasonable belief that the juvenile "has left the care of his parents, guardian or legal custodian without the consent of such person").

37   Child Abuse Prevention and Treatment Act, Pub. L. No. 93-247, 88 Stat. 4 (1974), *amended by* Keeping Children and Families Safe Act of 2003, Pub. L. No. 108-36, 117 Stat. 800 (codified in scattered sections of 42 U.S.C.).

38   *See, e.g.,* ME. REV. STAT. ANN. tit. 22, § 4002.

39   *See, e.g.,* CONN. GEN. STAT. § 46b-120(9).

40   *E.g.,* FLA. STAT. § 39.01(2).

41   *E.g.,* 55 PA. CODE § 3490.4 (a "child will not be deemed to be physically or mentally abused based on injuries that result solely from environmental factors that are beyond the control of the parent or person responsible for the child's welfare, such as inadequate housing, furnishings, income, clothing and medical care").

42   The author is aware of at least one instance where a state child welfare agency became involved with a family because of a provider report that the parents were assisting a youth to transition. The provider viewed the family's support of their transgender child as constituting child abuse and made a mandatory child abuse report. Upon reviewing the report, the child welfare worker initiated an investigation but did not remove the child from the home.

43   Arizona and California have particularly extensive lists of the rights of

children placed in foster care. Ariz. Rev. Stat. Ann. § 8-529; Cal.Welf. & Inst. Code § 16001.9.

44 *See* Caitlin Ryan et al., *Family Acceptance in Adolescence and the Health of LGBT Young Adults*, 23 J. Child & Adolescent Psychiatric Nursing 205 (2010), *available at* http://familyproject.sfsu.edu/files/FAP_Family%20Acceptance_JCAPN.pdf.

45 Doe v. Bell, 754 N.Y.S.2d 846 (N.Y. Sup. Ct. 2003).

46 *Cf.* Me. Rev. Stat. Ann. tit. 5, §§ 4553, 4553-A (specifically excluding gender identity from a statute pertaining to disability discrimination).

47 *See* Norfleet v. Ark. Dep't of Hum. Servs., 989 F.2d 289 (8th Cir. 1993); LaShawn A. v. Dixon, 762 F. Supp. 959, 993 (D.D.C. 1991).

48 *See, e.g.*, Karolyn Ann Hicks, *"Reparative" Therapy: Whether Parental Attempts to Change a Child's Sexual Orientation Can Legally Constitute Child Abuse*, 49 Am. U. L. Rev. 505 (1999).

49 *See, e.g.*, Banks v. Havener, 234 F. Supp. 27 (E.D. Va. 1964).

50 *See, e.g.*, Canell v. Lightner, 143 F.3d 1210 (9th Cir. 1998); R.G. v. Koller, 415 F. Supp.2d 1129 (D. Haw. 2006).

51 *See, e.g.*, Casey Family Programs, Mental Health, Ethnicity, Sexuality, and Spirituality Among Youth in Foster Care: Findings from the Casey Field Office Mental Health Study (2007), http://www.casey.org/Resources/Publications/pdf/MentalHealthEthnicitySexuality_FR.pdf. This particular study does not include findings from transgender youth because none of the youth in the survey that forms the basis of the publication identified as transgender or gender non-conforming. *Id.* at 24.

52 Nat'l Ct. Appointed Special Advocs. Ass'n, http://casaforchildren.org (last visited Sept. 5, 2011).

53 *See Sexual Orientation/Lesbian, Gay, Bisexual, Transgender, and Questioning (LGBTQ) Youth Issues Publications*, Child Welfare League of America, http://www.cwla.org/programs/culture/glbtqpubs.htm (last visited Oct. 20, 2011).

54 *See* ABA Ctr. on Children & the Law, *Opening Doors Project*, Am. Bar. Ass'n, http://www.americanbar.org/groups/child_law/projects_initiatives/opening-doors.html (last visited Oct. 20, 2011).

55 *Youth Publications and Downloads*, Nat'l Ctr. for Lesbian Rights, http://www.nclrights.org/youth (last visited Oct. 20, 2011). NCLR's Youth Project also provides guidance for group care facilities that serve transgender youth.

56 *See* Jody Marksamer, Nat'l Ctr. for Lesbian Rights, A Place of Respect: A Guide for Group Care Facilities Serving Transgender and Gender Non-Conforming Youth (2011), http://www.nclrights.org/site/DocServer/A_Place_Of_Respect.pdf?docID=8301; Shannan Wilber et al., Child Welfare League of America, Best Practice Guidelines: Serving

LGBT Youth in Out-of-Home Care (2006), *available at* http://www.nclrights. org/site/DocServer/bestpracticeslgbtyouth.pdf?docID=1322.

57   Angela Irvine, *"We've Had Three of Them": Addressing the Invisibility of Lesbian, Gay, Bisexual and Gender Non-Conforming Youths in the Juvenile Justice System*, 19 Colum. J. Gender & L. 675, 686 (2010). It is difficult to collect accurate data about the number of gender non-conforming youth in the juvenile justice system because many youth are afraid to reveal their identity. *Id.* at 679–80.

58   *Id.* at 689.

59   *In re* Gault, 387 U.S. 1 (1967).

60   *See* Jody Marksamer, *In Defense of LGBT Youth: Strategies to Help Juvenile Defenders Zealously Advocate for Their LGBT Clients,* 15 U.C. Davis J. Juv. L. Pol'y 403 (2011).

61   Katayoon Majd et al., Hidden Injustice: Lesbian, Gay, Bisexual, and Transgender Youth in Juvenile Courts 93 (2009), *available at* http://www. equityproject.org/pdfs/hidden_injustice.pdf.

62   *Doe v. Bell* is relevant in an incarceration context as well as a foster care context. *See Bell*, 754 N.Y.S.2d 846.

63   Majd et al., *supra* note 61, at 97.

64   Female-to-male transgender youth may be safer being housed in detention facilities based upon birth sex, however. An attorney should explain the consequences of these decisions to a client and ensure s/he understands all the implications of whether they are housed based on gender identity and expression or birth sex.

65   Youngberg v. Romeo, 457 U.S. 307 (1982).

66   *See, e.g.*, Alexander S. *ex rel.* Bowers v. Boyd, 876 F. Supp. 773, 788 (D.S.C. 1995).

67   For example, a transgender juvenile in the custody of New York's Office of Children and Family Services filed suit when she was denied her prescription hormone treatment. Rodriguez v. Johnson, No. 06-CV-00214 (S.D.N.Y. filed Jan. 11, 2006). The case was resolved by settlement in favor of the plaintiff.

68   Lambda Legal et al., National Recommended Best Practices for Serving LGBT Homeless Youth 3 (2009), http://data.lambdalegal.org/publications/downloads/bkl_national-recommended-best-practices-for-lgbt-homeless-youth.pdf.

69   Nicholas Ray, Nat'l Gay & Lesbian Task Force Pol'y Inst. & Nat'l Coal. for the Homeless, Lesbian, Gay, Bisexual and Transgender Youth: An Epidemic of Homelessness 58 (2006), *available at* http://www.thetaskforce. org/downloads/HomelessYouth.pdf.

70   *Id.*

71   *Id.* at 59.

72   Lisa Mottet & John M. Ohle, Nat'l Gay & Lesbian Task Force Pol'y Inst. & Nat'l Coal. for the Homeless, Transitioning Our Shelters: A Guide to Making Homeless Shelters Safe for Transgender People (2003), *available at* http://www.thetaskforce.org/downloads/reports/reports/TransitioningOurShelters.pdf.

73   20 U.S.C. § 1232g.

74   An eligible student is "a student who has reached 18 years of age or is attending an institution of postsecondary education." 33 C.F.R. § 99.3. A parent is "a parent of a student and includes a natural parent, a guardian, or an individual acting as a parent in the absence of a parent or a guardian." *Id.*

75   33 C.F.R. § 99.20.

76   *Id.*

77   *See, e.g.,* Haw. Rev. Stat. § 92F-24 (pertaining to the accuracy of agency records).

78   *See* 33 C.F.R. § 99.21.

79   *See* 33 C.F.R. § 99.22.

80   33 C.F.R. § 99.21(b)(2).

81   33 C.F.R. § 99.21(c).

82   33 C.F.R. § 99.30.

83   33 C.F.R. § 99.31. In addition, disclosures can be made to protect the health or safety of others. *Id.* An attorney should review the Code of Federal Regulations for a full list of permitted disclosures. 33 C.F.R. § 99.31 *et seq.*

84   33 C.F.R. § 99.37.

85   33 C.F.R. § 99.63 *et seq.*

86   For example, Colorado, Oregon, Washington, and Maine define sexual orientation as including gender identity. *See* Colo. Rev. Stat. §§ 22-32-109 (nondiscrimination in education), 24-34-401 *et seq.* (nondiscrimination in public accommodation, housing and employment); Me. Rev. Stat. Ann. tit. 5, § 4552 *et seq.* (nondiscrimination in employment, housing, public accommodation, credit and education); Or. Rev. Stat. §§ 10.030(1) (jury service), 101.115(3) (retirement communities), 174.100(6), 179.750(2) (state institutions), 240.306(1) (state employees), 418.648(10) (selection of foster parents), 430.550 (drug abuse diversion programs), 443.739(19) (adult foster care), 458.505(4)(h) (community service programs hosted by a community action agency), 659.850(2) (education), 659A.003 *et seq.* (nondiscrimination in public accommodation, employment, and housing), 744.382(4) (making life settlement contracts); Wash. Rev. Code §§ 48.30-300 (insurance), 49.60.175 (credit), 49.60.180 (employment), 49.60.190 (labor unions), 49.60.215 (public accommodation), 49.60.222 (housing).

87　*See, e.g.*, Cal. Civ. Code § 51 (public accommodations); Cal. Gov't Code § 12926 *et seq.* (nondiscrimination in employment and housing); Cal. Penal Code § 422.56.

88　However, be aware that some states specifically exclude gender identity from the definition of disability under public accommodations law. *See* Me. Rev. Stat. Ann. tit. 5, §§ 4553, 4553-A (specifically excluding gender identity from a statute pertaining to disability discrimination).

89　For example, the Maine Human Rights Commission provides a venue for the administrative investigation and adjudication of Maine discrimination cases, independent from the court system. *See About Us*, Me. Hum. Rts. Commission, http://www.maine.gov/mhrc/about/index.htm (last visited Oct. 20, 2011).

90　*See e.g.*, Schroer v. Billington, 577 F. Supp.2d 293 (D.D.C. 2008); Doe v. Yunits, No. 001060A, 2000 WL 33162199, at *6 (Mass. Super. Ct. Oct. 11, 2000).

91　*See, e.g.*, Freeman v. Realty Res. Hospitality, No. CV-09-199 (Me. Super. Ct. May 27, 2010) (order denying in part, and granting in part, defendant's motion to dismiss) (noting that the Maine Human Rights Act provided for gender identity discrimination claims in dismissing disability and sex discrimination claims by a transgender woman who was not permitted to use a female restroom, but upholding a claim based on sexual orientation discrimination where sexual orientation was defined as including gender identity).

92　*See, e.g.*, *Yunits*, 2000 WL 33162199 (finding grounds for an injunction requiring defendants to permit child to wear clothing appropriate to her gender identity to school based upon free speech and liberty interest claims under the Massachusetts Declaration of Rights).

93　Doe v. Clenchy, No. CV-09-201 (Me. Super. Ct. filed May 9, 2011). In this case, the school department originally permitted the youth to use the restroom consistent with her gender identity, and only after another student's legal guardian complained did the school require the transgender student to use a gender-neutral bathroom. The Penobscot County Superior Court rejected an argument that the school had an affirmative obligation to permit the youth to continue to use a gender appropriate bathroom. Doe v. Clenchy, No. CV-09-201 (Me. Super. Ct. Apr. 1, 2011) (order denying in part, and granting in part, defendant's motion to dismiss).

94　For recommendations about how to effectively advocate for transgender youth to be allowed to participate in sports according to their gender identity, see Pat Griffin & Helen J. Carroll, Nat'l Ctr. for Lesbian Rights et al., On the Team: Equal Opportunity for Transgender Student Athletes (2010), http://www.nclrights.org/site/DocServer/TransgenderStudentAthleteReport.pdf?docID=7901. Many FTM youth do not have problems being allowed to play on boys' teams because most boys' teams must allow girls to play on them, but may have problems with access to the locker room that is consistent with their gender identity.

95   Doe v. Yunits, No. 00-1060A, 2001 WL 664947 (Mass. Super. Ct. Feb. 26, 2001).

96   *Id.* at *5.

97   *Id.* at *17.

98   *Id.* at *21–22.

99   Individuals with Disabilities Education Act, Pub. L. No. 101-476, 104 Stat. 1103, 1142 (1990) (codified as amended in scattered sections of 20 U.S.C.).

100   34 C.F.R. § 300.320.

101   *See, e.g.*, Md. Code Ann., Educ. § 7-424.1 (requiring schools to develop a model policy that prohibits bullying, harassment, and intimidation in schools).

102   Vermont, for example, provides a private statutory right of action for harassment. *See* Washington v. Pierce, 895 A.2d 173 (Vt. 2005).

103   *See, e.g.*, 105 Ill. Comp. Stat. 5/27-23.7 (sexual orientation and gender identity); Iowa Code § 280.28 (same); Or. Rev. Stat. § 339.351 (sexual orientation).

104   Shore Reg'l High Sch. Bd. of Educ. v. P.S., 381 F.3d 194 (3d Cir. 2004).

105   20 U.S.C. § 1681.

106   Rehabilitation Act of 1973, Pub. L. No. 93-112, 87 Stat. 355 (codified as amended in scattered sections of 29 U.S.C.). For an example of a possible argument that might permit a FRA claim for gender identity, Justice Ralph D. Gants noted in footnote 6 of *Doe v. Yunits* that "even under the FRA, an individual with a gender identity disorder 'resulting from physical impairments' is not excluded from the definition of an 'individual with a disability.' In light of the remarkable growth in our understanding of the role of genetics in producing what were previously thought to be psychological disorders, this Court cannot eliminate the possibility that all or some gender identity disorders result 'from physical impairments' in an individual's genome." Doe v. Yunits, No. 00-1060A, 2001 WL 664947, at *5 n.6 (Mass. Super. Ct. Feb. 26, 2001) (internal citation omitted).

107   Rehabilitation Act, *supra* note 107.

108   *See* 29 U.S.C. § 794.

109   "For the purposes of Sections 791, 793, and 794 of this title, the term 'individual with a disability' does not include an individual on the basis of … transvestism, transsexualism, pedophilia, exhibitionism, voyeurism, gender identity disorders not resulting from physical impairments, or other sexual behavior disorders." 29 U.S.C. § 705(20)(F).

110   The World Professional Association for Transgender Health (WPATH) Standards of Care (SOC) provide recommendations for transition-related medical care for transgender youth. The Harry Benjamin International Gender Dysphoria Association, Standards Of Care For Gender Identity Disorders 8–11 (7th ed. 2011), *available at* http://www.wpath.org/documents/Standards%20

of%20Care%20V7%20-%202011%20WPATH.pdf. These standards are used by many, but not all, medical providers in making treatment decisions for transgender youth.

111   Appendix 8D includes a list of organizations, both national and regional, that serve transgender youth. Many of these organizations offer publications geared towards lawyers and non-lawyers.

Chapter 9: Intimate Partner Violence

Morgan Lynn, Terra Slavin, and Wayne A. Thomas Jr.

Introduction

Intimate partner violence is a social and public health epidemic that affects people of all classes, races, abilities, sexual orientations, religions, and gender identities. What little research that exists shows that transgender people are unsurprisingly not immune from the epidemic. Transgender clients presenting with family law issues may be survivors or they may be perpetrators of intimate partner violence. Few family law attorneys are prepared to ensure that clients who have faced intimate partner violence are appropriately represented and receive essential services to aid them in negotiating the biased judicial and non-judicial systems (including, for example, a shelter mediation program) they may encounter.

9.1 Intimate Partner Violence and Transgender Clients

9.1.1 Intimate Partner Violence Basics

For the purposes of this chapter, intimate partner violence is defined as a recurring and chronic pattern of behaviors where one person (the abuser) tries to control the thoughts, beliefs, and/or actions of her/his married or unmarried partner, someone s/he is dating, or someone with whom s/he had or has an intimate relationship (the survivor).[1] It is important for an attorney to focus on the pattern of behavior, rather than an isolated incident. While intimate partner violence or abuse can include physical assault, it is not limited to physical abuse. Abuse may be physical, emotional, sexual, economic, or related to a person's culture or identity. These are not discrete categories and instances of abuse may be in overlapping categories. Below are some examples of abusive behavior:

- emotional abuse: verbal abuse, lying, undermining self-esteem, humiliation, monitoring whereabouts, threats, and/or intimidation;

- physical abuse: pushing, hitting, punching, choking, withholding medications or hormones, sleep deprivation;

- sexual abuse: rape, coercing sex and/or sex with others, exposure to HIV or sexually transmitted infections;

- economic abuse: controlling money and resources, forcing to live above means, stealing, identity theft;

- cultural/identity abuse: threat of outing partner's sexual orientation, gender identity, sexual history or interests, HIV status, or any other personal information such as a partner's former name; using a partner's race, class, age, immigration status, religion, size, physical ability, language, and/or ethnicity against them.[2]

9.1.2 Intimate Partner Violence Involving a Transgender Spouse or Partner

9.1.2.1 Incidence of Abuse

There is a still small but growing body of research to assess the prevalence of intimate partner violence within transgender communities and to explore the experiences of transgender survivors. In *Injustice at Every Turn,* A Report of the National Transgender Discrimination Survey, the study of more than 6,000 transgender respondents revealed that:

> Nineteen percent (19%) of respondents have experienced domestic violence at the hands of a family member because of their transgender identity or gender non-conformity.

American Indian (45%), Asian (36%), Black (35%) and Latino/a (35%) respondents reported higher rates of domestic violence than the full sample, as well as undocumented non-citizens (39%), those earning under $10,000 annually (38%), those without a high school diploma (39%), the unemployed (30%), respondents who have lost jobs due to bias (35%) and those who worked in the underground economy (42%). MTF respondents endured family violence more often (22%) than FTM respondents (15%), while gender non-conforming respondents were victimized more often (21%) than their transgender peers (19%).[3]

In a report by The National Coalition of Anti-Violence Projects (NCAVP), research found that 50% of transgender and intersex respondents had been raped or physically assaulted by a romantic partner.[4] A study conducted by the Massachusetts Department of Public Health based on data collected in 2009 reported that 34.6% of transgender respondents had been threatened with physical violence by an intimate partner.[5]

While there has been some research on transgender survivors of intimate partner violence, there has been very little research on who perpetrates intimate partner violence. While many transgender individuals have experienced and will experience intimate partner violence, some transgender individuals are also abusers.

9.1.2.2 Tactics of Abuse and Hurdles to Assistance

Family law attorneys working with transgender individuals may well encounter clients and/or opposing parties who are survivors of intimate partner violence. Not all survivors present the same and many may not identify the abuse, victimization, or assault that they have experienced to be intimate partner violence. This occurs for a range of reasons: social and cultural images can distort people's understanding of intimate partner violence by narrowing the field of who can have such experiences to women in heterosexual relationships; internalized homophobia, biphobia, and/or transphobia can lead survivors to believe they deserve abuse; some survivors are too traumatized to talk about or acknowledge the abuse; and others may be too afraid of their abuser to speak out or take action, or they may have been threatened by their abuser about speaking to anyone. Transgender survivors may fear being "outed" (having their transgender identity disclosed against their will) to their family, friends, employers, or neighbors. For transgender survivors who work or have worked in illegal trades, such as sex work, their partners' knowledge of such work gives their partners an even greater amount of power over the survivor. Survivors who have engaged in sex work may be concerned about seeking police and court assistance for the abuse committed against them. This may be based on their own history with or legitimate concerns about interacting with law enforcement.

Given how small many transgender communities are, some survivors may be concerned about being identified as an intimate partner violence survivor. Furthermore, one partner identifying as a survivor and labeling her/his partner as an abuser within a small community may significantly affect the dynamic of the community. The survivor may have no interest in affecting that dynamic or fear s/he will lose her/his place within that community. For some transgender individuals, that community may be all the social support they have. Historically, LGBTQ communities have not always been fully supportive of intimate partner violence survivors and have not always been focused on holding abusers accountable for their actions. Given the political, social, and cultural battles over extending marriage equality and civil unions to same-sex couples, some in LGBTQ communities are considerably invested in promoting same-sex and LGBTQ relationships strictly as healthy relationships. This can add pressure to transgender survivors to stay silent about the abuse so as not to reflect negatively on the community.

Many transgender survivors are wary about interacting with the police and court system due to experienced or perceived concerns about harassment, discrimination, and bias. Police often respond inappropriately to calls involving physical assaults between intimate partners, particularly where one of the partners is transgender. If one of the parties is identifiably transgender, presents as masculine, is perceived to have been born male, or is physically larger than the other party, s/he may be more likely to be blamed for the incident or less likely to receive protection or be believed because of police bias or discrimination.[6] In some cases, the abuser will specifically disclose that her/his partner is transgender to law enforcement to leverage institutional bias. If the relationship presents to responding officers as a same-sex relationship, then police may respond by arresting both parties or neither party—believing that "boys will be boys," that it is not that serious if it is "between girls," that the fight is "fair," or that there could not be a survivor and an abuser where it is between two men or two women.[7] For these reasons, if an attorney is working with a person who has been arrested for intimate partner violence or against whom a protective order has been brought, it is important to understand that that person may not always be the abuser in the relationship and may in fact be the survivor.

An additional concern when working with transgender survivors is the possibility of mutual restraining orders. Mutual restraining orders, issued by a court for and against both parties, are mostly an inappropriate response to both parties seeking an order of protection. Referring back to the definition of intimate partner violence, one of the partners (the abuser) is using abusive tactics to obtain power and control over their partner (the survivor). Thus, only one of the parties is deserving of the restraining order. Mutual restraining orders and mutual arrests send a message that both parties are survivors and that both parties are abusers—a misleading message when only one partner holds power and control over the other. Mutual restraining orders empower the abuser while leaving the survivor feeling that the courts and law enforcement will not protect her/him.

Abusers prey on survivors, often using their fears—fear of disclosure of transgender identity or previous gender, police, violence, etc.—to keep survivors silent and under their control. A transgender person's fear that s/he might be treated in a way that is discriminatory or biased by the court system in an intimate partner violence-related or family court case is a fear that may be especially strong and is well-founded. Abusers may attempt to take advantage of such fear of, or actual, institutional bias against transgender individuals.

In addition to institutional bias from the police and court system, the broader community of intimate partner violence organizations and service providers have often either largely ignored the issue of intimate partner violence in transgender communities or replicated the kind of discrimination and prejudice transgender people experience in other areas of their lives. Some intimate partner violence programs see intimate partner violence exclusively through a lens in which men are abusers and women are survivors. As a result of this myopic view, survivors seeking services who present as, identify as, or were born male often are excluded from receiving intimate partner violence services, especially from shelter-providing organizations which may only provide housing to women and, then only to non-transgender women, and who may not serve transgender men or may insist that transgender men use their female name to access services.

Some tactics of abuse are more likely to be used against transgender survivors. In addition to institutional bias and capitalizing on the fears of survivors as discussed above, an abuser may engage in other forms of abuse that specifically target a transgender partner's gender identity, including: forcing her/him to dress consistent with her/his previous gender (including destroying or withholding access to her/his gender specific clothing or accessories), interfering with her/his gender transition (such as forcing her/him to stop taking hormones), withholding medications such as hormones or post-surgery drugs, refusing to use her/his post-transition name or pronoun (particularly in public), obstructing her/his access to transgender support groups and/or medical services related to gender transition, outing her/him as transgender, ridiculing her/his body, or challenging the authenticity of her/his gender identity.

Identity theft and other forms of economic abuse are other powerful tools in an abuser's arsenal. While electronic identity theft is increasing with the expansion of the Internet and wireless communications, old-fashioned impersonation in person and over the phone to make unauthorized financial transactions using the victim's stolen identity is easier when the identity thief presents as the same gender as the identity theft victim. A transgender survivor may be more vulnerable to this type of identity theft either because her/his partner is the same gender or because s/he has chosen a gender-neutral name that makes it easier for the identity thief to impersonate her/him. In addition, given the fact that many transgender individuals have difficulty finding stable, well-paying employment, an abuser can force her/his partner to become economically dependent on her/him as a way to exact control. For example, an abuser may run up charges on the survivor's debit/credit card(s) or empty out the survivor's bank accounts. For an additional list of abusive tactics used against and by transgender individuals, as well as the impact of transphobia on access to services, see the *Transgender Domestic Violence and Sexual Assault Resource Sheet* included in the resource list in Appendix 9A.

Unfortunately, as will be discussed below, while there may be protection under the law, not all transgender survivors will be able to benefit from that protection in court where bias and discrimination against transgender people are too often still the norm.

9.1.2.3 When the Abuser is Transgender

While much of this chapter is focused on working with a transgender survivor of intimate partner violence, it is important to acknowledge that transgender individuals can also be abusers. Transgender individuals who abuse their transgender or non-transgender partners may use some of the same abusive tactics mentioned above. They may also attempt to coerce their partner to stay in the relationship or not report the abuse because they, as a transgender person, would face institutional bias and/ or violence in the courts and justice system.

Sometimes attorneys may feel a tension between zealously representing their client's interests and not using an opposing party's identity against her/him. An attorney may achieve the client's goals without taking advantage of institutional biases against transgender, bisexual, and gay and lesbian people. Family law representation involving intimate partner violence should focus on behavior, not the parties' sexual or gender identities. When representing a transgender abuser, it is important to recommend that s/he seek assistance to stop such behavior.

9.1.3 Difference between BDSM and Abuse

As stated earlier, intimate partner violence is a recurring and chronic pattern of behaviors where one person tries to control the thoughts, beliefs, and/or actions of her/his partner, someone s/he is dating or someone with whom s/he has or had an intimate relationship. BDSM stands for bondage and discipline, dominance and submission, and sadomasochism. BDSM is the generally accepted umbrella term for a broad group of consensual behaviors that includes the giving and receiving of intense erotic sensation.[8] The behaviors used in BDSM are consensual, negotiated, and involve the communication of limits and the use of a safe word that can stop all action at any time.[9]

Because BDSM is a consensual dynamic, it is not abuse. Power is negotiated between "players"—who may or may not be partners/spouses outside the BDSM context—for the purpose of a "scene" only, and do not correlate to the players' relationships outside the BDSM context. In contrast, abuse is nonconsensual force, power over another, and/or actions that are meant to limit the survivor's choices and resources.

However, abusive behavior can manifest itself within negotiated interactions. For example, if one player's use of a safe word is ignored, that may indicate abusive behavior. Additionally, it is common for abusers to claim that abuse was really negotiated BDSM behavior. This is particularly true for transgender individuals whose sexuality is often eroticized. When analyzing an allegation of abusive behavior within a BDSM context, it is important to focus on the context, intent, and effect of the behavior, and not to rely on cultural stereotypes.

9.2 Impact of Intimate Partner Violence on Family Law

9.2.1 Impact of Intimate Partner Violence on Family Law Representation Generally

A client's experience as a survivor of intimate partner violence might dramatically affect an attorney's representation in family law matters. This section addresses the intersection of intimate partner violence and family law representation as it relates to custody determinations, divorce and relationship dissolution, and estate planning.

Determining whether a client is a survivor of intimate partner violence can be accomplished through adept client interviewing and case records searches. As discussed in Section 9.1.2.2, it is possible that a client will be reluctant to discuss abuse. S/he may not feel comfortable offering up sensitive information and may not think it is relevant to her/his case. It is also very likely that a client will not have reported the abuse to the police or sought some form of a civil protective order. When an attorney meets with a client, s/he can ask the client questions about her/his relationship's dynamics, specifically touching on issues of physical, sexual, economic, and emotional abuse. For additional information about how to screen for intimate partner violence, see the ABA's screening tool.[10]

9.2.2 Custody Remedies for Survivors

As described in Chapter 6, transgender clients may face barriers in securing custody of and visitation with their children in family dissolution cases. Transgender clients who are also survivors of intimate partner violence, though, may have some important legal protections in custody/visitation disputes that should not be overlooked.

Custody determinations are generally based on a best interests of the child(ren) standard. According to the American Bar Association's Commission on Domestic Violence, forty-two states and the District of Columbia explicitly take intimate partner violence into consideration in doing an assessment of the child's best interests.[11] Three states (West Virginia, South Dakota, Oklahoma) do not include it, and another five (Washington, Texas, Maryland, Louisiana, Arizona) do not explicitly consider it as a factor, but have some form of recognition that intimate partner violence between parents affects the emotional and physical health of the children and may consider the abuse in determining custody.[12] Intimate partner violence against a parent, particularly when witnessed by the child, can sometimes be strong evidence against the abusive parent getting full physical and legal custody. Sometimes, particularly in cases where intimate partner violence has been witnessed by the children or has involved them, abusers will be granted no physical custody and limited or supervised visitation. In fact, almost half of the states and the District of Columbia have some form of rebuttable presumption against custody for abusive parents or against joint custody when intimate partner violence has occurred.[13]

Clients who are survivors of intimate partner violence, depending on the specific jurisdiction's evidence requirements, may introduce evidence of past intimate partner violence perpetrated by the abuser against them or against the children involved in a custody case. Past civil protective orders, criminal cases, or other court documents may substantiate the client's claim. A client may also be called to testify about intimate partner violence and its impact on her/his capacity to share custodial rights (specifically around legal decision making and visitation) or on the mental and physical health and safety of the children. An expert witness may also be called to testify about the impact of intimate partner violence on children, including those who did not directly witness the abuse.

In establishing a visitation arrangement for a transgender client who is a survivor, it is important to consider the safety of the visitation arrangement as well as how appropriate and comfortable it is for a transgender parent. For example, spaces such as supervised visitation centers or police stations—which are often used for visitation in cases involving child abuse or intimate partner violence—are safe for many survivors, but might not be staffed by individuals who are respectful of transgender parents. Conversely, transgender community spaces or a known third party might be respectful of transgender parents, but not necessarily safe for survivors of intimate partner violence.

An attorney should also take abusive dynamics into consideration during custody and visitation negotiations. Some survivors will not feel comfortable or be able to fully assert their preferred options if forced to negotiate in the same room as their abuser. Some jurisdictions allow for an exception to mediation or negotiation if there is a history of intimate partner violence or if the mediators otherwise determine that mediation would not be productive or reliable as a result of relationship dynamics. Shuttle negotiation or some other process that does not require direct communication between a survivor and abuser is an option in some jurisdictions. In other jurisdictions, the only option may be to fully litigate the case before a judge or to conduct negotiations solely between attorneys (if both parties are represented).

9.2.3 Divorce and Relationship Dissolution for Survivors

Transgender individuals who are divorcing or legally separating from their spouse face legal hurdles (see Chapter 5) that may be exacerbated for individuals who are also survivors of intimate partner violence. A few of the areas where intimate partner violence intersects with divorce or dissolution are the mediation process, asset and debt distribution, alimony, and fault versus no-fault divorce assessment.

As noted in Section 9.2.2, mediation may not be safe for survivors of intimate partner violence. Abusive partners may use tactics of abuse to coerce a survivor into an agreement in mediation that is not in the survivor's best interest or that the survivor would not consent to if not in the same room with the abuser. Being unable to mediate or consent to a divorce, separation, or dissolution agreement may result in the case going to trial.

Asset and debt distribution may be impacted by intimate partner violence particularly where the abusive relationship included economic abuse. For example, a former partner may have withheld money, controlled household expenditures, forced a former partner not to work or contributed to her/him being fired from jobs, kept property titled in the abuser's name only, or worked to ruin the survivor's credit. This situation could be exacerbated for transgender persons who work in the majority of jurisdictions that have no express employment discrimination protections for transgender people. In equitable distribution states where courts consider factors in determining distribution of debt and/or property, a survivor's attorney could discuss the relevance of intimate partner violence and economic abuse to the reason for the relationship's termination or the cause for indebtedness. Similarly, an attorney may be able to provide evidence and arguments related to intimate partner violence or economic abuse to argue for alimony for a client in states that consider similar factors to determine alimony.[14]

While all states now have some no-fault grounds for proceeding with divorce, the majority still retain some combined form of fault/no-fault grounds. In many of the states that retain fault-based grounds for divorce, most include some form of physical or emotional cruelty as one of the grounds. Intimate partner violence, be it physical or emotional, can often count for this ground and should be considered in the assessment of whether the client should proceed under a fault or no-fault theory. A finding of fault in a divorce may impact distribution of marital assets as well as custody determinations.

9.2.4 Estate Planning

While intimate partner violence may be more apparent when a relationship is dissolving or during a custody dispute, estate planning attorneys should also be aware of and screen for intimate partner violence and other abusive dynamics when working with a couple who is engaged in estate planning. Attorneys may need to refer each spouse to a separate attorney and possibly provide the client with resources for intimate partner violence services when there are indicators of the presence of abuse. See Chapter 10 for guidance about transgender clients and estate planning.

9.3 Specific Intimate Partner Violence-Related Legal Remedies

9.3.1 Protective Orders

One of the main legal remedies that a survivor of intimate partner violence may access is a civil protective order.[15] These orders, which are governed by the states' intimate partner violence statutes, typically provide broad discretion to a judge to direct the behavior of the abuser (respondent), which includes orders that the respondent must stop harassing, threatening, and abusing the survivor (petitioner). Additionally, these orders can require that the abuser have no contact with the survivor at her/his home, school, and/or workplace; that s/he stay a specific distance away from the survivor; move out of the home; obey temporary child custody orders; pay financial obligations, including child and spousal support; and other orders as deemed appropriate. A violation of a protective order usually carries a criminal penalty and the existence of a protective order can increase the likelihood that law enforcement will intervene if called to the location of a future incident. While the grounds to qualify for a protective order vary from state to state, in most jurisdictions, there must be threats of or actual physical or sexual violence or seriously harassing behavior.

9.3.1.1 Availability for Transgender Survivors

While the majority of states have gender-neutral intimate partner violence protective orders, some states explicitly exclude same-sex couples,[16] which could affect a transgender survivor's eligibility depending upon how the state regards an individual's legal sex (see Chapter 2) and whether the relationship is considered a same-sex or different-sex relationship (see Chapter 3).[17] Currently, the two states that explicitly exclude survivors in same-sex relationships from accessing intimate partner violence protective orders are South Carolina and

Montana,[18] although if a couple shares a child in common in Montana, a survivor may still be eligible.[19]

Another challenge is that different states have different requirements for what types of relationships qualify in order for someone to be eligible for a protective order. Some states require that the parties live together or be related by blood or have children in common, others require that they only be in a dating relationship, some allow for victims of stalking and sexual assault to obtain protective orders against people to whom they are not related, and still others may only require that the petitioner be a roommate of the abuser.

Where an individual is not eligible for an intimate partner violence protective order, s/he may be eligible for a different order, including a civil harassment order, where available.

9.3.1.2 Challenges for Transgender Survivors

Although the majority of states either explicitly or through gender neutral language allow LGBTQ individuals to seek protective orders, it remains to be seen whether this remedy, that has historically been framed in a heterosexual context, can adequately protect the interests of transgender survivors who may be facing threats of abuse that are unique to this population. One of the more prevalent threats used by an abusive partner is to threaten to publicly disclose a person's gender identity. The threat of public disclosure can also be used in the context of a person's sexual orientation. While this threat can have real repercussions, it is uncertain whether threats of public disclosure qualify as abuse for purposes of obtaining a protective order under state statutes.[20] Attorneys are advised to closely review the specific statutory language that describes the type of harm that must be demonstrated to qualify for a protective order. Even if a threat of public disclosure is probably not sufficient to qualify as an offense legally worthy of a protective order, it is possible that such a threat in conjunction with other threats or actions could constitute a crime such as stalking or harassment.

The case of *Richardson v. Easterling* is one to which parallels may be drawn.[21] In this case, a gay male petitioner sought a protective order on the grounds that his same-sex abuser had threatened to contact the police and falsely accuse him of knowingly spreading communicable diseases;

had contacted the District of Columbia's Board of Medicine, multiple colleagues, and his secretary, and divulged his sexual orientation, information about his sex life, and falsely accused him of knowingly spreading communicable diseases; and had forged and attempted to pass a check on a closed financial account in his name, resulting in a criminal investigation by Maryland authorities. [22]

The petitioner received a temporary protective order which included a provision prohibiting the respondent from contacting the petitioner's colleagues.[23] The respondent challenged the protective order, arguing that petitioner was HIV positive and that nothing petitioner alleged fell under the acts covered by the particular statute.[24] The trial court agreed with the respondent stating that "neither abuse nor violence has been alleged."[25] The matter was appealed and reversed on the grounds that the allegations could have constituted stalking, emotional violence, or intentional infliction of emotional distress, but noting that had the respondent only defamed him, there would have been no criminal conduct to invoke the act.[26] This case is instructive because even at the appellate level the court was resistant to protect the petitioner from statements that could be seen as defamatory, i.e., the threats to disclose his HIV status and sexuality, because they were not seen as crimes committed by the respondent against the petitioner's person.

Another challenge for transgender survivors is that there may be little to no evidence of the abuse. Given the historically difficult relationship between transgender individuals and law enforcement, many members of the transgender community are reluctant to involve law enforcement or other service providers. This fear is regularly reinforced by abusers who proclaim that their transgender partner will not be believed, will be arrested, or will experience violence by the very institutions that are meant to help. As a result, there are often no police reports, and where there are reports, they may have been misclassified as another crime or contain narratives that place blame on the survivor. Transgender individuals may also be reluctant to access medical care given past experiences of discrimination, disrespect, or mistreatment by health care providers. The absence of medical documentation may make it hard to prove the abuse. Where these documents do not exist, an attorney should be ready to argue about the barriers to accessing these traditional services and explain the absence of medical documentation.

Because proof beyond testimony is often unavailable, the credibility of each party is a pivotal issue in most protective order hearings. Attorneys working with transgender clients may have to overcome biased or discriminatory misinformation offered to the court by opposing parties. Attorneys may want to consider bringing in expert witnesses to overcome some of these barriers.

The following is a list of some things for attorneys to keep in mind when assisting a transgender client who is a survivor of intimate partner violence:

- A protective order is not always the best solution, and in fact, in certain circumstances could increase the dangerousness of the situation. (See Section 9.4.1 Safety Planning discussion below).

- Attorneys working with survivors of intimate partner violence are urged to be sensitive and work towards empowering the survivor, by first listening to her/his story, informing the survivor of her/his various options, asking what s/he wants, and then respecting that decision. People who have been abused have had the power to make their own decisions taken away from them; regaining that power is an important step in healing.

- Survivors frequently struggle with the shame, hurt, and fear that come with being a survivor of intimate partner violence. These feelings may be compounded for a transgender survivor because s/he has to "come out" to a legal system that in many ways negates or disrespects both her/his relationship and her/his identity. When representing transgender survivors, an attorney should make sure that the survivor's post-transition name, pronoun, and gender are used where legally possible. An attorney should be vigilant when a judge, clerk, bailiff, or opposing counsel uses, for instance, male pronouns when referring to the abuser, when the abuser is actually a transgender woman, or uses female pronouns when referring to the survivor, when the survivor is actually a transgender man. If the wrong pronoun or name is being used to identify a client, the attorney should politely inform the speaker of the correct pronoun or name. To provide effective representation, an attorney should be comfortable using the client's pronoun and name and be consistent in references to the client. There is more guidance about providing culturally competent representation in Chapter 1.

- An attorney should be prepared for the possibility that the legal system will trivialize a transgender client's case. Judges and/or court personnel may encourage the attorney to settle the matter or they may be less willing to grant the protective order or more likely to grant mutual protective orders, which is an inappropriate option that often leaves a survivor in a more dangerous situation and more vulnerable to arrest. It also reaffirms the survivor's experience that the abuser will not be held accountable for her/his actions. An attorney representing a transgender client should research and prepare arguments in advance to counter these barriers.

- An attorney should also ensure that a client's preferred name and pronoun are included in the court record and paperwork in a way that matches the client's desires while recognizing the legal requirements of the record and other legal documents. For example, it may be difficult to have a protective order enforced unless the petitioner's name matches the petitioner's legal and identification documents (e.g. license, passport, lease). If a client wishes for her/his post-transition name to be used in the hearing and in the documents and her/his post-transition name is different from her/his legal name, her/his attorney should consider adding both names to the protective order (e.g. Petitioner AB a.k.a. Petitioner DC versus Respondent) and stating the client's post-transition name on the record.

- Communicating respectfully to a survivor client that s/he is not alone and that intimate partner violence exists in all forms of relationships helps reassure a client that s/he is not to blame and that the attorney is supportive of her/his gender identity.

9.3.2 Criminal Advocacy

Family law attorneys may be called upon to provide advocacy for clients in the criminal justice system. As discussed above, there can be significant barriers for transgender individuals in accessing law enforcement. Family law attorneys may need to advocate or petition that a police report be taken or amended. Often, police reports involving transgender victims of crime misstate the victim's name, gender, and relationship to the other party. An attorney may also need to advocate that a protective order that has been violated be enforced. Where possible, it is helpful for attorneys working in these systems to build relationships with local prosecutors and police departments, particularly ones with liaisons to the LGBTQ community.

A family law attorney may also need to address a transgender client's legitimate fear of interacting at all with the criminal justice system, including filing a police report, seeking a protective order, or participating as a witness in a criminal matter. Abusers typically threaten a transgender survivor that if s/he accesses these systems and protections, s/he will be arrested and incarcerated. For many transgender people, the fear of being incarcerated in a sex-segregated facility is extreme and justified. Therefore, an attorney should counsel transgender clients about the reality of interacting with the system (e.g. you will not be locked up solely for filing a protective order, but you may be locked up if the police are called to the scene of an intimate partner violence incident and even wrongly determine that you have committed a crime against your partner). Also, attorneys should counsel a client who is working with a prosecutor that the prosecutor is not her/his attorney and that the prosecutor can use admissions to crimes against her/him.

9.3.3 Immigration Remedies for Survivors of Intimate Partner Violence

Immigration status may be used as a tool by an abuser to try and maintain power and control, and many survivors are unaware that there are specific domestic violence remedies that can be used by immigrant survivors.[27] As discussed in Chapter 3, a transgender client may or may not be eligible for family-based immigration remedies, such as marriage-based petitions or fiancé/ée visas. However, the transgender client, if s/he is a survivor of intimate partner violence, may have access to additional, and very significant, immigration remedies.

Two immigration remedies that are available to some survivors of intimate partner violence are a Violence Against Women Act (VAWA) Self-Petition and a Battered Spouse Waiver. An individual who is or was previously legally married to a citizen or a lawful permanent resident and who survived abuse may be eligible to apply without her/his spouse for lawful permanent residence pursuant to VAWA.[28] To apply for lawful permanent residence without a spouse/abuser a client would file a VAWA Self-Petition. This option is available for survivors while they are married and for up to two years after they divorce. Generally, an individual is eligible to file as a VAWA Self-Petitioner if 1) s/he entered into a good faith marriage to a United States Citizen or Lawful Permanent Resident, 2) s/he experienced battering or extreme mental cruelty (a pattern of abusive power and control) during said marriage, and 3) s/he is a person of "good moral character."[29] An individual may be eligible for this form of relief irrespective of how s/he entered the United States.

A Battered Spouse Waiver is another immigration remedy that is available to an individual with Conditional Lawful Permanent Residence (as evidenced by a two-year green card) who is or was previously legally married to a United States Citizen and who survived abuse.[30] A Battered Spouse Waiver allows a noncitizen to remove the conditions on her/his green card without the joint participation of her/his United States Citizen Spouse.

Both VAWA Self-Petitions and Battered Spouse Waivers are only available to individuals who are legally married according to the federal government, so a transgender client's eligibility depends upon whether or not the federal government considers her/him to be legally married to a different-sex spouse. See Chapter 3 for guidance about assessing whether a transgender client's marriage is likely to be considered a valid marriage between different-sex individuals. Note, it is not clear yet what the February 2011 Department of Justice announcement about its decision not to defend the federal Defense of Marriage Act will have on family-based immigration remedies for individuals legally married to a same-sex spouse.

Marriage-based immigration remedies, including the ones described above, may not be an option for transgender individuals who are deemed to be in a "same-sex" relationship because the federal government does not recognize marriages between persons of the same sex pursuant to DOMA. However, the "U Visa" protects individuals regardless of their sexual orientation or gender identity who are victims of certain crimes, including intimate partner violence and sexual assault.[31] To be eligible, the crime must have occurred in the United States and the victim must have suffered substantial emotional or physical harm and be willing and able to cooperate with the government's prosecution of the crime. The U Visa is dependent on the victim's status as a crime victim, and does not depend upon the existence of a recognized marriage or on the immigration status of the abuser. A client may be eligible for a U Visa even if the client entered the country without documentation or if the client has some criminal activity on her/his record. Transgender clients who have survived abuse and who work with the police, prosecutors, or other governmental agencies by filing police reports, participating in hearings as witnesses, etc., may be eligible. As discussed earlier in this chapter, transgender people may have reasonable fears about reaching out to and working with the police or other parts of the justice system. An attorney may be in a good position to help make connections between a client and these systems to ensure that the client interacts with people who will not discriminate against her/him because s/he is transgender. Since evidence of abuse is required to obtain a U Visa, it is important for an attorney to encourage a transgender client to document the abuse and keep records wherever possible. U Visas provide noncitizens with lawful residency and a work permit for four years and the ability to petition for permanent residency after three years.[32]

Transgender survivors of intimate partner violence may also be eligible for asylum status if they are unable to return to their home country out of fear of persecution because of their membership in a particular social class (potentially including survivors of extreme intimate partner or sexual violence, people who are gay, lesbian, bisexual and/or transgender, or people with HIV/AIDS) or their race, religion, nationality or political opinion.[33] Asylum applications must be filed within one year of entry into the United States (with some exceptions). Asylees are granted lawful residency and a work permit and are eligible to petition for lawful permanent residence (a green card) after one year.

9.4 Safety Planning and Other Issues

9.4.1 Safety Planning

One of the most important aspects of successfully providing legal services for a transgender survivor of intimate partner violence is to adequately ensure that her/his safety remains a priority throughout the legal process. Attorneys who have not had training on safety planning and the unique safety dynamics for transgender clients should consider contacting or being trained by a service provider with such expertise. Appendix 9A includes a resource list that includes a safety planning worksheet.

9.4.2 Screening Questions

If an attorney reaches out to local intimate partner violence agencies as potential resources, s/he should consider asking the following screening questions to evaluate whether the service is appropriate for transgender survivors:

- Does your agency have experience working with transgender survivors, and if not, does your agency partner with any local organization with experience working with transgender survivors?

- What services is a transgender client eligible for?

- What are the shelter's policies in regard to sex-segregated services and housing transgender clients?

- Will your program staff be respectful of my transgender client's gender identity?

- Does your organization have a nondiscrimination policy in place? Is gender identity or expression included as a protected category? Is the nondiscrimination policy provided to residents or other program participants? Is it posted in a visible place? How is it enforced?

9.4.3 Sex-Segregated Services/Facilities and Intimate Partner Violence

The reality is that too often transgender survivors are unable to access traditional intimate partner violence resources because such services, particularly housing, are sex-segregated and often have access policies based on biology, physiology, or birth sex, rather than gender identity. Even where a sex-segregated facility, such as a shelter, will allow a transgender individual admittance based on her/his gender identity, it is very possible that the other clients and staff may create a hostile environment.[34]

If taking refuge at a shelter is not an option for a client for any reason, one alternative is accessing Victims of Crime Compensation.[35] This money can be used to cover the cost of a hotel or the cost of relocating and can also help pay for medical bills and counseling. To have access to these funds an individual is typically required to cooperate with law enforcement.

9.4.4 Resources for Abusers

While there are few resources for transgender survivors, there are even fewer resources for transgender abusers. The best option for an attorney working with a transgender abuser is to call the resources for survivors and ask whether they have referrals for abusers. If an attorney knows that s/he is working with an abuser, the attorney should not refer her/him to survivor-focused resources. Resources for transgender abusers may also be available through the local court offender services agency. An attorney working with a transgender abuser can contact the court agency to determine whether they would be safe and competent to work with transgender participants.

---

1   The term "intimate partner violence" is used in this chapter to denote the most common type of relationship in which abusive behaviors may occur and the most common type of relationship in a family law context. Other terms such as "domestic violence," "domestic abuse," "battering," etc. may sometimes be used interchangeably to communicate the same type of behaviors. Abusive behaviors in relationships between children and their parents, siblings, roommates, individuals who have never been involved in an intimate relationship together, or caregiver

and patient may not be remedied, however, in a family law context, depending on the particular state's law (although criminal sanctions may be available).

2   *What is Partner Abuse?*, The Network, http://tnlr.org/about-partner-abuse/what-is-partner-abuse/ (last visited Sept. 14, 2011).

3   Jaime M. Grant et al., Nat'l Ctr. for Transgender Equal. & Nat'l Gay & Lesbian Task Force, Injustice at Every Turn: A Report of the National Transgender Discrimination Survey 100 (2011), *available at* http://www.thetaskforce.org/downloads/reports/reports/ntds_full.pdf.

4   Diana Courvant & Loree Cook-Daniels, *Trans and Intersex Survivors of Domestic Violence: Defining Terms, Barriers, and Responsibilities, in* 1998 Nat'l Coal. Against Domestic Violence Conference Handbook, *available at* http://www.survivorproject.org/defbarresp.html.

5   Mass. Dep't of Pub. Health, The Health of Lesbian, Gay, Bisexual, and Transgender (LGBT) Persons in Massachusetts 11 (2009), http://www.mass.gov/eohhs/docs/dph/commissioner/lgbt-health-report.pdf.

6   "When police do attempt to identify the abuser in an LGBT domestic violence situation, reports to [Amnesty International] suggest that transgender and gender variant survivors, immigrant survivors, survivors of color, the person perceived to be of lower socioeconomic status or the biggest and youngest person are reportedly often assumed to be the abusers and arrested." Amnesty International, Stonewalled: Police Abuse and Misconduct Against Lesbian, Gay, Bisexual and Transgender People in the U.S. 129 (2005), *available at* http://www.amnesty.org/en/library/info/AMR51/122/2005.

7   *See* Sommi v. Ayer, 744 N.E.2d 679 (Mass. App. Ct. 2001); Press Release, Gay & Lesbian Advocates & Defenders, Appeals Court Decides Cases of Domestic Violence Involving Gay Men (Mar. 28, 2001), http://www.glad.org/current/pr-detail/appeals-court-decides-cases-of-domestic-violence-involving-gay-men/.

8   *Is It S/M or Abuse?*, The Network, http://tnlr.org/about-partner-abuse/sm-v-abuse/ (last visited, Sept. 14, 2011).

9   *Id.*

10   ABA Commission on Domestic Violence, *Tool for Attorneys to Screen for Domestic Violence, in* Lesbian, Gay, Bisexual, and Transgender Domestic Violence Toolkit for Attorneys (2005), http://www.americanbar.org/content/dam/aba/migrated/domviol/screeningtoolcdv.authcheckdam.pdf.

11   *See* ABA Commission on Domestic Violence, Child Custody and Domestic Violence By State (2008), http://www.americanbar.org/content/dam/aba/migrated/domviol/docs/Custody.authcheckdam.pdf. This statutory summary chart details the child custody and domestic violence statutes in the fifty states.

12   *See id.*

13   *See id.*

14   There's a good deal of variation in the factors that can be considered for alimony/support. In states with fault divorce, marital fault can usually be considered and intimate partner violence would likely be relevant to that analysis. *See Family Law in the 50 States: Chart 1: Alimony/Spousal Support Factors*, 44 Fam. L.Q. 510 (2011), *available at* http://www.americanbar.org/content/dam/aba/publishing/family_law_quarterly/vol44/4404_win11_chart1alimony.pdf.

15   Civil protective order is a broad term which varies depending on the jurisdiction. Other names may include an order of protection or a domestic violence restraining order.

16   *See* ABA Commission on Domestic Violence, Domestic Violence Civil Protection Orders by State (2009), http://www.americanbar.org/content/dam/aba/migrated/domviol/pdfs/dv_cpo_chart.authcheckdam.pdf. This statutory summary chart details the domestic violence civil protection order statutes in the fifty states.

17   *See id.*

18   *Id.*

19   Mont. Code Ann. § 45-5-206(2)(b).

20   Shannon Little, *Challenging Changing Legal Definitions of Family in Same-Sex Domestic Violence*, 19 Hastings Women's L.J. 259, 269 (2008).

21   Richardson v. Easterling, 878 A.2d 1212 (D.C. 2005).

22   *Id.* at 1214.

23   *Id.*

24   *Id.* at 1214–15.

25   *Id.* at 1216.

26   *Id.* at 1217–18. The D.C. protective order statute requires "an act punishable as a criminal offense committed by an offender upon a person," which was the reasoning for the criminal analysis. *See id.* at 1216.

27   In general, a non-citizen client who has a prior deportation order, any criminal history, or has left and reentered the country should exercise particular caution before applying for any immigration remedies and is well-advised to consult with an immigration attorney before doing so.

28   Violence Against Women Act of 1994, Pub. L. No. 103-322, 108 Stat. 1902 (codified as amended in scattered section of 8, 18, 28, 42 U.S.C.).

29   *See* 8 U.S.C. § 1154.

30   *See* 8 U.S.C. § 1186a.

31   *See* 8 U.S.C. § 1101(a)(15)(U). *See generally* Greta D. Stoltz, *The U Visa: Another Remedy for Battered Immigrant Women*, 7 Scholar 127 (2004).

32   *See* 8 U.S.C. §§ 1184(p), 1255(m).

33   *See* Hernandez-Montiel v. INS, 225 F.3d 1084 (9th Cir. 2000).

34   *See* Lisa Mottet & John M. Ohle, Nat'l Coal. for the Homeless & Nat'l Gay & Lesbian Task Force Pol'y Inst., Transitioning Our Shelters: A Guide to Making Homeless Shelters Safe for Transgender People (2003), *available at* http://www.thetaskforce.org/downloads/reports/reports/TransitioningOurShelters.pdf. While this guide focuses on homeless shelters, many of the issues, challenges, and policies are also applicable to intimate partner violence shelters.

35   42 U.S.C. § 10602. *See* Nat'l Assoc'n of Crime Victim Comp. Bds., http://www.nacvcb.org/ (last visited Sept. 15, 2011).

Chapter 10: Estate Planning and Elder Law

Michelle B. LaPointe

Introduction

Transgender clients and their spouses or partners are likely some of the most vulnerable clients with whom an estate-planning or family law attorney will have the opportunity to work. Transgender clients and their spouses or partners may have the validity of their marriages or relationships challenged, either during life or after their death, even in circumstances where family members appeared to be supportive of the transgender client's transgender status and the relationship. For this reason, it is critically important that all estate-planning measures taken for transgender clients and their spouses or partners are carefully tailored to their unique history, identity, and personal needs. Likewise, attorneys should exercise an abundance of caution in ensuring that the wishes of a transgender client and her/his spouse or partner are carried out with respect to the management of her/his property, personal and medical care, and testamentary wishes.

10.1 Surviving Spouse's or Partner's Ability to Inherit

10.1.1 Intestacy

In a best case scenario, a transgender client and her/his spouse or partner will execute a will and other testamentary instruments prior to her/his death. Estate planning and the execution of legal instruments is the best way to ensure that a transgender client's and her/his spouse's or partner's intentions will be respected subsequent to her/his death. See Section 10.1.3 below for guidance about which testamentary instruments an attorney should advise her/his clients to execute.

If an individual dies without a valid will, inheritance of all probate property is subject to intestacy law. Intestacy is established by state statute and therefore varies from state to state. According to the Uniform Probate Code, a spouse's right to inherit if her/his spouse dies intestate is limited.[1] A surviving spouse only receives the entirety of the decedent's estate if the decedent has no living parents or children.[2] It is important to consider that the client may own property in multiple states which would then subject the property to intestate distribution in each state with differing results.

10.1.2 Probate Process

Some notice of the probate is required, even if the partners were married. Notice includes mailing a citation to all heirs at law. In some instances, the petitioner may be required to give notice of probate proceedings by publishing the details of the probate matter in the local newspaper.[3] Such notice is quite literally an invitation to object to the proceedings and may be particularly problematic for transgender people because of the perceived invitation to challenge a proper designation, not necessarily because it is legally problematic, but rather, because relatives or others may have some opposition to the person's transgender identity or because death may be the first time some learn of the fact of a transgender person's identity.

The Uniform Probate Code provides a hierarchy of those individuals who should be appointed to administer an intestate estate. First priority is given to the surviving spouse.[4] If the decedent was unmarried, all heirs are eligible to be appointed.[5] An unmarried surviving partner can only be appointed to administer an estate if, after formal proceedings, the court determined that all heirs with priority had been given proper notice of such proceedings and had failed to bring a petition for appointment of their own, or if assented to by the heirs.[6]

10.1.3 Considerations for Transgender Clients

A surviving spouse's ability to inherit under intestacy law is contingent upon the recognition of the validity of the marriage.[7] In states that do not recognize marriages between same-sex individuals, the validity of the marriage may depend upon legal recognition of the transgender spouse's post-transition sex. In addition, some states have case law that addresses the validity of transgender people's marriages. See Chapter 3 for guidance about counseling your transgender client regarding state recognition of her/his marriage.

The potential obstacles to inheritance underscore the importance of formalizing the relationship and testamentary wishes of a transgender individual and her/his spouse. Section 10.1.4.1 includes detailed recommendations for drafting and executing a document that recognizes the transgender spouse's transgender status. Likewise, strategies for formalizing the clients' testamentary wishes are discussed throughout Section 10.1.4. The probate process is, by definition, a public process that invites anyone interested in the decedent's estate to be heard. Despite this emphasis on openness, the probate process fails to fully recognize relationships between unmarried individuals. The Uniform Probate Code makes no provision for unmarried partners and therefore, even in instances where partners have been legally married, there is a risk for transgender individuals that if their marriage is invalidated, the surviving partner will not inherit the deceased partner's property. For this reason, it is critical that even married couples with one or more transgender partners execute the appropriate documents to increase the likelihood that their testamentary wishes will be carried out.

Particularly if a transgender person and her/his spouse reside in a jurisdiction where their marriage may be invalidated, or members of the couple's families are believed to be likely to challenge their testamentary wishes, an attorney should advise the couple to pursue non-probate approaches to inheritance, such as trusts, joint assets, and beneficiary designations for non-probate assets. These strategies are discussed in Sections 10.1.4.4 and 10.1.4.5 below.

10.1.4 Practice Recommendations: Disposition of Property at Death

10.1.4.1 Transgender Clients Who Marry, Enter Civil Unions, or Other Marital Equivalents

An attorney should advise transgender clients who intend to marry about whether the state is likely to recognize the marriage as valid. See Chapter 3 for more specific guidance about how to access the validity of a transgender client's marriage. Consideration should also be given to any issues that may cause a detriment if married, such as taxes, insurance, and future benefits.

In addition, clients who marry or enter civil unions or domestic partnerships should execute some form of acknowledgement of the transgender spouse's transgender status. In the event a couple is already married and one spouse intends to transition to a different sex, a similar acknowledgement should be executed by both spouses. The purpose of the acknowledgement is to demonstrate that there is no fraud or misrepresentation by the transgender spouse as to her/his identity should that issue ever be raised by a spouse, heir, or third party. By affirmatively acknowledging that the details of the transgender spouse's status are known, the other spouse will hopefully be estopped from attempting to invalidate the marriage or diminish the transgender spouse's rights to property or child custody by bringing an equitable claim of fraud or misrepresentation at a later date.[8]

An acknowledgement of the transgender spouse's transgender status can be accomplished in a formal prenuptial or postnuptial agreement. However, unless there are other financial or custody issues to establish before or after the marriage, including inheritances, a formal prenuptial or postnuptial agreement is not necessary and may be unlikely. In the absence of a prenuptial or postnuptial agreement, both clients should execute an affidavit or agreement, acknowledging the spouse's transgender status. Such affidavit or agreement should:

- acknowledge the transgender spouse's transgender status and transition history, including sex designation at birth;

- affirmatively state the parties' intention to undertake the responsibilities and obligations of marriage;

- acknowledge the transgender spouse's or spouses' ability to procreate;

- affirmatively state that both parties repudiate any claims for dissolution of marriage or denial of rights based on the transgender status of one or both spouses; and

- acknowledge that the transgender spouse has fully disclosed all information related to her/his gender identity to the fullest extent possible.[9]

10.1.4.2 Avoiding Challenges Based on Mental Incapacity or Undue Influence

Even the best estate plan can be invalidated by a relative who claims that the testator/testatrix did not have the mental capacity to execute her/his documents or that the testator/testatrix was unduly influenced by a friend, partner, or other relative.

If the client suffers from any mental illness or cognitive impairment, s/he should be advised to undergo an examination by a physician and obtain a written opinion of competence as close to the date of signing as possible prior to executing testamentary instruments. Because the psychological elements of gender identity are often misunderstood and misconstrued by the public and by jurists unfamiliar with transgender people, a transgender client who anticipates a potential challenge to her/his testamentary wishes may wish to undergo such an examination even if s/he does not have a history of mental illness or cognitive impairment. As with all clients, if a will contest is anticipated, extra care should be taken, such as audio recording or videotaping of the will.

Additionally, as with all clients, when a transgender client wishing to execute estate-planning documents is accompanied by a nonclient partner, friend, or relative, the attorney must spend time alone with the client to verify her/his wishes. The attorney should document that when alone, the client reaffirmed her/his wishes as expressed earlier, or that the client voiced that s/he would rather proceed differently.

Before drafting estate-planning documents, the attorney should prepare for the client's specific family dynamics. This requires a frank conversation with the client about her/his family relationships. In the event one or more family member(s) is known to be likely to challenge the will or disposition of the client's property or the validity of the marriage, it is important to take every step possible to neutralize any potential claim. The will or trust should clearly state the client's intention to disinherit relatives s/he does not wish to benefit in order to demonstrate that there is no oversight. Most states recognize an *in terrorem* clause in a will. An *in terrorem* clause cancels any bequest to a beneficiary who brings a challenge as to the validity of the will in court. A client may wish to make a nominal gift to a potentially troublesome family member, so that s/he has something to lose under the *in terrorem* clause if s/he brings a challenge to the will.

10.1.4.3 Drafting and Executing a Will

In *In re Gardiner*, the Kansas Supreme Court denied J'Noel Gardiner the right to inherit her deceased husband's property on the basis that she was born male, and therefore, the marriage was held to be invalid.[10] J'Noel's post-transition sex was not recognized by the court despite the fact that she had undergone sex reassignment surgery, legally changed her birth certificate to reflect her post-transition sex, and established that her late husband was aware of her transgender status.[11] Had J'Noel's late husband executed a valid will acknowledging J'Noel's transgender status and his desire to benefit her regardless of whether their marriage was deemed valid, the case would likely have been decided differently.

Thus, if the client is married, the will should include language clearly stating the desire to benefit the spouse of the testator/testatrix regardless of whether their marriage is considered valid at the time of death. This is particularly important in states where the validity of transgender individuals' marriages has been challenged. However, couples residing in more tolerant states may very well move out of state at a later date for work or family obligations. Therefore, it is wise to include such protective language in wills for all couples made up of one or more transgender spouses.

As with all estate-planning documents, a will should clearly state all names by which the testator/testatrix has ever been known. This minimizes the chance that the will can be challenged as to the identity of the testator/testatrix, and will make it easier for the executor to marshal all assets of the estate, including any which may still be titled under a prior name. This is especially important for transgender clients, many of whom have changed their names. Likewise, if the client's will names anyone else who has changed her/his name, the will should list all names the beneficiary has ever been known by as well as current addresses. A sample partial will is included in Appendix 10C.

10.1.4.4 Will Substitutes

Establishing and funding a trust during the client's lifetime is an effective way to avoid the probate process and its required notice and scrutiny. A revocable trust, where the client serves as trustee and the trust assets are treated as belonging to her/him for income tax purposes, can be a relatively seamless way to control assets during the client's lifetime and after the client's death. The client will have the flexibility to amend or revoke the trust at any time, allowing for the fluid management and distribution of assets and provision for beneficiaries during the client's life and after her/his death.

A trust can still be challenged on equitable grounds. As with a will, the practitioner should take all steps that are appropriate to establish that the client is acting freely and with a full understanding of the effects of the trust. This may include an affidavit, careful notes by the practitioner, or in some cases, a statement by the client's physician attesting to the client's competence, all similar to a will execution.

> **Practice Tip**: The income, gift, and estate tax treatment of assets held in trust is of the utmost importance, even for clients without considerable wealth. An attorney should seek the advice of an experienced estate-planning attorney before drafting and funding a trust.

10.1.4.5 Non-testamentary Dispositions

By designating the beneficiary of non-probate assets, such as life insurance policies, retirement accounts, and some investment and bank accounts, the client can avoid the delay and scrutiny of the probate process. Non-probate assets pass directly to the beneficiary immediately upon proper proof of death, without any need for court involvement or potential challenges from heirs. A transgender client who anticipates that family members may challenge probate proceedings that recognize her/his partner's right to inherit would greatly benefit from the opportunity to transfer assets directly to her/his partner immediately upon death.

Regardless of how confident the client may be that her/his beneficiary designations properly name her/his intended beneficiaries, it is critical that the practitioner urge the client to double-check, particularly in instances where the client or her/his beneficiaries have changed their names. Financial institutions routinely lose or incorrectly transcribe beneficiary designations. Further, where an employer offers several different planning vehicles, such as insurance policies and retirement benefits, it is not uncommon for the company to fail to apply updated beneficiary designation wishes to all policies and accounts. Similarly, if a company is taken over by a new owner, employee benefits may change and new forms may need to be completed. It is far easier to correct these errors during the life of the client. Once the client dies or becomes incapacitated and an incorrect designation is given effect, correcting the error will likely result in costly litigation.

In addition to beneficiary designations, the client may want to grant joint ownership in a bank or investment account or in real property to her/his desired beneficiary. With respect to the personal residence, the practitioner should examine state statutes related to homestead protection, with particular attention to strategies for protecting the property against the creditors of both partners if the clients are unmarried or if the marriage could be invalidated posthumously. For some bank accounts, it may be possible to designate a beneficiary after the account owner's death by retitling the account as "payable on death" or "in trust for." The rules for such designations will vary by state and by financial institution.

> **Practice Tip**: Certain lifetime transfers may have income, gift, or estate tax consequences for the client or the recipient. Consideration should be given to whether a transfer should occur pre- or post-marriage. In addition, transfers made to or from an individual who receives, or may in the future receive, government benefits, including Supplemental Security Income or Medicaid, can cause disqualification. It is important to consult with an experienced estate-planning

and/or disability law practitioner in these circumstances. The attorney should also pay careful attention to the terms of the loan when changing title to mortgaged real property to be sure the transfer does not trigger due on sale provisions.

10.2 Medical Decision Making

10.2.1 Overview

Transgender individuals can be extremely vulnerable during medical emergencies and in hospitals or skilled nursing environments. It is critical to ensure that the client's partner, relative, or a trusted friend who understands the client's identity, medical needs, and preferences, has the authority to make medical decisions on her/his behalf. This is accomplished most effectively by advising the client to execute a power of attorney or a health care proxy, known in some states as a power of attorney for health care or an advance medical directive. For ease of discussion, this type of medical decision-making document will be referred to as a health care proxy herein.

In the event of a medical crisis that renders the client unable to make medical decisions, if s/he has not had the foresight to execute a health care proxy, her/his partner, relative, or friend will instead be forced to go to court to seek guardianship. This is a public process that requires the petitioner to notify all interested parties and invite them to contest the appointment.[12] Such interested parties may include the parents and/or siblings of the incapacitated person. As with executors or administrators of probate estates, the Uniform Probate Code establishes a hierarchy of individuals who may be appointed guardian of an incapacitated person. According to this hierarchy, a spouse has the highest level of priority. However, a parent takes priority over "an adult with whom the respondent has resided for more than six months before the filing of a petition."[13] The effect of this provision is that a parent will be appointed instead of an unmarried partner, regardless of the incapacitated person's wishes. On the contrary, unless a guardian or temporary guardian has already been appointed, the individual nominated in the incapacitated person's health care proxy takes priority over all other petitioners.[14]

10.2.2 Health Care Proxy or Power of Attorney for Health Care

A health care proxy is an effective tool for the client to control who will have the authority to make medical decisions on her/his behalf in the event of incapacity. Such a document is particularly advisable when the client is unmarried or there is any potential question as to the recognition of her/his marriage. A sample health care proxy is included in Appendix 10D.

An effective health care proxy will, in most instances, obviate the need for a guardianship. The agent under a health care proxy will avoid the court oversight and reporting requirements to which guardians are subject. In addition, the guardianship process can be time consuming, expensive, emotionally draining, and unnecessarily public.

Each state has different rules and technical requirements related to health care proxies. A practitioner should be sure to review state statutes on the subject. Failure to strictly comply with statutory requirements undermines the strength of the instrument and threatens to leave a client, or principal, unprotected at the time when s/he is the most vulnerable. The client should carefully choose the agent s/he would like to appoint and should be advised to discuss her/his health care preferences with the designated agent. The primary role of the agent is to be an advocate and decision maker for the client when the client is unable to manage her/his own medical care. Transgender clients are well advised to inform the designated agent of the fact of their transgender identity and the legal and medical history relating to their transition. Although lack of information about the principal's transgender identity should not be grounds for invalidating or challenging the designation of an agent, it could be strategically misused and call into question the validity of the designation, particularly where a challenge is taking place in a court unfamiliar with transgender people.

10.2.2.1 Practice Recommendations: Drafting a Health Care Proxy or Power of Attorney for Health Care

The form and content of health care proxies vary from state to state. As with all estate-planning documents, it is critical that the instrument comply with the statutory formalities of execution in the client's state, such as whether witnesses or notarization are required. It is advisable to execute all estate-planning documents, including a health care proxy, with two witnesses and a notary, even if such formalities are not required. The client should provide a copy of the health care proxy to all treating physicians and medical providers and to the agent named in the document. In the event the client resides in multiple jurisdictions, consideration should be given to having separate documents prepared for each state or one document that conforms to both states' laws.

In states where a power of attorney for health care, rather than a health care proxy or an advanced medical directive, is recognized, the document should be a "durable" power of attorney for health care, meaning the language of the document specifies that it shall remain effective regardless of any illness or incapacity of the principal.

The client should state in the document that s/he is transgender and wishes to be treated as male or female. If the client has particular grooming preferences or is undergoing hormone therapy, s/he should clearly indicate that s/he wishes for such grooming or therapy to continue while receiving medical treatment.

The health care proxy should identify a nominee, and possibly a backup, whom the client would choose to be appointed as her/his guardian if guardianship should become necessary. Such a nominee, if otherwise qualified to serve as guardian, will take priority over any other petitioners.[15]

The health care proxy should specifically identify the client's partner or any friends s/he wishes to have unlimited visitation rights in a hospital or nursing home. In the event the client has difficult family relationships, it may be equally important to identify individuals who should *not* have the right to visit in a hospital or nursing home. A simple way to facilitate this wish may be to identify a trusted friend or a partner as the "gatekeeper." This individual will be identified in the document as the person with the authority to determine whether or not a visitor shall be given access to the client in a hospital or nursing home. This allows for changing family dynamics and removes the stress and responsibility of setting visitation boundaries from the patient.

In addition to including hospital visitation instructions in her/his health care proxy, the client may wish to execute a separate, stand-alone hospital visitation authorization. This may be a particularly attractive strategy for a client who has included all of the details related to her/his transgender status and ongoing treatments in her/his health care proxy, but does not wish for these details to be widely circulated upon every hospitalization. However, a hospital visitation authorization should not be executed in lieu of a properly drafted health care proxy, but in addition to such a document.

Should a medical institution refuse to honor the client's hospital visitation wishes, the state statute related to health care proxies will provide a statutory basis for demanding that her/his wishes be honored. The nature of a health care proxy is that it identifies an agent who has the authority to handle medical decision making. By putting hospital visitation decisions within the scope of this authority, the client is appointing a medical advocate with the legal authority to enforce her/his wishes when s/he cannot.

10.2.3 The Health Insurance Portability and Accountability Act (HIPAA)

Identifying which individuals can access the client's medical information is as important as appointing a medical decision maker, particularly for transgender clients who have been and wish to remain private about the fact of their transition and transgender identity. The primary source of medical privacy is the Health Insurance Portability and Accountability Act of 1996.[16]

HIPAA imposes civil penalties on entities and individuals who knowingly or unknowingly release protected health information. These penalties range from $1,000 to a maximum of $1,500,000.[17] Because the penalties associated with HIPAA privacy violations can be so severe, many medical institutions and practitioners appropriately err on the side of caution with respect to releasing protected medical information, particularly where there are any obvious family conflicts.

It is essential that all clients, particularly those who are transgender, execute an effective HIPAA authorization, identifying the individuals who should have access to their medical records and the scope of records to be released. In many states, a health care proxy does not take effect until the principal is no longer able to make decisions for herself/himself. This creates an effective "Catch-22" for the appointed decision maker who cannot find out enough information from medical personnel to determine whether or not the principal is incapacitated. Without knowledge as to whether the health care proxy has been activated as a result of incapacity, the agent cannot begin to act on behalf of the principal. Arming the health care agent with access to medical records under a HIPAA authorization enables the agent to find out enough medical information to begin to act immediately when the principal becomes incapacitated. A sample HIPAA authorization is included in Appendix 10E.

10.2.3.1 Practice Recommendations: Drafting a HIPAA Authorization

As discussed above, it is extremely important that every transgender client executes an effective HIPAA authorization to provide access to health information to her/his partner, spouse and/or trusted friends. In order to be effective, a HIPAA authorization must contain several "core elements."[18] These core elements include, but are not limited to:

- a description of the information to be disclosed ("all health information" is preferred);

- identification of the specific persons or class of persons that are authorized to receive protected health information;

- an affirmative statement that the client has the right to revoke the authorization; and

- a statement from the client acknowledging that when medical information is used or disclosed pursuant to the authorization, it may be subject to redisclosure and is no longer protected by HIPAA.

In order for a HIPAA authorization to encompass psychotherapy notes, the authorization must affirmatively state the individual's desire for such information to be disclosed.[19]

The client should state all legal or informal names s/he has been known by. This will help to ensure that access will be granted to older medical records that identify the client by a previously used name.

As with the health care proxy, the client should provide a copy of this authorization to all treating physicians and/or medical providers.

10.2.4 Practice Recommendations: Drafting End-of-Life Decision-Making Documents

All clients should be advised to express their wishes with respect to end-of-life medical decision making. Unlike health care proxies or powers of attorney for health care, many states do not have statutes recognizing living wills or advance directives. Without statutory recognition, doctors or medical institutions may refuse to honor the terms of the instrument. In such states, practitioners should bootstrap the living will or advance directive by incorporating it, by reference, into the health care proxy or power of attorney for health care. In so doing, the health care agent can force the recognition of the principal's wishes by arguing that s/he has the authority to direct end-of-life care under the health care proxy or power of attorney for health care. The transgender client should include all names s/he has been known by, her/his preference that s/he be treated as male or female, and any hormone treatment or grooming that s/he prefers be continued in the event s/he is not able to do so herself/himself. A sample living will and advance directive is included in Appendix 10F.

10.3 Financial Decision Making

Even in instances where a couple is legally married, they should not take for granted that each spouse will have access to the other's assets in a time of need. Simply identifying one's spouse or partner as a person who is authorized to discuss accounts with a financial institution does not necessarily grant that spouse or partner legal access to the funds. Moreover, because there could be a challenge to the validity of a transgender person's marriage, ensuring access to assets where desired may be especially important for transgender clients.

All clients should be advised to execute a durable power of attorney identifying the individual or individuals they would like to have access to their assets in the event of incapacity and the scope of that authority.

If the client has not effectively appointed someone to manage her/his financial affairs in the event of incapacity, it will be necessary for someone to petition the probate court for conservatorship. As with a guardianship, a conservatorship is a public and uncertain process. Family members of the incapacitated person must be notified of a petition for conservatorship and will have an opportunity to intervene and block the appointment. As with guardianship, the parent is given first priority to serve as conservator when the incapacitated person is unmarried or her/his marriage is treated as invalid. Therefore, avoiding conservatorship is especially critical for unmarried partners or married couples where one or more spouse is transgender, particularly in a jurisdiction or family circumstance where the validity of the marriage may be subject to challenge.

10.3.1 Durable Power of Attorney

A power of attorney enables the client, or principal, to identify whom s/he would like to appoint as an agent to make financial decisions for her/him, and establish the scope of the agent's authority, without the need for probate court intervention. This authority is only effective during the lifetime of the principal.[20]

The purpose of a power of attorney is to empower a partner, relative, or trusted friend with the authority to manage the principal's finances when the principal is incapacitated or otherwise unable to manage her/his affairs. A "durable" power of attorney refers to a power of attorney that remains in effect after the principal becomes incapacitated or disabled.[21] Because incapacity and disability are the circumstances under which the effectiveness of a power of attorney is most critical, it is important to be sure that the instrument is properly drafted as a durable power of attorney. The elements of such designation are detailed in Section 10.3.1.1 below. However, the format and execution of a durable power of attorney vary from state to state. It is important to carefully review state statutes for the required format, contents, and formalities of execution.

Nominating a guardian or conservator within the power of attorney makes her/him the presumptive guardian or conservator, assuming the court finds that s/he is otherwise fit to serve.[22]

Further, as described below in greater detail, a power of attorney document may also be an appropriate place for a parent to establish her/his wishes for custody of her/his children in the event of incapacity. A sample durable power of attorney is included in Appendix 10G.

10.3.1.1 Practice Recommendations: Drafting a Durable Power of Attorney

The form and content of powers of attorney vary state by state. An attorney should always begin with a careful examination of the relevant state statutes. As with all estate-planning documents, it is critical that the document meets the statutory formalities of execution for the client's state or states, such as whether witnesses or notarization are required. Given that requirements vary by state, it is advisable to execute all estate-planning documents with two witnesses and a notary. This increases the likelihood that the document will be valid in another jurisdiction if the client needs it while traveling out of state.

The power of attorney should clearly acknowledge the client's transgender status and all names the client, or principal, has ever been known by. Likewise, if the named agent has changed her/his name, the document should include all names the agent has ever been known by.

In some states, a power of attorney must specifically address each power the principal wishes to grant to the agent. A simple statement that the agent should have "all of the powers held by the principal" is not necessarily sufficient. Yet, even if a specific description of powers is not required, it will make use of the document easier, particularly when dealing with large financial institutions, most of which are reluctant to act at the direction of an agent. Accordingly, the document should identify whether or not the agent has the authority to sell or transfer real estate, make gifts of the principal's property, name beneficiaries of retirement accounts and life insurance policies, establish revocable or irrevocable trusts, and whether the agent has the authority to "self-deal," or to take actions that benefit herself/himself.

In order for the document to be effective after the disability or incapacity of the principal, it must be titled "durable power of attorney." Further, the terms of the document must state, "this power of attorney shall not be affected by subsequent disability or incapacity of the principal, or lapse of time."[23]

A principal may make the agent's authority contingent upon a finding that the principal is incapacitated.[24] This "springing" type of durable power of attorney is often preferable to clients who do not have a spouse, partner, or trusted friend to serve because it minimizes the chances that the agent will abuse her/his power to steal or mismanage the principal's assets. Although it is often difficult to strike a balance between protecting a client from financial abuse and maximizing ease of use of the power of attorney by the agent, it is important to keep in mind that financial institutions are very wary of potential liability for honoring the authority of an agent. Any limitations placed on the agent's authority will likely create obstacles to accessing retirement, investment, or brokerage accounts. Ultimately, this balance must be struck by discussing the client's specific assets, her/his level of trust in her/his proposed agent, and the likelihood that the agent will need to serve.

Within the power of attorney, the principal should nominate the individual or individuals whom s/he would like to serve as conservator and guardian for herself/himself and for her/his children, if appropriate, in the event court-appointed fiduciaries become necessary. The agent or agents nominated under the power of attorney, if otherwise fit to serve, will take priority over all other petitioners for appointment as guardian or conservator.[25]

The principal should execute two or three duplicate powers of attorney. This enables the principal to furnish originals to financial institutions, courts, or registries without fear that it will be lost or that her/his authority will be hampered while waiting for an original to be returned.

10.4 Estate Planning for Clients Who Are Disabled or Terminally Ill

It is very important for a transgender parent to firmly establish her/his wishes with respect to guardianship of her/his children. Families with one or more transgender parents are particularly vulnerable because the validity of the marriage may be challenged and the authority of a transgender parent may be challenged based on a claim of deceit or unfitness as a parent. This issue becomes even more critical in the event of the disability or illness of the parent.

10.4.1 Standby Guardianship Laws

The Uniform Probate Code provides several ways in which a parent's wishes with respect to guardianship of her/his children can be recognized. Parents facing a major disability or illness should consider obtaining formal court recognition of these wishes in advance of their incapacity or death. This process is referred to as a "standby guardianship."

During her/his lifetime, the appointing parent may petition for court confirmation of a standby appointment.[26] The parent first brings a petition requesting that the court confirm the appointment.[27] In order to confirm the appointment, the court must find that the parent is likely to become unable to care for the child within two years.[28] Additionally, the court will order standard notice to interested parties, who may then object.[29] Once affirmed by the court, the appointment becomes effective upon:

- death of the appointing parent;
- adjudication that the parent is incapacitated; or
- a written determination by an examining physician that the parent is no longer able to care for the child.[30]

Once effective, the guardian must file an acceptance of appointment within thirty days.[31] However, because notice has already been issued, interested parties are barred from objecting to the agent's appointment at this stage.[32]

The process of establishing a standby guardian can be an emotionally and logistically difficult approach for an ill parent. In addition, it entails public probate proceedings. The parent would be required to publicly identify and discuss her/his impairment to some degree, such as disclosing her/his HIV status to the court, which the parent may wish to avoid. However, a standby guardianship provides the parent with confidence that her/his wishes with respect to her/his minor child will be carried out. Likewise, it is a fluid option that can carry through illness and then beyond the parent's death without the risk of any interruption in the guardianship arrangement.

An alternative to a full standby guardianship in the case of a disabled or ill parent is the temporary delegation of guardianship authority.[33] This may be a more appropriate approach when an illness is likely to be temporary or the child will soon be of majority age. The parent can delegate "any power regarding care, custody or property of the minor."[34] Such appointment can be made for up to six months, or longer if necessary, with a renewal required every six months.[35] The parent can identify the agent and the powers to be delegated in her/his power of attorney. The agent must file a petition and provide notice to all interested parties in order to receive appointment.[36]

10.4.2 Appointment after the Death of the Parent

A parent can nominate a future guardian for her/his child to take effect in the event of death or disability. The nomination can be made by will or by another signed statement, including a power of attorney.[37] As with a pre-established standby guardianship, such guardianship becomes effective upon the death of the parent or submission of a signed statement by the treating physician that the parent is no longer able to care for the child.[38] Although the guardian can begin to act immediately, within thirty days of effective appointment, the nominee must file a petition to affirm the guardianship with the probate court.[39] Notice will then be issued and any interested party may object to the appointment.[40] The family of the deceased parent, who will receive notice and be given an opportunity to intervene in the guardianship, may be likely to object to the appointment due to the transgender status of the parent or the nominated guardian.

10.4.3 Guardianship Considerations

In the event that more than one guardianship nomination is made in various wills or powers of attorney, the most recent nomination will likely be treated as the parent's wish. For this reason, it is a good idea to be sure that the client's power of attorney, will, and any other document nominating a guardian are consistent and up to date.

It is important to inform a client that no guardianship nomination or appointment may supersede the guardianship authority of the other parent if the other parent has custody of the child.[41]

If the client anticipates that a minor child will inherit assets upon the parent's death, the client should be advised to consider establishing a trust. The trust will operate outside the probate process, eliminating the need for court oversight and reporting. Unlike a conservatorship under the review of the probate courts, a trust does not end when the minor reaches majority. This enables the parent to ensure that the child doesn't suddenly obtain full ownership of her/his inheritance at eighteen years old, which may be before s/he is mature enough to responsibly manage the funds.[42]

> **Practice Tip**: If the parent's estate contains retirement benefits, be aware that there are significant pitfalls to funding a trust with qualified retirement funds. Placing retirement benefits into a trust may automatically trigger liquidation of the account upon the death of the testator/testarix and cause income taxes to be realized. Drafting a trust that allows the beneficiary to "stretch out" the retirement benefits during her/his lifetime is a challenging task. One should seek the advice of an experienced gift and estate tax planning attorney.

10.5 Postmortem Instructions

Postmortem instructions should be stated clearly in a "directive as to remains" (or similar document) and repeated in the client's will and possibly a health care proxy. Although a will is unlikely to be obtained, filed, and allowed quickly enough to dictate the funeral and burial process, in the event of any controversy, having these wishes memorialized in the will creates a venue and a process for the petitioner to obtain a court order enforcing these wishes.

Often, the state statutes and regulations regarding which party has the authority to consent to cremation or burial ambiguously identify "family" or "next of kin." Particularly where there are challenging family dynamics or religious differences, it is critical that the principal clearly state whether s/he wishes to be cremated, and whom s/he would like to have the authority to take possession of the remains. If the client anticipates that her/his family might object to the involvement of a partner or spouse in funeral and burial procedures because the client or her/his spouse is transgender, it is critical that all documentation related to funeral and burial wishes clarify the transgender status of the principal or her/his spouse, as well as all names s/he may have ever been known by.

Because these are decisions that must take place under the stress of grief within a very limited period of time, the more clearly the client's funeral and burial wishes are stated the better. The principal may also wish to include instructions as to her/his preferred name and gender to be used in an obituary, service, and/or burial marker. A client may prearrange their own funeral arrangements which may include signing a cremation authorization. A sample directive as to remains is included in Appendix 10H.

10.6 Housing for Transgender Elders

10.6.1 Bias or Discrimination in Elder Housing

Once elders become more frail and as their assets diminish, they commonly move from their privately-owned or rented homes to subsidized senior housing, assisted living, or a skilled nursing facility.

Transgender elders are significantly more likely than their non-transgender peers to experience discrimination in seeking senior housing and in obtaining care and services once placed in such an environment. This negative treatment stems from pervasive bias and discrimination as well as lack of knowledge and information available to the provider community about transgender people and transgender people's lives. Unfortunately, because of their vulnerability and reliance on others, transgender elders may be less likely to speak out about discrimination or abuse. While this is true of all elders, transgender elders seeking to maintain privacy or discretion about their transgender status may be particularly reluctant to publically acknowledge that they have been discriminated against on that basis. In addition, although transgender elders are afforded some protection under federal and state nondiscrimination laws, elders are often less likely to have the resources to identify these protections and to access the advocates necessary to help assert them.

Subsidized senior housing facilities, assisted living facilities, and nursing homes are all subject to The Fair Housing Act of 1968 (FHA).[43] While the FHA does not explicitly protect against discrimination based on gender identity or expression, federal sex and disability discrimination prohibitions should, at least theoretically and conceptually, protect transgender elders from discriminatory treatment.[44] The United States Department of Housing and Urban Development (HUD) recently explained that discrimination based on gender identity and expression falls under the FHA.[45]

The Nursing Home Reform Act of 1987 ("Act") establishes standards of care and certain basic rights for nursing home residents.[46] Although the Act does not specifically address the rights of transgender nursing home residents, the Act calls for dignity, quality of life, and patient-directed care in nursing homes, and creates a cause of action for enforcement.[47]

10.6.2 Advocacy

The threshold issue for a transgender elder entering subsidized housing, assisted living, or a nursing home is whether s/he wishes to identify herself/himself to the staff and fellow residents as transgender. As in all circumstances, this decision is a personal one and is ultimately up to the client. However, in a nursing home where a client is likely to receive skilled nursing care, s/he may not be afforded privacy or have the physical capacity to maintain autonomy. In such a situation, it may be wise for the client to disclose her/his transgender status to appropriate administrative employees and staff upfront. This may allow a transgender elder to determine what information is important for them to convey and what educational materials to provide along with the information. It is critical for an elder to know, upon entering a nursing home, that s/he will be treated with dignity and compassion, particularly at times when s/he may be physically or emotionally vulnerable, and to know what her/his rights are and who to contact if her/his rights are violated.

If a transgender client does experience discrimination or mistreatment in a nursing home, a complaint should be made directly to the state attorney general's office. The attorney general is responsible for enforcing patient's rights under health care and consumer rights laws and regulations.

The stressful choices of where to live and how to interact with other residents and patients will be much easier if the transgender elder has an advocate, such as a geriatric care manager or attorney, particularly one who is sensitive and knowledgeable about transgender people's lives. The advocate can be more direct and assertive than the client may feel comfortable being. Before a transgender elder moves into an assisted living facility or nursing home, her/his advocate should ask direct questions about how a transgender elder will be treated and how the staff will ensure her/his privacy, and, if the elder wishes, advocate for recognition of her/his gender identity. The advocate should prepare the administration and direct care staff to use the transgender resident's preferred name and appropriate pronoun.

In an assisted living facility or nursing home, the client is likely to share a room with another resident. The facility should place the client with an appropriate roommate based on the transgender client's gender identity. For example, in a sex-segregated assisted living or nursing home facility, a transgender woman should be placed with a female roommate and a transgender man should be placed with a male roommate. The transgender resident's advocate should work with the administration and the staff to help ensure that the roommate will observe the client's privacy. The advocate should put the onus on the administration to demonstrate a concrete plan for communicating with the staff and other residents, remain actively involved in ensuring that the plan is being properly carried out, and ensure that there are consequences for residents or staff who fail to provide the transgender elder with the respect, care, and comfort s/he deserves.

---

1   Although the Uniform Probate Code does not illustrate the laws of every state, it has been adopted in whole or in part in nineteen states. Further, in states that have not adopted the Uniform Probate Code in whole or in part, statutes related to probate procedures are often relatively similar to the Uniform Probate Code. The Uniform Probate Code is used as the standard throughout this chapter. Practitioners are advised to review their own state statutes on each topic discussed herein, even in states where the Uniform Probate Code has been adopted, as there will likely be some deviation in implementation.

2   Unif. Probate Code § 2-201A(a)(1).

3   Unif. Probate Code §§ 3-306, 1-401(a).

4   Unif. Probate Code § 3-203(a).

5   Unif. Probate Code § 3-203(a).

6   Unif. Probate Code § 3-203(e).

7   In addition, some transgender clients may be unable or choose not to marry their partner. In such circumstances, a transgender client who wants to protect her/his property rights in case a non-marital relationship dissolves may want to execute a cohabitation agreement. See Appendix 10A for a sample cohabitation

agreement.

8   *See* Kantaras v. Kantaras, 884 So. 2d 155 (Fla. Dist. Ct. App. 2004).

9   There is a sample affidavit acknowledging a transgender spouse's transgender identity included in Appendix 10B.

10   *In re* Estate of Gardiner, 42 P.3d 120 (Kan. 2002).

11   *See id.*

12   Unif. Probate Code § 5-309.

13   Unif. Probate Code § 5-310(a)(7).

14   Unif. Probate Code § 5-310(a)(2)-(3).

15   Unif. Probate Code § 5-310(a)(3).

16   Health Insurance Portability and Accountability Act of 1996, Pub. L. No. 104-191, 110 Stat. 1936 (codified in scattered sections of 29 U.S.C.).

17   45 C.F.R. § 160.402(a).

18   45 C.F.R. § 164.508(c).

19   45 C.F.R. § 164.508(a)(2).

20   Although a durable power of attorney is only legally effective during the life-time of the principal, the actions of an agent acting in good faith without knowl-edge that the principal has died are binding. Unif. Probate Code § 5-504(a).

21   Unif. Probate Code § 5-502.

22   Unif. Probate Code § 5-413(a).

23   Unif. Probate Code § 5-501.

24   *Id.*

25   Unif. Probate Code §§ 5-413(a)(2), 5-310(a)(2), 5-105.

26   Unif. Probate Code § 5-202(b).

27   *Id.*

28   *Id.*

29   Unif. Probate Code §§ 5-202(b), 5-205(a).

30   Unif. Probate Code § 5-202(c).

31   Unif. Probate Code § 5-202(d).

32   Unif. Probate Code § 5-202(b).

33   Unif. Probate Code § 5-105.

34   *Id.*

35   *See* Unif. Probate Code § 5-105 cmt.

36   Unif. Probate Code § 5-105.

37   Unif. Probate Code § 5-202(a).

38   Unif. Probate Code § 5-202(c).

39   Unif. Probate Code § 5-202(d).

40   Unif. Probate Code § 5-205(a).

41   Unif. Probate Code § 5-202(g).

42   Technically, the Uniform Probate Code does allow a conservator to establish a trust under a conservatorship that extends beyond the ward's eighteenth birthday. Unif. Probate Code § 5-407(c)(1). However, this process is cumbersome and subject to court oversight, and carries the obligation to notify all interested parties.

43   42 U.S.C. §§ 3601–3631; Hovsons, Inc. v. Twp. of Brick, N.J., 89 F.3d 1096, 1101–02 (3d. Cir. 1996); United States v. Lorantffy Care Ctr., 999 F. Supp. 1037, 1044 (N.D. Ohio 1998).

44   42 U.S.C § 3631.

45   *Housing Discrimination Against Lesbian, Gay, Bisexual, and Transgender Individuals and Families*, U.S. Dep't Housing & Urban Dev., http://portal.hud.gov/hudportal/HUD?src=/program_offices/fair_housing_ equal_opp/LGBT_Housing_Discrimination (last visited Oct. 19, 2011) (includes information about which states include gender identity and expression in housing nondiscrimination policies).

46   Nursing Home Reform Act of 1987, Pub. L. 100-203, §§ 4201–4218, 101 Stat. 1330-160 to 1330-220 (codified as amended in scattered sections of 42 U.S.C.).

47   *See id.*

Contributors

Kylar W. Broadus is a professor, attorney, activist, and public speaker. He is an associate professor of business law at Lincoln University of Missouri and maintains a general law practice in Columbia, Missouri. Kylar is a Division Director of the American Bar Association's Section of Individual Rights and Responsibilities and co-chairs the ABA's Committee on Sexual Orientation and Gender Identity. He founded the Trans People of Color Coalition and is a founding board member of the Transgender Law and Policy Institute. Kylar speaks and lobbies on the national, state, and local levels in the areas of transgender and sexual orientation law and advocacy.

Patience Crozier is a partner at Kauffman Crozier LLP in Cambridge, Massachusetts. Her practice includes all areas of family law, particularly adoption, divorce, child custody, assisted reproductive technology, paternity and guardianship, with a focus on serving lesbian, gay, bisexual, and transgender people and non-traditional families. Patience has served as co-chair of the Massachusetts LGBTQ Bar Association, and she has been recognized by the National LGBT Bar Association as one of the "Best LGBT Lawyers Under 40" (2011), by Boston College Law School with the Daniel G. Holland Recent Graduate Award (2010), by *Massachusetts Lawyers Weekly* as an Up & Coming Lawyer (2010), and as a Rising Star by *Super Lawyers* (2009-2011).

Benjamin L. Jerner is the managing shareholder of Jerner & Palmer, P.C. He has practiced law in Pennsylvania and New Jersey for over 15 years, concentrating his practice on adoption, estate planning, probate, and legal issues affecting lesbian, gay, bisexual, and transgender clients. Benjamin has served on the boards of directors of the Philadelphia Bar Association's Committee on the Legal Rights of Lesbians and Gay Men, the Gay and Lesbian Lawyers of Philadelphia, and the National LGBT Bar Association.

Michelle B. LaPointe is a partner at Wade Horowitz LaPointe LLC, a firm specializing in LGBT estate planning. Prior to beginning her legal career, Michelle worked on several local, state, and federal political campaigns, served on the board of the LGBT Political Alliance of Massachusetts, and worked at the Massachusetts Chapter of the Alzheimer's Association. She is a member of the National Academy of Elder Law Attorneys and the LGBT Aging Project. She speaks regularly on issues surrounding long-term care planning with a focus on special needs trusts.

Jennifer L. Levi is the director of the Transgender Rights Project at Gay & Lesbian Advocates & Defenders, where she has served as lead counsel in a number of precedent setting cases establishing basic rights for transgender people. Jennifer was also co-counsel in the case of *Goodridge v. Department of Public Health* which established the right of same-sex couples to marry in Massachusetts. Jennifer is a law professor at Western New England University. She serves on the Legal Committee of the World Professional Association for Transgender Health, and is a founding member of both the Transgender Law & Policy Institute and the Massachusetts Transgender Political Coalition.

Morgan Lynn is a supervising attorney and manager of the LGBTQ Program at Washington (formerly, Women) Empowered Against Violence, Inc. (WEAVE) in Washington, DC, where she represents LGBTQ survivors in civil protection order cases and related family law and immigration matters. Morgan conducts outreach and education on LGBTQ domestic violence in the DC area and nationally and coordinated the launch of "Show Me Love DC!" a campaign about healthy LGBTQ relationships and resources for survivors. She also served on the advisory committee for the American Bar Association's Legal Assistance and Education for LGBT Victims of Domestic Violence Project and is a faculty member for the ABA's Commission on Domestic Violence. Morgan helped found the Rainbow Response Coalition, which addresses LGBTQ intimate partner violence in the DC area.

Shannon Price Minter is the legal director for the National Center for Lesbian Rights, one of the nation's leading advocacy groups for lesbian, gay, bisexual, and transgender people. Shannon was lead counsel for same-sex couples in the California marriage case and has represented LGBT people in many other family law cases around the country. He is a co-editor of *Transgender Rights* (University of Minnesota Press, 2006) and a co-author of *Family Law for Lesbian, Gay, Bisexual, and Transgender People* (West, 2010). Shannon serves on the boards of Equality California, Faith in America, Gender Spectrum, and FORGE.

Elizabeth E. Monnin-Browder was a staff attorney at Gay & Lesbian Advocates & Defenders (GLAD) and is now a litigation associate in the Boston office of Ropes & Gray LLP. While at GLAD, Elizabeth contributed to litigation challenging the Defense of Marriage Act and worked with GLAD's Transgender Rights Project. Elizabeth is the co-chair of the Massachusetts LGBTQ Bar Association's Committee on Transgender Inclusion. She is a member of the Massachusetts Transgender Political Coalition and a founding member of Massachusetts Transgender Legal Advocates, which provides free legal services to poor transgender Massachusetts residents.

Zack M. Paakkonen is the co-founder of West End Legal, LLC, a general practice firm that concentrates on representation for the transgender, lesbian, gay, bisexual, intersex, queer, and allied communities in Maine. His practice includes family law, bankruptcy, criminal defense, discrimination law, and civil litigation. Zack is a member of the Maine Rainbow Business and Professional Association and belongs to the National LGBT Bar Association. He also serves as a guardian ad litem in the Maine courts.

Terra Slavin is the lead staff attorney and project manager of the Domestic Violence Legal Advocacy Project at the Los Angeles Gay & Lesbian Center. Terra served on the advisory board of the American Bar Association's Legal Assistance and Education for LGBT Victims of Domestic Violence Project, and participated in a Standards of Practice Working Group sponsored by the ABA and Office of Violence Against Women to develop national standards of practice in civil protection order cases. Terra co-chairs the LGBT DV Issues Committees of the City of Los Angeles Domestic Violence Task Force and Los Angeles County Domestic Violence Council, and serves on the Governance Committee of the National Coalition of Anti-Violence Programs.

Wayne A. Thomas Jr. created the GLBT Domestic Violence Attorney Program in Boston, Massachusetts, where he practices as the managing attorney. He primarily handles civil protection order cases and family law matters, provides advocacy to victims and witnesses in criminal matters and represents clients in discrimination cases. Wayne served on the advisory board of the American Bar Association's Legal Assistance and Education for LGBT Victims of Domestic Violence Project from 2007-09. He is a former co-chair of the GLBT Domestic Violence Coalition in Boston and currently is working on a committee addressing LGBT issues in a redrafting of the Violence Against Women Act.

Deborah H. Wald is the founder of Wald & Thorndal, P.C. Her primary practice areas include parentage litigation, adoption, and assisted reproduction law. She teaches "Topics in Contemporary Family Law" as an adjunct professor at the University of San Francisco School of Law. Deborah is a member of the American Academy of Assisted Reproductive Technology Attorneys, and the Academies of California Adoption and Family Formation Lawyers. She chairs the National Family Law Advisory Council for the National Center for Lesbian Rights, and is a member of the Family Law Sections of the American Bar Association and the State Bar of California, as well as the National LGBT Bar Association.

Janson Wu is a staff attorney at Gay & Lesbian Advocates & Defenders, where he works on a variety of litigation and legislative efforts around transgender rights throughout New England. He serves on the American Bar Association's Commission on Sexual Orientation and Gender Identity, as a vice chair of the Sexual Orientation/Gender Identity Committee of the Individual Rights and Responsibilities Section of the ABA, and on the Legal Committee of the World Professional Association for Transgender Health. Janson was recently named a 2011 "Best LGBT Lawyer Under 40" by the National LGBT Bar Association.

Appendix

1A. 10 Things to Do to Make a Law Office Safe, Respectful, and Welcoming for Transgender Clients, Staff, and Visitors

1. Educate staff and colleagues about transgender people. Everyone in the office should understand that there are many gender identities and expressions and that confidentiality and discretion may be especially important for transgender people.

2. Modify the client intake form to be welcoming, respectful, and inclusive of transgender people's identities and life experiences.

3. Avoid using gendered language—including terms like "sir" or "ma'am"—until a person's gender identity is known.

4. Refer to transgender clients by their post-transition name and pronoun in all interactions, including when calling the client's name in the waiting room, in communications with the client, and in court documents and appearances, unless a client decides to use a different name, pronoun, and/or gender expression in some or all of these contexts.

5. Implement procedures to ensure that special instructions regarding client contact are adhered to.

6. Ask questions about a client's transgender identity and transition only if the information is relevant to the representation. Avoid asking unnecessary questions out of curiosity.

7. Adopt and implement a restroom policy that allows people to use the facility that is consistent with their gender identity or expression. Educate all staff about the policy.

8. Address any barriers for transgender people that are specific to the office space. For example, if building security requires clients and visitors to show identification prior to entrance, take steps to ensure that this will not be a problem for transgender clients and visitors whose identification may not match their gender identity or expression.

9. Include sexual orientation and gender identity and expression in the office nondiscrimination policy.

10. Offer comprehensive benefits for LGBTQ employees, such as health insurance for domestic partners and coverage for transition-related health care expenses.

1B.   Sample Transgender-Inclusive Family Law Client Intake Questionnaire

Today's Date: _____

YOUR INFORMATION:

Current Full Legal Name (please do not use abbreviations or nicknames):

First	Middle	Last

Name You Prefer to be Called (if different from your legal name):

First	Middle	Last

Name Given at Birth (please do not use abbreviations or nicknames):

First	Middle	Last

Other Names/Aliases You Have Used: _____

Date of Birth: _____ / _____ / _____

Gender: _____   Preferred Pronoun: _____

Your Current Home Address:

Street	Apartment Number

City	County	State	Zip Code

Your Current Mailing Address (if different from your home address):

Street	Apartment Number

City	County	State	Zip Code

May we send written correspondence to your mailing address? Yes / No

E-mail: _____   May we contact you via e-mail? Yes / No

INTAKE FORM
PAGE 1 OF 4

Home Phone: _____ May we contact you via home phone? Yes / No

May we leave a message at your home phone number? Yes / No

Cell Phone: _____ May we contact you via cell phone? Yes / No

May we leave a message at your cell phone number? Yes / No

Work Phone: _____ May we contact you via work phone? Yes / No

May we leave a message at your work phone number? Yes / No

Name you prefer we use when contacting you: _____

Special instructions regarding contact with you by our office:

_____

_____

_____

Employer: _____ Position: _____

Employer Address: _____

Salary: _____ Length of Time at Job: _____

FAMILY INFORMATION:

Relationship Status: _____ Partner's Gender: _____

Partner's Full Legal Name:

_____	_____	_____
First	Middle	Last

Partner's Preferred Name (if different from legal name):

_____	_____	_____
First	Middle	Last

Partner's Name Given at Birth (please do not use abbreviations or nicknames):

_____	_____	_____
First	Middle	Last

INTAKE FORM
PAGE 2 OF 4

Other Names/Aliases Partner Has Used:_____

Partner's Date of Birth: _____/_____/_____

Partner's Gender:_____Partner's Preferred Pronoun: _____

Do you and your partner have any of the following? (check box if yes)	Date signed	Place signed
Prenuptial or Postnuptial Agreement		
Pre-Civil Union, Pre-Domestic Partnership, or Cohabitation Agreement		
Acknowledgment of Transgender Spouse's Transgender Identity		
Parenting or Co-parenting Agreement		
Durable Power of Attorney		
Health Care Proxy		
HIPAA Authorization		
Living Will		
Will		
Directive as to Remains		
Written property agreement or trust		
Court order concerning property or parentage		

Describe your previous relationships that have been legally recognized in any city, state or country (such as marriage, domestic partnership, civil union), including: date and place where entered into, date when officially dissolved, name and gender of former partner(s):

_____

_____

_____

Do you have any children? Yes / No

Does your partner have any children? Yes / No

Please provide the following information regarding each child of you or your partner:

1. _____
   Name   Date of Birth   Legal Parents

2. _____
   Name   Date of Birth   Legal Parents

3. _____
   Name   Date of Birth   Legal Parents

Have you ever been represented by a lawyer before? Yes / No

If yes, please state the lawyer's name and the reason for the representation: _____

_____

Is there anything else you would like us to know about your family or your legal concerns?

_____

_____

THANK YOU!

INTAKE FORM
PAGE 4 OF 4

1C. Legal Organizations with a Focus and Expertise in Transgender Law

American Civil Liberties Union (ACLU) LGBT Rights Project http://www.aclu.org/lgbt-rights/transgender

The ACLU, a national civil liberties legal group, includes LGBTQ rights as one of its key issue areas. As part of the LGBT Rights Project, the organization works to include gender identity in non-discrimination laws and brings lawsuits to challenge statutes that discriminate against transgender people in employment, schools, and public accommodations.

Gay & Lesbian Advocates & Defenders (GLAD) Transgender Rights Project (TRP) http://www.glad.org/

GLAD is New England's leading legal rights organization dedicated to ending discrimination based on sexual orientation, HIV status, and gender identity and expression. Through the Transgender Rights Project (TRP), GLAD puts its litigation, legislative, and educational assets to work in a focused way to establish clear legal protections for the transgender community. GLAD's website contains in-depth resources on transgender legal issues in New England.

Immigration Equality http://www.immigrationequality.org/

Immigration Equality is a national organization that advocates for equality under U.S. immigration law for LGBTQ and HIV-positive individuals. The organization provides information about immigration law, runs a pro bono asylum project, maintains a list of LGBTQ/HIV-friendly immigration attorneys, and provides assistance to attorneys working on sexual orientation, gender identity, or HIV-based asylum and immigration cases.

Lambda Legal http://www.lambdalegal.org/

Lambda Legal is a national legal organization committed to achieving full recognition of the civil rights of LGBTQ individuals and those with HIV through impact litigation, education, and public policy work. The organization maintains a collection of publications and fact sheets discussing employment, parenting, and relationship recognition laws that impact LGBTQ and HIV-positive individuals in each state.

National Center for Lesbian Rights (NCLR) http://www.nclrights.org/

NCLR is a national legal organization committed to advancing the civil and human rights of LGBTQ people. NCLR represents transgender adults, families, and youth on a wide range of issues including nondiscrimination, immigration, and family law. The organization also provides technical assistance to attorneys representing transgender clients, in addition to maintaining a list of publications discussing past and current transgender legal issues and cases nationwide.

LEGAL ORGANIZATIONS
PAGE 1 OF 2

National Center for Transgender Equality (NCTE) http://www.transequality.org

NCTE is a national nonprofit organization dedicated to advancing equality for transgender people through advocacy, collaboration, and empowerment. Based in Washington, D.C., NCTE tracks federal activity related to transgender issues and maintains an online database of issue-specific publications, many of which provide an overview and analysis of current or pending federal policies, programs, and regulations.

Servicemembers Legal Defense Network (SLDN) http://www.sldn.org/

SLDN is the nation's sole legal aid and advocacy organization assisting members of the U.S. Armed Forces harmed by the "Don't Ask, Don't Tell" policy and related forms of intolerance. SLDN is a national nonprofit legal services, watchdog, and legal organization dedicated to ending discrimination against and harassment of military personnel based on sexual orientation, gender identity or gender expression.

Sylvia Rivera Law Project (SRLP) http://srlp.org/

The New York-based SRLP works to guarantee that all people are free to determine their gender identity and expression, regardless of income or race, and without facing harassment, discrimination, or violence. SRLP is a legal services organization that seeks to increase the political voice and visibility of low-income people and people of color by improving access to respectful and affirming social, health, and legal services for these communities.

Transgender Law Center (TLC) http://transgenderlawcenter.org/cms/

The TLC is a California-based organization working to make the state one in which everyone can fully and freely express their gender identity. TLC's website includes many resources, including step-by-step guides. Legal information can be requested via the website, and its publications offer practical advice, including how-to guides about changing one's identification.

The Transgender Law and Policy Institute (TLPI) http://www.transgenderlaw.org/

TLPI is a national nonprofit organization dedicated to engaging in effective advocacy for transgender people. The TLPI brings experts and advocates together to work on law and policy initiatives designed to advance transgender equality. The TLPI website provides information about laws, regulations, policies and cases affecting transgender persons.

Transgender Legal Defense and Education Fund (TLDEF) http://www.transgenderlegal.org/

The TLDEF works nationally to end discrimination based on gender identity and expression and to achieve equality for transgender people through public education, test-case litigation, direct legal services, community organizing, and public policy efforts. The organization also operates a New York City-based initiative called The Name Change Project, aimed at assisting people in getting legal recognition for their names.

2A.   Sample Petition for Change of Legal Sex

STATE OF MAINE   SUPERIOR COURT
                                                       CIVIL ACTION
                                                       DOCKET NO.

IN RE: JOHN DOE	)
	) PETITION FOR ORDER OF LEGAL
	) CHANGE OF SEX
	)

NOW COMES the Petitioner John Doe, through undersigned counsel, and respectfully petitions this Court, pursuant to its equitable powers under 4 M.R.S.A. §105 and 14 M.R.S.A. §6051, to grant an order of legal change of sex. In support of his petition, the Petitioner states the following:

JURISDICTION

1.   The Petitioner is a resident of XXX, XXX County, State of Maine.

2.   This Court has equitable jurisdiction pursuant to 4 M.R.S.A. § 105 and 14 M.R.S.A. 6051(13) to grant the requested relief.

FACTUAL BACKGROUND

3.   The Petitioner was born in XXX, XXX County, State of New Hampshire in XXX.

4.   In XXX, the Petitioner moved to Maine, where he currently resides.

5.   From XXX to XXX, the Petitioner received counseling from a licensed clinical social worker, who made a diagnosis of Gender Identity Disorder and Transsexualism. Beginning in XXX, the Petitioner began endocrinological (hormonal) treatments to medically change his sex from female to male. He also underwent a surgical procedure on XXX to medically change his sex. As a result of these medical procedures, the Petitioner is medically male, as attested to by his physicians. Affidavits from the Petitioner's counselor and physicians are attached hereto as Exhibits 1, 2 & 3.

SAMPLE PETITION
PAGE 1 OF 2

6. For all factual and medical purposes, the Petitioner is male. Overall, his medical changes are permanent and irreversible.

7. On his New Hampshire birth certificate, the Petitioner is designated as female. New Hampshire law requires a court order recognizing a change of sex before amending a person's birth certificate. N.H. REV. STAT. ANN. § 5-C:87(V) (2006).

8. Prior to beginning endocrinological treatments, the Petitioner legally changed his name on XXX to John Doe through a proceeding in XXX County Probate Court. Such certification of legal change of name is attached hereto as Exhibit 4.

WHEREFORE, the Petitioner respectfully requests that this Court exercise its equity jurisdiction and grant the following relief:

1. An order recognizing Petitioner's legal change of sex to male;

2. Any and all other relief deemed reasonably necessary by this Court.

Date:_____   Respectfully submitted,

John Doe
By his Attorney,

_____
XXX

2B.   Sample Order for Change of Legal Sex

STATE OF MAINE   SUPERIOR COURT
                                                 CIVIL ACTION
                                                 DOCKET NO.

)
IN RE: JOHN DOE   )   ORDER OF LEGAL
)   CHANGE OF SEX
)

Upon the pleadings, evidence, affidavits and all other documents entered in this action, as well as opportunity for hearing and argument, this Court hereby finds that Petitioner has demonstrated that he completed the medical treatment for sex-reassignment and that his sex is for all medical and legal purposes permanently and irreversibly changed to male. Accordingly, this Court hereby orders that Petitioner's sex is hereafter and for all purposes male.

Date: _____   BY THE COURT

                                          _____

2C.   Sample Memorandum for Change of Legal Sex

STATE OF MAINE		SUPERIOR COURT CIVIL ACTION DOCKET NO.

	)))))	
IN RE: JOHN DOE		MEMORANDUM IN SUPPORT OF PETITION FOR ORDER OF LEGAL CHANGE OF SEX

INTRODUCTION

John Doe, a resident of Maine, respectfully requests this Court to issue an order of legal change of sex under its equitable powers. Mr. Doe is an individual who was born in New Hampshire but has resided in Maine since XXX. Mr. Doe has completed the medical process of sex reassignment and has lived exclusively as a male in all aspects of his life for XXX years. He seeks this legal order to arrange his legal affairs to accurately reflect his current sex. In particular, he seeks an order stating that he has legally changed his sex to male, which will enable him, among other things, to obtain a corrected birth certificate from New Hampshire. Like New Hampshire, Maine permits a transgender person who has completed sex-reassignment to obtain a new birth certificate. *See* CODE ME. R. § 10-146 ch. 2, § 11 (2005). This statute evidences the clear public policy of this state, which is to recognize the existence of transgender persons and facilitate their integration into society in their corrected sex. Although the statutory procedure itself is limited to persons born in Maine, the statute provides a substantive legal standard that can and should be applied to determine the legal sex of all transgender persons residing in this state, regardless of their place of birth. Accordingly, having met the standard articulated in Code Me. R. § 10-146 ch. 2, § 11, Mr. Doe asks this Court to issue his requested order pursuant to its equity jurisdiction.

FACTS

Mr. Doe is a transgender individual who was born in New Hampshire but has resided in Maine since XXX. In XXX, Mr. Doe was medically diagnosed as transsexual and has since completed the

SAMPLE MEMORANDUM
PAGE 1 OF 8

medical process of sex-reassignment. Declaration of XXX. Transsexualism is a severe form of Gender Identity Disorder (GID). Declaration of XXX. GID is a serious medical condition recognized as such in both the International Classification of Diseases-10 (ICD-10) and the Diagnostic and Statistical Manual of Mental Disorders (DSM-IV) published by the American Psychiatric Association.[1] *Id.*

Transsexualism is defined by an intense discomfort with one's assigned sex and with one's primary and secondary sex characteristics. Declaration of XXX. For people who suffer from profound GID, there is a conflict between the person's body and the person's psychological identity as male or female. *Id.* This conflict creates intense emotional pain and suffering. *Id.* If left untreated, this condition can result in dysfunction, debilitating depression and, for some people without access to medical care and treatment, suicide and death. *Id.* To avoid these results, it is vitally important that transgender people seek out appropriate medical treatment. *Id.*

Mr. Doe has undergone both surgical and endocrinological (hormonal) treatment to medically change his sex to male. Declaration of XXX. He was referred to Dr. XXX for sex-reassignment surgery in XXX after having undergone extensive hormonal and psychological treatment. Declaration of XXX. On XXX, Dr. XXX performed sex reassignment surgery on Mr. Doe to permanently and irreversibly correct his anatomy and appearance, thereby effecting a permanent change in his sex. Declaration of XXX. In addition, Mr. Doe has been treated since XXX, by his primary care physician, Dr. XXX. Declaration of XXX. As a result of these medical procedures, Mr. Doe is medically male and has been living as a male for the last XXX years. Declaration of XXX. Overall, the changes he has experienced are permanent and irreversible. Declaration of XXX.

---

[1] While GID is presently listed as a "mental disorder" in the DSM-IV, recent medical research into the etiology of the condition has concluded that there is rigorous scientific evidence that the condition has a neurobiological etiology. See Jaing-Ning Zhou, et al., A Sex Difference in the Human Brain and Its Relation to Transsexuality, 378 Nature 68-70 (1995); F.P. Kruijver, et al., Male-to-Female Transsexuals Have Female Neuron Numbers in a Limbic Nucleus, 85(5) J. Clin. Endocrinology & Metabolism, 2034-41 (2000); F.P. Kruijver, Sex in the Brain, Netherlands Institute for Brain Research, Publisher, ISBN: 90-808705-2-8, October 2004.

Mr. Doe has already sought and received an order legally changing his name on XXX. He now seeks an order from this Court to legally change his sex so that he may, among other things, amend his New Hampshire birth certificate to correctly reflect his sex as male.[2]

ARGUMENT

I.   THE MAINE SUPERIOR COURT HAS EQUITABLE JURISDICTION OVER THE MATTER.

By statute, the Superior Court is granted equity jurisdiction in a variety of specifically enumerated cases, and "according to the usage and practice of courts of equity, in all other cases where there is not a plain, adequate and complete remedy at law." 14 M.R.S.A. § 6051. These equitable powers are both broad and indifferent to the novelty of the wrong to be righted:

> It is a well-known maxim that equity will not suffer a wrong without a remedy, and absence of precedents does not prevent the application of equitable doctrines. "The absence of precedents, or novelty in incident, presents no obstacle to the exercise of the jurisdiction of a court of equity, and to the award of relief in a proper case. It is the distinguishing feature of equity jurisdiction that it will apply settled rules to unusual conditions and mold its decrees so as to do equity between the parties." 30 *C.J.S. Equity*, §12.

Unity Tel. Co. v. Design Service Co. of New York, 179 A.2d 804, 811 (Me. 1962). Relevant to Mr. Doe's case, no Maine statute or regulation specifically provides a remedy for transgender persons residing in Maine but born in another state. Mr. Doe therefore lacks an adequate remedy at law. *See Usen v. Usen*, 13 A.2d 738, 748 (1940) ("One has no plain, adequate remedy at law if no remedy at law is afforded him in the domestic court of the state where he resides").

In addition, equity provides a remedy where doing so accords with existing statutory or common law rights but no formal remedy exists. *See Rossi Bros. v. Commissioner of Banks*, 283 Mass. 114, 119 (1933). Such is the case in Maine. Transgender persons born in Maine have the right to a legal change of sex under the laws of Maine. Indeed, as discussed in Section II below, Maine's Department of Health and

---

[2]   Under New Hampshire law, "Upon receipt of a certified copy of a certified copy of a court order advising that such individual born in the state of New Hampshire has had a sex change, a new birth record shall be prepared to reflect such change." N.H. REV. STAT. ANN. § 5-C:87(V) (2006). The court order must be furnished to the "clerk of the town or city of birth occurrence by a personal visit or letter from the requesting party." *Id.*

Human Services has promulgated regulations with regard to changing one's sex on a Maine birth certificate. *See Bangor Baptist Church v. State of Me., Dept. of Educational and Cultural Services*, 576 F.Supp. 1299, 1321 (D.C. Me.1983) ("legislative rules are binding on courts"); *Central Steel Supply Co., Inc. v. Planning Bd. Of Somerville*, 447 Mass. 333, 342 (Mass. 2006) ("[p]romulgated regulations have the force of law"); 73 C.J.S. PUBLIC ADMINISTRATIVE LAW AND PROCEDURE § 175. Among other things, this requires the presentation of a physician's affidavit to the Office of Vital Statistics. CODE ME. R. §10-146, ch. 2, §11 (2005). As such, the Department of Health and Human Services' standard for allowing a change of sex on a birth certificate evidences Maine's policy to recognize a transgender person's post-transition sex.

Moreover, Maine's recognition of this right comports with English common law. *Petition of Carson*, 39 A.2d 756 (Me. 1944) (Maine has adopted common law "just so much. . . as suited [its] purpose"). In early English common law, courts had the authority to classify a person of ambiguous gender as either male or female. Saru Matambanadzo, *Engendering Sex: Birth Certificates, Biology and the Body in Anglo American Law*, 12 Cardozo J.L. & Gender 213, 239 (Fall 2005); *see also* 1 E. Coke, *The First Part of the Institutes of the Laws of England* 8.a. (1st Am. Ed. 1812); 2 Bracton, *On the Laws and Customs of England* 31 (Samuel E. Thorne trans., 1968). "It is a basic principle that only so much of the English common law has been adopted as is compatible with our views of liberty and sovereignty, or as is adaptable to the peculiar conditions and circumstances of each state or to the wants and necessities of institutions." 15A Am. Jur. 2d Common Law §12 ("Adoption—Selective or limited adoption") (2005). Indeed, in *Davis v. Scavone*, 149 Me. 189, 100 A.2d 425 (1953), the Law Court held that a specific principle of English common law would govern, despite the absence of an express recognition by Maine laws acknowledging such principle as law, so long as it was compatible with the "new state and condition of the colonists." 149 Me. at 195.[3]

---

[3]   As explained in *Hilton v. State*, 348 A.2d 242, 244 (Me. 1975), "In *Davis v. Scavone*, [citation omitted], this Court painstakingly analyzed the process by which those who settled the Colony of the Massachusetts Bay brought with them, and adopted as their law, the 'common law of England,' [citation omitted], which in turn,

Considering Maine's already existing public policy of recognizing a transgender person's post-transition sex when s/he is born in Maine, *see* CODE ME. R. §10-146, ch. 2, §11 (2005), a common law right to a legal change of sex for persons born elsewhere is consonant with Maine's laws and public policies and should be allowed. Therefore, in keeping with the legal and common law recognition of a transgender person's right to a legal change of sex, equity is best suited to provide the specific remedy requested by Mr. Doe.

Finally, section 6051(13) vests the Superior Court with proper authority to issue the requested order. 14 M.R.S.A. §6051(13). Neither the Maine District Court nor the Maine Probate Court have jurisdiction to grant such relief. *See* ME. REV. STAT. ANN. tit. 4, §§152, 251-52 (2005) (limiting jurisdiction of district and probate court); *see also In re Perry*, 845 A.2d 1153 (Me. 2004) ("The Probate Court is a creature of statute and only has such authority as the Legislature has granted it."). As such, it is both proper and consistent with Maine law that this Court exercise its equity jurisdiction to grant Mr. Doe the relief that he requests.

II. MAINE PUBLIC POLICY RECOGNIZES TRANSGENDER PERSONS' POST-TRANSITION SEX.

Maine law provides that birth certificates may be amended "in accordance with such regulations as the [Department of Health and Human Services] may adopt to protect the integrity of vital statistics records." 22 M.R.S.A. §2705. One such regulation provides that:

> [a]ny person born in this State whose sex has been changed by surgical procedure and whose name has been changed by judicial decree from a court of competent jurisdiction may present a certified copy of the notification form, ... a notarized affidavit by the physician who performed the surgical procedure to the Office of Vital Statistics and a form VS-7 requesting that his or her birth certificate be amended accordingly.

CODE ME. R. § 10-146 ch. 2, § 11 (2005).

The existence of a clearly defined standard and procedure for a transgender person to change one's birth certificate indicates an established statewide policy recognizing transsexualism as a medical

---

became the common law of the Commonwealth of Massachusetts by operation of the Massachusetts Constitution and, subsequently, the common law of the State of Maine by force of the Act of Separation and Article 10, Section 3 of the Constitution of Maine."

condition and recognizing the importance of treating people humanely and facilitating their integration and acceptance in society. Transgender persons who were born outside of Maine but who are legal residents of this state have the same need to benefit from this policy and to obtain appropriate documentation of their corrected sex. Likewise, Maine has a strong interest in applying a uniform standard to all transgender persons living within its borders; it would be irrational, and lead to absurd results, for Maine to withhold legal recognition to long-time Maine residents who have completed sex-reassignment, simply because they were not born here.[4] Such a result would thwart the humanitarian public policy in Code Me. R. § 10-146 ch. 2, § 11, by relegating transgender persons not born in Maine to a permanent legal limbo.

III.   OTHER JURISDICTIONS, INCLUDING NEW HAMPSHIRE, SIMILARLY HAVE ESTABLISHED PUBLIC POLICIES OF RECOGNIZING A TRANSGENDER PERSON'S POST-TRANSITION GENDER.

Maine is not alone in legally recognizing a transgender person's post-transition gender. New Hampshire, where Mr. Doe was born, has a similar public policy of recognizing a transgender person's post-transition gender. Statutory and regulatory authorities in New Hampshire provide a mechanism for transgender persons to revise government issued documents. Under New Hampshire law, "Upon receipt of a certified copy of a court order advising that such individual born in the state of New Hampshire has had a sex change, a new birth record shall be prepared to reflect such change."[5] N.H. REV. STAT. ANN. § 5-C:87(V) (2006). The court order must be furnished to the "clerk of the town or city of birth occurrence by a personal visit or letter from" Mr. Doe. N.H. REV. STAT. ANN. § 5-C:87(I). Most relevant to Mr. Doe's request, the New Hampshire statute requires a court order, which order Mr. Doe requests from this court.

---

[4]   Moreover, such denial of legal recognition to non-native Maine residents only may have constitutional implications on Petitioner's fundamental right to travel. *See Saenz v. Roe*, 526 U.S. 489, 505 ("[T]he right to travel embraces the citizen's right to be treated equally in her new State of residence").

[5]   Within the arena of vital records, New Hampshire considers a sex change to be "a surgical procedure changing the anatomical structure of a person to that of his/her opposite sex." N.H. Code Admin. R. Ann. Dept. of Health & Human Serv. He-P 7002.68.

Moreover, courts around the country have issued orders such as the one requested by Mr. Doe, demonstrated both by the sample from Colorado, attached hereto as Exhibit A, and by the contemplation of the issuance of such orders in state statutes and regulations. *See, e.g.*, ALA. CODE §22-9A-19(d) (2004); ARK. CODE ANN. §20-18-307(d) (2003); COLO. REV. STAT. §25-2-115(4) (2004); CON. GEN. STAT. §19a-42b (2003); DEL. ADMIN. CODE 40 700 049; GA. CODE ANN. §31-10-23(e) (2004); MD. CODE ANN. §4-214(b)(5) (2004); MO. ANN. STAT. §193.215(9) (2004); MONT. ADMIN. R. 37.8.106(6) (2004); NEV. ADMIN. CODE. CH. 440, §130 (2004); OR. REV. STAT. §432.235(4); VA. CODE ANN. §32.1-269(E) (2004); D.C. CODE ANN. §7-217(d); WYO. RULES AND REG. ch. 102 4(e)(iii) (2004); *see also In re Heilig*, 816 A.2d 68, 70 (Md. 2003) (holding that the Maryland Circuit Court has equitable jurisdiction to "determine and declare that a person has changed from one gender to another"); *In re Taylor*, 2003 WL 22382512 at *5 (D.C. Super., March 17, 2003) (observing that legal recognition of one's gender identity after transition is "a matter of public policy," and thus "most courts will approve a sex change on a birth certificate if the legislature has authorized such a change by statute").

IV.   MR. DOE MEETS THE STANDARD NECESSARY FOR THIS COURT TO ISSUE THE REQUESTED ORDER.

Mr. Doe has met the standard in Maine for a legal change of sex by showing that he has: (1) legally changed his name; and (2) changed his sex through surgical procedure. *See* ME. STAT. REV. ANN. tit. 22, § 2705. First, he legally changed his name to John Doe in XXX, as evidenced by the XXX County Probate Court Order attached to his Petition as Exhibit 4. In addition, as attested to by both his current primary care physician and the surgeon to whom he was referred for sex reassignment surgery, Mr. Doe successfully completed the medical process of sex reassignment on XXX. Declaration of XXX. As such, Mr. Doe is entitled to an order of legal change of sex in accordance with the standard set out by the State of Maine and pursuant to this Court's equitable powers.

CONCLUSION

Because he satisfies the standard articulated under Maine law for amending government records to reflect the process of sex reassignment and because Mr. Doe has no remedy at law to obtain the requested order, this Court in an exercise of its equity jurisdiction should issue the requested order of legal change of sex.

Date:_____

Respectfully submitted,
John Doe

By his Attorney,

....
XXX

Jennifer L. Levi & Elizabeth E. Monnin-Browder

2D. **Sample Primary Care Doctor Affidavit**

DECLARATION OF XXX, M.D.

1.   My name is Dr. XXX. I am a physician licensed in the state of Maine.

2.   I have been the primary care physician for XXX since XXX.

3.   I attach as Exhibit A my *curriculum vitae* setting forth my qualifications.

4.   As XXX's primary care physician, I am aware and knowledgeable of XXXs medical history, including his history of endocrinological treatments and sex reassignment surgery to medically change his sex to male.

5.   Overall, this change is irreversible and permanent.

6.   It is my medical opinion that his sex is now male.

7.   I am completing this notarized Affidavit to support XXX's request for an order of legal change of sex.

I declare under penalty of perjury that the foregoing is true and correct.

_____   _____
Date   Name

2E. Sample Social Worker Affidavit

DECLARATION OF XXX, LCSW

1. My name is XXX. I am a licensed clinical social worker (LCSW) licensed in the state of Maine.

2. I was the primary counselor for John Doe between XXX and XXX.

3. I attach as Exhibit A my *curriculum vitae* setting forth my qualifications.

4. As Mr. Doe's counselor, I diagnosed Mr. Doe with and provided treatment for Gender Identity Disorder (GID) and Transsexualism. I am also aware and knowledgeable of John Doe's medical history, including his diagnosis of history of endocrinological treatments and sex reassignment surgery to medically change his sex to male, which I had recommended to his respective physicians.

5. Overall, this change is irreversible and permanent.

6. It is my opinion that his sex is now male.

7. Any designation on Mr. Doe's official government documentation, including any birth records, to the contrary is incorrect.

8. I am completing this notarized Affidavit to support Mr. Doe's request for an order of legal change of sex.

I declare under penalty of perjury that the foregoing is true and correct.

....
Date   Name

2F.   <u>Sample Surgeon Affidavit</u>

<u>**DECLARATION OF XXX, M.D.**</u>

1.   My name is Dr. XXX, M.D., FACS. I am a physician licensed to practice in the State of XXX.

2.   I provided care and treatment, including surgery, for my patient John Doe during XXX.

3.   I attach as Exhibit A my *curriculum vitae* setting forth my qualifications.

4.   A significant part of my surgical practice is focused on the care and treatment of persons diagnosed with Gender Identity Disorder ("GID"). I have been involved in this practice for XXX years.

5.   GID is a serious medical condition recognized as such in both the International Classification of Diseases-10 (ICD-10) and the Diagnostic and Statistical Manual of Mental Disorders (DSM-IV) published by the American Psychiatric Association.[1]   Transsexualism is a severe form of GID.

6.   Transsexualism is defined as an intense discomfort with one's assigned sex and an intense discomfort with one's primary and secondary sex characteristics. For people who suffer from profound GID, there is a conflict between the person's body and the person's psychological identity as male or female. This conflict creates intense emotional pain and suffering. If left untreated, this condition can result in dysfunction, debilitating depression and, for some people without access to medical care and treatment, suicide, and death. To avoid these results, it is vitally important that transsexual people seek out appropriate medical treatment.

---

[1]   While GID is presently listed as a "mental disorder" in the DSM-IV, recent medical research into the etiology of the condition has concluded that there is rigorous scientific evidence that the condition has a neurobiological etiology. See Jaing-Ning Zhou, et al., A Sex Difference in the Human Brain and Its Relation to Transsexuality, 378 Nature 68-70 (1995); F.P. Kruijver, et al., Male-to-Female Transsexuals Have Female Neuron Numbers in a Limbic Nucleus, 85(5) J. Clin. Endocrinology & Metabolism, 2034-41 (2000); F.P. Kruijver, Sex in the Brain, Netherlands Institute for Brain Research, Publisher, ISBN: 90-808705-2-8, October 2004.

SURGEON AFFIDAVIT
PAGE 1 OF 3

7.   The World Professional Association for Transgender Health ("WPATH") is the leading, international, professional organization devoted to the understanding and treatment of gender identity disorders, and is actively involved in supporting, educating, and advocating on behalf of individuals diagnosed, or undiagnosed, with gender identity disorder. The organization's membership includes licensed professionals in the disciplines of medicine, internal medicine, endocrinology, plastic and reconstructive surgery, urology, gynecology, psychiatry, nursing, psychology, neuropsychology, and other disciplines.

8.   I have been an active member of WPATH for XXX years.

9.   WPATH has established internationally accepted Standards of Care ("SOC") for the treatment of people with GID. The SOC are designed to promote the health and welfare of persons with GID and are recognized within the medical community, as they are titled, to be the standard of care for treating transsexual persons. A true and correct copy of the WPATH Standards of Care for Gender Identity Disorders, Seventh Version (2011) is attached hereto as Exhibit B.

10.   Pursuant to the SOC, for individuals who pass a clinical threshold for profound GID, the recommended treatment is sex reassignment. Sex reassignment is highly effective in alleviating the distress people experience from the severe GID and in enabling them to lead healthy, productive lives.

11.   The current WPATH SOC provide that, "[i]n persons diagnosed with transsexualism or profound GID, sex reassignment surgery, along with hormone therapy and real-life experience, is a treatment that has proven to be effective. Such a therapeutic regimen, when prescribed or recommended by qualified practitioners, is medically indicated and medically necessary." The treatment described in the SOC is often referred to as "triadic therapy."

12.   The SOC require treating physicians to consider the individual needs of each patient and

SURGEON AFFIDAVIT
PAGE 2 OF 3

253

recognize that no single course of treatment is correct for every patient.

13.   Physicians treating persons with GID must prescribe the medical treatments that are necessary for a patient to achieve genuine and lasting comfort with his or her gender, based on the person's individual needs and medical history. There is no single treatment that is necessary in every case; however, the great majority of transsexual persons require hormone therapy and surgical treatment to alleviate their GID.

14.   John Doe was referred to me for treatment of GID in XXX after having undergone extensive hormonal and psychological treatment. I was aware at the time of the referral that Mr. Doe had been diagnosed with GID, had initiated hormone therapy and had been living full-time as male.

15.   On XXX, I performed surgery on Mr. Doe for the purposes of his change of sex from female to male, thereby permanently and irreversibly correcting his anatomy and appearance. Any designation on Mr. Doe's official government documentation, including any birth records, to the contrary is incorrect.

16.   I am completing this notarized Affidavit to support Mr. Doe's request for an order of legal change of sex.

17.

I declare under penalty of perjury that the foregoing is true and correct.

_____   _____
Date   Name

SURGEON AFFIDAVIT
PAGE 3 OF 3

4A. Sample Assisted Reproduction & Co-Parenting Agreement

This Agreement is made on DATE, between NAME 1 (hereafter referred to as "FIRST NAME 1") and NAME 2 (hereafter referred to as "FIRST NAME 2"), and is made with reference to the following facts:

A.   FIRST NAME 1 and FIRST NAME 2 are a married couple, who have been together for approximately XXX years. They were married in CITY, STATE, as husband and wife, on DATE.

B.   FIRST NAME 2 is a transgender man. FIRST NAME 2 underwent irreversible gender reassignment surgery on DATE, and legally changed his name and sex in NAME OF COUNTY County Superior Court on DATE, prior to the marriage.

C.   For as long as they have been together, FIRST NAME 2 and FIRST NAME 1 have known they wanted to have children together. Because FIRST NAME 2 is transgender, the couple is biologically unable to conceive a child together. They therefore have obtained donor sperm from SPERM BANK NAME AND LOCATION, and will be pursuing conception through artificial insemination at CLINIC in CITY, assisted by REPRODUCTIVE ENDOCRINOLOGIST and her/his staff.

D.   FIRST NAME 2 and FIRST NAME 1 chose the sperm donor together, with a primary consideration being finding a donor whose physical characteristics most closely resemble FIRST NAME 2's physical characteristics. The donor they chose has similar eye color, hair color, skin tone and facial bone structure to FIRST NAME 2, and also shares common interests and tastes in books and music with FIRST NAME 2. FIRST NAME 2 is consenting to FIRST NAME 1's insemination with the sperm of their chosen donor, with the understanding that FIRST NAME 2 will be the legal parent of any child conceived through the insemination process. FIRST NAME 1 also intends that FIRST NAME 2 will be the other legal parent of any child she conceives through the assisted inseminations. FIRST NAME 1 is voluntarily and knowingly agreeing to give up her/his exclusive constitutional parental rights to the child by sharing those rights with FIRST NAME 2.

E.   The purpose of this Agreement is to settle the rights and obligations of FIRST NAME 1 and FIRST NAME 2 with regard to the parties' children, including paternity, custody, visitation, and child support, consistent with the children's best interests. The parties intend by this Agreement to guide a court, should it become involved, in determining the best interests of the children. However, it is the parties' further intent by way of this Agreement to facilitate the resolution of disputes without the involvement of courts.

THEREFORE, for good and valuable consideration including, without limitation, the mutual promises, conditions and agreements set forth herein, the parties agree as follows:

ASSISTED REPRODUCTION & CO-PARENTING AGREEMENT
PAGE 1 OF 3

1. <u>PATERNITY:</u> FIRST NAME 2 shall be the father of the parties' children. FIRST NAME 1 will not challenge FIRST NAME 2's parental status based on the lack of a biological or legal tie to the child. If, for any reason, FIRST NAME 2's paternity is ever challenged on the ground that he is not legally a man, then it is the intention of both parties that he nevertheless be recognized as the second legal parent of any children born to FIRST NAME 1 as a result of the artificial insemination process.

2. <u>CUSTODY:</u> FIRST NAME 2 and FIRST NAME 1 will share joint legal and physical custody of their children. Each of the parties acknowledges and agrees that all major decisions regarding the children's residence, support, education, medical care, religious training, etc. shall be made jointly by the parties.

3. <u>GUARDIANSHIP:</u> The parties agree that in the case of either of their deaths, the children shall live with the other party. The surviving party agrees that s/he will allow liberal visitation between the children and the other parents' family, to the extent that the children developed actual relationships with the family while the deceased parent was still alive. Both parties agree to prepare estate planning documents including, at minimum, a nomination of guardian, whereby they will both appoint CHOSEN GUARDIAN as guardian of the minor children in the case of the death or incapacity of both parents.

4. <u>DIVORCE OR DISSOLUTION OF THE PARTIES:</u> Both parties agree that they will honor the other party's parental relationship with the children, regardless of any break-up of their marriage. Further, both parties agree that any new intimate relationships–including new marriages–into which either party may enter will not alter the fundamental terms of this Agreement. Any new partner of either party will be a step-parent to the children, and will not replace either party as a parent absent the full consent of that party to adoption of the children by the new partner.

5. <u>APPLICABLE LAW:</u> This Agreement is executed in STATE and shall be subject to and interpreted under the laws of STATE. Subsequent changes in STATE law or federal law through legislation or judicial interpretation that creates or finds additional or different rights and obligations of the parties shall not affect this Agreement.

6. <u>ENTIRE AGREEMENT:</u> This Agreement contains the entire understanding and agreement of the parties, and there have been no promises, representations, warranties, or undertakings by either party to the other, oral or written, of any character or nature, except as set forth herein.

7.   DECLARATION OF UNDERSTANDING: Each party hereby acknowledges that, prior to the execution of this Agreement, s/he has read this Agreement and has had the opportunity to have it fully explained by her/his own counsel and is fully aware of its contents and of its legal effect. Each of the parties has given full and mature thought to the making of this Agreement and to each and all of the obligations contained herein, and each party understands and agrees that the covenants and obligations assumed herein may be enforced in a court of law.

8.   SEVERABILITY: If any term, provision or condition of this Agreement is held by a court of competent jurisdiction to be invalid, void or unenforceable, the remainder of the provisions shall remain in force and effect and shall in no way be affected, impaired, or invalid.

9.   CONFLICT RESOLUTION: It is possible that, in the future, the parties may have disagreements with one another concerning the interpretation of this Agreement, or concerning modification of provisions of this Agreement. Notwithstanding any such disagreements, the parties wish to avoid going to court before reasonable non-court alternatives have first been attempted. The parties agree, therefore, that it is in their best interests——and in the best interests of their children——to try to resolve informally any disputes that may arise in the future as set forth below, except in the case of urgent or emergency situations which would reasonably prevent such resolutions or make them impracticable:

A.   As a first step in resolving future differences, if any, the parties will attempt in good faith to confer with one another orally.

B.   If speaking with one another is unsuccessful, then as the second step the parties will try to achieve resolution in writing, with each of them presenting to the other a proposed modification to and/or implementation of this Agreement.

C.   If there is no resolution at the end of the second step, as a third step the parties agree to hire a Mediator, or to each retain Collaborative Attorneys and convene a collaborative process to resolve the dispute. Both parties agree to participate in the mediation or collaborative process in good faith and to attend at least three mediation sessions and/or collaborative negotiation sessions prior to resorting to litigation.

D.   If there is no resolution at the third step, either party may commence contested court proceedings.

IN WITNESS WHEREOF, the parties have executed this Assisted Reproduction & Co-Parenting Agreement on the date set forth on the first page of this Agreement.

_____   _____
NAME 1   NAME 2

ASSISTED REPRODUCTION & CO-PARENTING AGREEMENT
PAGE 3 OF 3

6A. Checklist of Facts Potentially Relevant to Client's and Other Parent(s)'s Legal Relationship with Child

These are facts that an attorney should ask a client about to determine the client's and the other parent(s)'s legal relationship with a child.

I have:	Yes	No
Children with my partner/spouse		
Children from another relationship		
Guardianship of children		
Child support obligation from a prior relationship		
Sperm stored for me/my partner		
Donor eggs stored for me/my partner		
Embryos stored for me/my partner		
Parentage orders for my children		
Spousal support obligation from a prior relationship		
Court order concerning property/parentage		

I have:	Place signed	Date signed
Parenting Agreement(s)		
Egg Donation Agreement(s)		
Donor Agreement(s)		
Carrier Agreement(s)		

6B. **Questions for Potential Guardians Ad Litem**

<u>General Questions</u>

1. What is your hourly rate?

2. Do you have a CV online or that you can send me?

3. What is your investigatory process in a nutshell?

4. How long do investigations generally take?

5. How many investigations do you perform each year?

6. How long have you been doing investigations?

7. Do you have any experience working with (opposing counsel)? What has your experience been?

8. When are you available to start your work?

<u>Questions to Assess Experience With Transgender People</u>

9. How many cases have you worked on as a guardian ad litem where one parent is transgender?

10. How many cases have you worked on as a therapist where a patient is transgender?

11. How many cases have you worked on as a parent coordinator where a patient is transgender?

12. How many cases have you worked on as an expert witness or consultant where a party is transgender?

13. How did you approach those cases?

14. Have your worked on cases involving lesbian, gay, or bisexual people? How do you think that cases involving transgender people may differ from those involving lesbian, gay, or bisexual people?

15. How does a person's transgender status relate to their ability to parent?

16. If a parent is in the process of transitioning, how do you think a parent's transition affects their children?

17. In the event of a parent's transition, what can both parents do to make the transition comfortable for children?

18. What is your experience with transgender children?

19. How many cases have you worked on where a child is transgender or gender non-conforming?

20. How did you approach those cases?

21. Have your worked on cases involving lesbian, gay, bisexual, or gender queer children? How do you think those cases may differ from one involving a transgender child?

22. How do you define transgender?

23. If you had questions about transgender issues, what resources would you consult?

24. I am trying to build my pool of knowledgeable practitioners, so can you please share the names of colleagues who have experience with transgender parents or children?

QUESTIONS FOR POTENTIAL GUARDIANS AD LITEM
PAGE 2 OF 2

8A. Resources for Practitioners Representing Transgender Youth

The following is a list of resources and publications for attorneys who work with transgender youth. This is not a complete list, but rather a starting point for research. Attorneys should contact the organizations listed in Appendix 8D or visit their websites for more resources and publications.

Resources for Parents

Stephanie Brill & Caitlin Ryan, Nat'l Ass'n of Soc. Workers, *How Do I Know If My Child Is Transgender?*, SOCIAL WORKERS, http://www/helpstartshere.org/kids-and-families/early-childhood-development/early-childhood-development-your-options-how-do-i-know-if-my-child-is-transgender.html (last visited Nov 11, 1011).

Florence Dillon, *Why Don't You Tell Them I'm a Boy? Raising a Gender-Nonconforming Child*, MINN. PARENT, Mar. 1999, at 29, *available at* http://www.safeschoolscoalition.org/whydontyoutellthem.pdf.

JUST EVELYN, MOM, I NEED TO BE A GIRL (1998), *available at* http://aixecs.umich.edu/people/conway/TS/Evelyn/Mom I need to be a girl.pdf.

TRANSGENDER NETWORK, PARENTS, FAMILIES & FRIENDS OF LESBIANS AND GAYS, OUR TRANS CHILDREN (4th ed. 2004), *available at* http://www.pflag.org/fileadmin/user upload/TNET/Our Trans Children Version 4.pdf.

General Resources

JAIME M. GRANT ET AL., NAT'L CTR. FOR TRANSGENDER EQUAL. & NAT'L GAY & LESBIAN TASK FORCE, INJUSTICE AT EVERY TURN: A REPORT OF THE NATIONAL TRANSGENDER DISCRIMINATION SURVEY (2011), *available at* http://www.thetaskforce.org/downloads/reports/reports/ntds full.pdf.

Gerald P. Mallon, *Practice with Transgendered Children*, 10 J. GAY & LESBIAN SOC. SERVS. 49 (2000).

B.W.D. Reed et al., *Medical Care for Gender Variant Young People: Dealing with the Practical Problems*. 17 SEXOLOGIES 258 (2008), *available at* http://www.gires.org.uk/assets/Sexologies/sexologies-print.pdf.

Sonja Shield, *The Doctor Won't See You Now: Rights of Transgender Adolescents to Sex Reassignment Treatment*, 31 N.Y.U. REV. L. & SOC. CHANGE 361 (2007).

Non-Discrimination Laws that Include Gender Identity and Expression, TRANSGENDER LAW & POLY INST., http://transgenderlaw.org/ndlaws/index.htm (last visited Nov. 11, 2011).

YOUTH RESOURCES
PAGE 1 of 3

Foster Care

CASEY FAMILY PROGRAMS, MENTAL HEALTH, ETHNICITY, SEXUALITY, AND SPIRITUALITY AMONG YOUTH IN FOSTER CARE: FINDINGS FROM THE CASEY FIELD OFFICE MENTAL HEALTH STUDY (2007),
http://www.casey.org/Resources/Publications/pdf/MentalHealthEthnicitySexuality FR.pdf.

ROB WORONOFF ET AL., CHILD WELFARE LEAGUE OF AM. & LAMBDA LEGAL DEF. & EDUC. FUND, OUT OF THE MARGINS: A REPORT ON REGIONAL LISTENING FORUMS HIGHLIGHTING THE EXPERIENCES OF LESBIAN, GAY, BISEXUAL, TRANSGENDER, AND QUESTIONING YOUTH IN CARE (2006), *available at* http://www.cw la.org/programs/culture/outofthemargins.pdf.

COLLEEN SULLIVAN ET AL., LAMBDA LEGAL DEF. & EDUC. FUND ET AL., YOUTH IN THE MARGINS: A REPORT ON THE UNMET NEEDS OF LESBIAN, GAY, BISEXUAL, AND TRANSGENDER ADOLESCENTS IN FOSTER CARE (2001), *available at*
http://www.jimcaseyyouth.org/filedownload/266.

Nat'l Ct. Appointed Special Advoc. Ass'n, *Addressing the Needs of LGBTQ Youth in Foster Care*, THE CONNECTION, Fall 2009, at 6, *available at*
http://nc.casaforchildren.org/files/public/site/publications/TheConnection/Fall2009/Cover Story.pdf.

Medical Treatment and Clinics

The Division of Adolescent Medicine Transgender Program
5000 Sunset Blvd. 4th Floor
Los Angeles, CA 90027
(323) 361-2153

Provides medical services for youth between ten and twenty-five, including evaluation of patients who are gender questioning for overall health and readiness for cross sex hormone replacement or puberty suppression.

Gender Management Service (GeMS) Clinic
Children's Hospital Boston
300 Longwood Avenue
Boston, MA 02115
(617) 355-6000

Treats children with disorders of sexual differentiation and also treats transgender children. Dr. Norman Spack is co-director and runs a specialized transgender clinic.

Juvenile Justice and Shelters

KATAYOONMAJD ET AL., HIDDEN INJUSTICE: LESBIAN, GAY, BISEXUAL, AND TRANSGENDER YOUTH IN JUVENILE COURTS (2009) *available at* http://www.equityproject.org/pdfs/hiddeninjustice.pdf.

LISA MOTTET & JOHN M. OHILE, NAT'L GAY & LESBIAN TASK FORCE POL'Y INST. & NAT'L COAL. FOR THE HOMELESS, TRANSITIONING OUR SHELTERS: A GUIDE TO MAKING HOMELESS SHELTERS SAFE FOR TRANSGENDER PEOPLE (2003), *available at* http://www.thetaskforce.org/downloads/reports/reports/TransitioningOurShelters.pdf

LAMBDA LEGAL ET AL., NATIONAL RECOMMENDED BEST PRACTICES FOR SERVING LGBT HOMELESS YOUTH (2009), http://data.lambdalegal.org/publications/downloads/bld national-recommended-best-practices-for-lgbt-homeless-youth.pdf.

Schools

Dear Colleague Letter from Russlynn Ali, Assistant Sec'y for Civil Rights, Office for Civil Rights, U.S. Dep't of Educ. (Oct. 26, 2010), *available at* http://www2.ed.gov/about/offices/list/ocr/letters/colleague-201010.pdf.

JOSEPH G. KOSCIW ET AL., GAY, LESBIAN & STRAIGHT EDUC. NETWORK, THE 2009 NATIONAL SCHOOL CLIMATE SURVEY: THE EXPERIENCES OF LESBIAN, GAY, BISEXUAL AND TRANSGENDER YOUTH IN OUR NATION'S SCHOOLS (2010), *available at* http://www.glsen.org/binary-data/GLSEN ATTACHMENTS/file/000/001/1675-2.pdf.

8B. Sample Insurance Appeal Letter

Date

Patient Name
Insurance Plan Name
ID # 12345678

Group # 9999

To Whom It May Concern:

I am writing to appeal your decision to deny coverage of my child's treatment for NAME OF DIAGNOSIS *(practice note: before appealing the denial, the attorney should first confirm that the diagnosis is not categorically excluded from the insurance plan's coverage)* on DATE. Payment was denied for services provided at DOCTOR'S NAME at OFFICE on DATE. Your billing code indicates that you denied this claim because treatment was not medically necessary.

Contrary to your assertions that the treatment was not medically necessary, my child has been receiving treatment from DOCTOR since DATE, and DOCTOR has clearly indicated that this treatment is medically necessary. I have attached statements from DOCTOR certifying that these treatments are medically necessary for my child's health. Therefore, since this treatment is medically necessary, I request that you reverse your denial decision and cover this treatment for my child.

Alternately, I hope to hear from you regarding your specific reasons as to why you believe, contrary to DOCTOR's medical opinion, that my child's treatment is not medically necessary and thus should not be covered by your insurance plan. I believe that your decision is in error and I request a review. I will forward you information needed for your review upon request.

I look forward to hearing from you soon regarding your decision.

Sincerely,

Insured Name
Street Address
City, State, Zip
E-mail Address
Phone

8C. Sample FERPA Correction Letter

Date

Dr. William James, School
Psychologist Jane Doe's School
Anytown, State ZIP

Re: FERPA Request to Correct Information in Jane Doe's Record

Dear Dr. James,

I am writing on behalf of Jane Doe's parents, PARENTS' NAMES, to correct information in Jane's record that is inaccurate, misleading, or in violation of her privacy rights. I am entitled to correct this record under The Family Education Rights and Privacy Act, 34 C.F.R. § 99.20 (FERPA).

I am writing to correct Jane Doe's student record so that it reflects her current name, Jane Doe, and sex, female. You currently have Jane enrolled under her former name, John. She has changed her name to Jane. I am enclosing a copy of her legal name change order. You also have Jane incorrectly enrolled as male. I request that you correct her enrollment to reflect that she should be enrolled as Jane Doe and female, as required by federal law. If you require further information to make these changes, I can provide it for you under separate cover, or I will discuss the information with you at your convenience.

Making these requested changes will help keep Jane Doe safe at school and will reduce the risk that she will be bullied or harassed. These changes will also help maintain her privacy.

This letter is not subject to FERPA disclosure because it does not constitute "educational information" within the purposes of FERPA. In addition, disclosure of this letter to others would violate Jane's rights of privacy. Please limit access to this letter only to school administrators who require access to it in order to make the requested changes and please ensure that this letter is placed in a secure location and not in her general file.

Please forward a complete copy of Jane's amended record to my attention after you have made the requested amendments and deleted any instances of her former name and sex. I would be willing to pay a reasonable fee not to exceed the cost of reproduction, if a fee is required. Thank you in advance for your cooperation. If you have any questions, please do not hesitate to contact me.

Sincerely,

Name of Attorney
Attorney at Law
Street Address
Phone E-mail
Address

8D.   Organizations that Advocate for Transgender Youth

The organizations listed below publish resources that may be useful for a practitioner working with transgender youth. This is not an exhaustive list of organizations that advocate for transgender or gender non-conforming youth.

American Civil Liberties Union (ACLU) LGBT Rights Project www.aclu.org/lgbt-rights/transgender

The LGBT Rights Project is a division of the national ACLU with a focus on advocacy for the LGBTQ population. The ACLU's website contains information about ongoing litigation and issue-specific publications, as well as a section devoted to concerns of LGBTQ youth.

Gay & Lesbian Advocates & Defenders (GLAD) www.glad.org

GLAD is New England's leading legal rights organization dedicated to ending discrimination based on sexual orientation, HIV status, and gender identity and expression. Through its Transgender Rights Project and its Youth Initiative, GLAD works to achieve a more just and affirming environment for the transgender community and all LGBTQ youth.

Gay, Lesbian & Straight Education Network (GLSEN) www.glsen.org

GLSEN is a national organization with many local chapters that works to create school environments where every student is valued, whatever her/his sexual orientation and gender identity and expression. GLSEN issues a yearly school climate survey that details the experiences of transgender students.

Lambda Legal Defense and Education Fund www.lambdalegal.org

Lambda Legal is a national legal organization committed to achieving full recognition of the civil rights of LGBTQ people and those with HIV, through impact litigation, education, and public policy work. Lambda Legal works to set standards for fair and equal treatment of LGBTQ youth across the country.

National Center for Lesbian Rights (NCLR) www.nclrights.org

NCLR is a national legal organization committed to advancing the civil and human rights of LGBTQ people and their families. The NCLR youth project advances the rights of LGBTQ youth through education, public policy, and precedent-setting casework.

National Gay and Lesbian Task Force (NGLTF) www.ngltf.org

NGLTF is a national political organization working for the civil rights of gay, lesbian, bisexual, and transgender people. NGLTF's website features publications on a variety of youth-specific issues, including homelessness, campus organizing, and the activities of ex-gay ministries targeting LGBTQ youth.

National Center for Transgender Equality (NCTE) www.transequality.org

NCTE is a national social justice organization dedicated to advancing the equality of transgender people through advocacy, collaboration, and empowerment. NCTE publishes the *National Transgender Discrimination Survey* and other resources focused on homelessness among transgender youth.

National Parents, Friends, & Families of Lesbians & Gays (PFLAG) www.pflag.org

PFLAG is a national nonprofit organization offering support to family members of the LGBTQ community. The organization is headquartered in Washington, DC and has a network of local chapters. In addition, PFLAG maintains a database of resources specifically tailored to parents, friends, and allies of transgender individuals.

National Youth Advocacy Coalition (NYAC) www.nyacyouth.org

NYAC is a national social justice organization that advocates for and with young people who are lesbian, gay, bisexual, transgender, or questioning in an effort to end discrimination against these youth and to ensure their physical and emotional well-being. NYAC's website has resources for both youth and organizations working with youth.

TransActive www.transactiveonline.org

TransActive is a Portland, Oregon-based organization that provides support to improve the quality of life for transgender and gender-nonconforming children and youth and their families through education, services, advocacy, and research. TransActive's website contains resources for family members of transgender youth, including legal, medical, and general information.

Trans Youth Family Allies (TYFA) www.imatyfa.org

TYFA empowers transgender children and youth and their families by partnering with educators, service providers, and communities to develop supportive environments in which gender may be expressed and respected. TYFA maintains a database of information on transgender issues for parents, youth, healthcare practitioners, and educators.

Trans Youth Equality Foundation (TYEF) www.transyouthequality.org

TYEF provides education, advocacy, and support for transgender and gender-nonconforming children and youth and their families. TYEF serves the New England area and its website includes information about transgender youth and schools, in addition to suggested reading for children, adolescents, and adults.

YOUTH ORGANIZATIONS
PAGE 2 OF 2

9A. **Intimate Partner Violence Resources for Family Law Practitioners Representing Transgender Clients**

Organizations

American Bar Association (ABA) Commission on Domestic Violence
http://www.americanbar.org/groups/domestic_violence.html

The ABA Commission on Domestic Violence mobilizes the legal profession to increase access to justice for victims of domestic violence, sexual assault, and stalking.

The GLBT Domestic Violence Attorney Program in Boston, MA
http://www.probono.net/dv/oppsguide/organization.264432-
GLBT_Domestic_Violence_Attorney_Program

The GLBT Domestic Violence Attorney Program provides direct representation, advice, and referrals to LGBTQ survivors of domestic violence in Massachusetts.

National Coalition of Anti-Violence Programs (NCAVP)
http://www.avp.org/ncavp.htm

NCAVP is a good place for an attorney representing transgender clients to start when researching local services. NCAVP is a coalition of forty-two agencies across the United States focused on LGBTQ crime victimization.

For Ourselves, Reworking Gender Expression (FORGE)
http://www.forge-forward.org

FORGE is a member of NCAVP and is a program specifically focused on working with transgender survivors of intimate partner violence and sexual assault.

The LGBTQ Program at Washington Empowered Against Violence, Inc (WEAVE) in Washington, DC
http://www.weaveincorp.org/programs-services/lgbtq-program/

WEAVE is a service organization providing legal representation and counseling to victims of domestic violence, sexual violence, dating violence, and stalking. The LGBTQ Program addresses the specific legal needs of LGBTQ survivors, ensuring that clients have access to appropriate holistic support.

The Domestic Violence Legal Advocacy Project (DVLAP) at the Los Angeles Gay & Lesbian Center
http://laglc.convio.net/site/PageServer?pagename=Legal_Services_DV

The DVLAP provides culturally competent legal assistance to LGBTQ domestic violence survivors and addresses systemic barriers that impede the full and equal access to justice by LGBTQ survivors.

Publications

A Sample Safety Planning Tool, NAT'L NETWORK TO END DOMESTIC VIOLENCE (2006), http://www.lcadv.org/SafetyPlan.pdf.

ABA COMMISSION ON DOMESTIC VIOLENCE, STANDARDS OF PROOF FOR DOMESTIC VIOLENCE CIVIL PROTECTION ORDERS BY STATE (2009), http://www.americanbar.org/content/dam/aba/migrated/domviol/pdfs/Standards_of_Proof_by_State.authc heckdam.pdf.

FORGE, TRANSGENDER DOMESTIC VIOLENCE AND SEXUAL ASSAULT RESOURCE SHEET (2011), *available at* http://forge-forward.org/wp-content/docs/TransDV-SA_2011-02.pdf.

MORGAN LYNN, AM. BAR ASS'N & THE NAT'L LGBT BAR ASS'N, TOOL FOR ATTORNEYS WORKING WITH LESBIAN, GAY, BISEXUAL, AND TRANSGENDER (LGBT) SURVIVORS OF DOMESTIC VIOLENCE, *available at* http://www.americanbar.org/content/dam/aba/multimedia/domestic_violence/publications/lgbttoolkit_aba _lgbt_tools_final.authcheckdam.pdf.

Nancy Glass et al., *Risk for Reassault in Abusive Female Same-Sex Relationships*, 98 AM. J. PUB. HEALTH 1021 (2008), *available at* http://www.dangerassessment.org/uploads/Risk_for_Reassault_in_%20Abusive_Female_Same_Sex_Rela tionships-Glass.pdf.

10A. Cohabitation Agreement

COHABITATION AGREEMENT

This Cohabitation Agreement ("Agreement") is made this _____ day of _____, [year], by and between Jordan ("Jordan") of _____, and Lesley ("Lesley") of _____.

I.   PURPOSE AND RECITALS

Jordan and Lesley desire to enter into this Agreement to determine, in advance, the economic consequences of any termination of their relationship. They agree that this Agreement shall control even in the event that future developments in the law of [state], or of any jurisdiction to which they may be subject, establishes that their relationship creates an entitlement to the property or income of the other. The parties intend to fix and determine any and all rights and claims that have or may accrue between them and to accept the terms of this Agreement in full discharge, settlement and satisfaction of any past, present or future rights and claims as a result of their relationship.

Each party specifically acknowledges that s/he:

1.   Owns certain property at the present time and has made full disclosure to the other party of the approximate value of such property (See Exhibits A and B);

2.   Recognizes that although the other party has made every effort to make a full financial disclosure that some of the parties' assets are by their nature difficult to value and that the values reported may not reflect the full current fair market value of the assets and that the future value of the assets is speculative and may increase;

3.   Has, in light of his or her respective age, health, occupation, educational background and training, the capability to be fully self-supporting and the ability to acquire income and assets;

4.   Intends that, except as provided by this Agreement, their relationship shall not create any claims or rights in either of them against the other or in the assets or income of the other event though the contribution of personal skills, services and efforts of either may have directly or indirectly enriched the other or enhanced the value of the property of the other;

5.   Understands and consents to all of the provisions of the Agreement, believes the Agreement to be fair and reasonable, enters into this Agreement freely and voluntarily, and has had the opportunity to review the Agreement with independent counsel of his or her choosing; and

6.   Is committed to a stable and healthy relationship of emotional support and companionship for their mutual benefit and that sexual services are not consideration in the making of this Agreement.

II. GENERAL PROVISIONS

Therefore, in consideration of the mutual covenants contained herein, the parties agree as follows:

1. **Joint Personal Property:** The parties may acquire and retain property jointly during the relationship. "Joint Property" shall include (a) any bank or brokerage accounts titled in joint name, (b) any property that is titled in joint name or otherwise designated as joint property in a writing signed and acknowledged by both parties, and (c) the real property located at _____ and referenced below. For the purposes of this Agreement, any property other than property described in (a) – (c) above shall be presumed to be the separate property of the party who furnished the consideration.

2. **Real Property:**

   a. On [date], the parties purchased the property located at [address] (hereinafter "the property"). The purchase price for said property was $ _____ , the parties invested $ _____ in the property, and the mortgage is currently $ _____ . The parties hold title as _____. The parties equally contributed to the purchase of the property, including down payment and closing costs. The parties acknowledge title shall be held in the manner described above until the parties' written mutual agreement otherwise or upon dissolution of this agreement or until either party's death, whichever first occurs. The parties agree to maintain a detailed schedule of monies invested by each party toward the purchase and improvement of the property.

   b. Any renovations or capital improvement desired by either party shall be decided upon jointly by the parties, and the parties shall agree in writing prior to embarking on any renovation or capital improvement. The parties shall share equally the cost of any renovations or capital improvement. For purposes of this agreement, any repair over the amount of $500.00 shall be considered a capital improvement unless the parties agree in writing otherwise. Documentation of payment for a renovation or capital improvement shall be maintained in a file by each party. Both parties must agree before any non-emergency repair costing more than $500.00 may be performed. Emergency repairs may be authorized unilaterally by either party.

   c. The parties shall continue to share payment of the mortgage (principal, interest, and insurance) and condominium fees equally, with each paying 50% of the monthly payments. The parties also shall share equally all other regular household expenses, including but not limited to utilities, telephone expenses, and groceries. [Name] shall manage the household bills and their payment and shall be responsible for keeping records in an orderly fashion, including keeping all receipts, and making same available for [Name's] inspection. The parties have a joint checking account for the purpose of paying joint household expenses and other joint bills, into which each shall contribute the same amount each month.

COHABITATION AGREEMENT
PAGE 2 OF 7

d. In light of their equal contributions to the purchase of the property and to the ongoing costs of maintaining the property, the parties agree that each owns a Fifty Percent (50%) share of the property.

3. **Separate Property:** During the relationship, each party shall retain sole and separate ownership, control and use of all of his or her separate property. Such separate property shall mean any property other than Joint Property, as defined in this Agreement in paragraph II.1 and II.2, both real and personal, wherever situated, and whether now owned or acquired after this Agreement legally or equitably by either party. The parties further agree that separate property shall include all professional degrees and licenses; all interests in professional partnerships and professional corporations; all interests in business or other joint ventures in which a party is engaged; all interests in pensions, individual retirement accounts, deferred compensation plans, profit-sharing plans and any other retirement vehicle; all income of whatever nature earned by a party; all property acquired and owned jointly with persons other than Jordan or Lesley; all property received by a party, whether before, during or after the relationship, by gift, legacy, bequest, devise, descent or inheritance from any source; appreciation of any separate property; proceeds received from the sale of any separate property; and income generated from separate property. Each party releases unto the other party all right, title and interest in the other party's separate property. Each party shall have the right at all times to dispose of any or all of his or her separate property by sale, gift, deed, will or otherwise, without claim or interference by the other party.

4. **Liabilities:** All debts incurred by a party individually shall remain the sole responsibility of the party who incurred the debt. Any debt incurred relating to joint property shall be the joint responsibility of the parties. Neither party shall incur any debt in the other's name or encumber the property of the other or joint property unless expressly agreed otherwise by both parties in writing.

5. **Gifts/Transfers:** This Agreement is not intended to prevent either party from voluntarily purchasing gifts or providing funds to the other; however, such gifts or transfers shall create no obligation for any claims or rights of support, past, present or future. Each party shall be entitled to keep any gifts given by the other.

6. **Termination:** Any obligations under this Agreement shall continue until the Agreement is terminated as defined herein. The Agreement shall be deemed terminated upon the first to occur of the following events:

    a. Legal marriage of the parties to one another or to another person;

    b. Death of either party;

    c. Execution of a notarized written statement of both parties indicating their mutual desire to terminate the Agreement; or

    d. One hundred and twenty (120) days following written notice by one party to the other of his or her desire to terminate the Agreement. During the notice period, each party agrees not to disrupt any of the various households maintained by Jordan and Lesley or remove any tangible property beyond clothing and personal necessities unless the parties otherwise mutually agree in writing.

7. **Provisions on Termination:** If this Agreement terminates for any reason other than marriage of the parties to one another, the parties or their estates, as applicable, agree to work together in good faith to ensure a smooth termination of the relationship and further agree as follows:

    a. Each party shall retain his or her separate property.

    b. With regard to any real property [insert here].

    c. The parties' joint personal property shall be divided equally, after taking into account any liabilities and tax implications associated with such jointly owned property. However, if the Agreement terminates due to the death of a party prior to written notice of termination, then the parties' joint personal property shall pass to the survivor.

    d. Any tangible personal property without title but purchased with joint funds shall be disposed of at termination as the parties mutually agree. If they cannot agree, then any disputed tangible property shall be sold and the proceeds divided equally between the parties or their respective estates. Furthermore, if the Agreement terminates due to the death of a party prior to written notice of termination, then the joint tangible personal property shall pass to the survivor. The deceased party may designate, in a writing, that certain items of tangible personal property be given to third parties, and the survivor shall work in good faith with the deceased's estate to ensure those wishes are respected.

    e. Lesley, or his estate, shall make a required payment to Jordan ("required payment") pursuant to the following terms [insert here].

8. **Provisions on Termination upon marriage of the parties to each other:** If this Agreement will terminate because the parties intend to marry each other, the parties agree as follows:

    a. Each party shall retain his or her separate property.

    b. With regard to any real property [insert here].

    c. Any joint property shall continue to be held jointly unless the parties mutually agree otherwise.

    d. They shall work together in good faith to negotiate a prenuptial agreement in advance of their marriage to determine their rights and obligations upon marriage.

9. **Waiver of support:** Each party waives any right to or claim for support or maintenance or other payments or transfers of property in addition to or in lieu of said support during their relationship or in the event of termination of their relationship. Each party further agrees that, in the event of termination, neither party shall seek to have any support for himself or herself ordered by any court. In the event of termination, it is expressly understood that neither party commits himself or herself to providing support to the other, past, present or future, and expressly waives any rights at law or equity to palimony or other transfers of assets growing out of the nature of the

COHABITATION AGREEMENT
PAGE 4 OF 7

relationship which may be implied or imposed by court order. No transfers pursuant to this Agreement are intended as alimony or palimony.

10. **Waiver of health insurance:** Each party waives any right or claim for the provision of health insurance or other related payments during their relationship or in the event of termination of their relationship. Each party acknowledges that he or she currently has health insurance and intends to maintain health insurance independently of the other.

11. **Waiver of estate provisions:** The parties hereby disclaim and renounce any and all interest, whether testate or intestate, in the estate of the other except for: (a) provisions specifically set forth in this Agreement which allow for distribution of assets upon the death of one party. Nothing in this Agreement is intended to or shall constitute a waiver by either party of any rights or claims either may have against the other or the other's estate by reason of breach of this Agreement. Nothing in this Agreement is intended to or shall constitute a waiver by either party of any testamentary provisions that the other may voluntarily make in a will or other instrument that is executed, ratified or confirmed after the date of this Agreement.

12. **Dispute Resolution:** If, after good faith efforts, the parties cannot agree to any interpretation, implementation or modification of this Agreement, then the parties agree to submit the matter to mediation with the cost of mediation to be shared equally. Either party may request in writing that the parties participate in mediation. Prior to filing any contested legal proceeding, each party agrees in good faith to attempt mediation and to engage in at least three (3) sessions in an attempt to resolve any dispute. In the event that mediation proves unsuccessful, a dispute regarding the Agreement may be presented to any court of competent jurisdiction for resolution. In any court proceeding, each party shall pay his or her own attorneys' fees and costs, unless otherwise agreed by the parties or ordered by the court.

13. **Notice:** All notices required to be given hereunder shall be in writing and deemed duly given when received in hand or by certified or registered mail, return receipt requested, postage and registration and certification charges prepaid, addressed to the other party at their address as provided herein, or to such address or addresses as may from time to time be designated to either party by written notice to the other, provided that any written notice actually received by the designated party by any method shall be deemed in compliance with this provision.

14. **Waiver:** The failure of either party to insist in any instance on the strict performance of any of the provisions of this Agreement shall not be construed as a waiver of the terms of this Agreement, and the Agreement shall nevertheless continue in full force and effect.

15. **Severability:** In the event that any part of this Agreement shall be held invalid, such invalidity shall not affect the whole Agreement, but the remaining provisions of this Agreement shall continue to be valid and binding to the extent that such provisions continue to reflect fairly the intent and understanding of the parties.

16. **Governing Law:** This Agreement shall be construed and governed according to the laws of [state]. The Parties are aware of the decision in Wilcox v. Trautz, 427 Mass. 326 (1998), and its

COHABITATION AGREEMENT
PAGE 5 OF 7

recognition of the validity of a written agreement between two unmarried cohabitants which defines the rights of the parties as to their finances and property.

17. **Effective Date:** This Agreement shall be effective as of the day it is executed by both parties.

18. **Modification:** This Agreement shall not be altered except by a written instrument signed and executed with the same formality exercised in the execution of the original Agreement.

19. **Heirs and Assigns:** This Agreement is intended to bind the parties, their estates, heirs, beneficiaries, executors, administrators, assigns and personal representatives.

20. **Indemnification:** Each party agrees to indemnify the other party and hold him or her harmless against any loss which may be incurred by as a result of a violation of any legal obligation or duty arising by reason of his or her ownership, management or control of joint or separate property or violation of any part of this Agreement.

21. **Legal Fees:** The parties agree that each shall be responsible for his or her own legal fees associated with this Agreement and its enforcement.

22. **Reliance:** Each party hereto acknowledges that he or she has entered into this Agreement in reliance on the information set forth herein, inclusive of the Exhibits, and further acknowledges that such information is an integral and important part of this Agreement.

23. **Confidentiality:** The parties intend and agree that this Agreement and the financial information they have provided to each other shall be kept confidential. Each party agrees not to disclose any financial information provided to them by the other without the other party's prior written consent, except as necessary to enforce the Agreement.

24. **Independent Counsel:** Jordan and Lesley have each had the opportunity to consult independent counsel of his or her own choosing prior to execution of the within Agreement, and each acknowledges that he or she has read the agreement line by line and has been fully informed of his or her respective rights and responsibilities pertaining to the Agreement.

25. **Voluntary Execution:** Each party acknowledges that he or she fully understands the Agreement and its legal effects and that he or she is signing the Agreement freely and voluntarily. Each party acknowledges that he or she has executed this Agreement in the absence of any duress, coercion, undue influence or illegal consideration.

26. **Counterparts:** This Agreement is executed in several counterparts, each of which shall be deemed to be an original instrument.

IN WITNESS WHEREOF, the parties set their hands and seals on this _____ day of _____ [year].

_____   _____

JORDAN   LESLEY

COHABITATION AGREEMENT
PAGE 6 OF 7

[state]

COUNTY OF _____

Then personally appeared the within-named JORDAN who proved to me by _____ that she is the person whose name is signed on this Agreement, and acknowledged the foregoing instrument to be her free act and deed, before me this ___ day of _____ [year].

_____

Notary Public:

My Commission Expires:

[state]

COUNTY OF _____

Then personally appeared the within-named LESLEY, who proved to me by _____ that he is the person whose name is signed on this Agreement, and acknowledged the foregoing instrument to be his free act and deed, before me this ___ day of _____ [year].

_____

Notary Public:

My Commission Expires:

COHABITATION AGREEMENT
PAGE 7 OF 7

10B. **Acknowledgment of Transgender Spouse's Transgender Identity**

AFFIDAVIT IN THE MATTER OF THE MARRAGE OF

_____

AND _____

STATEMENTS MADE UNDER OATH:

1. [Transgender client's post-transition name] was born [transgender client's birth name] in [birth city and state] on [birth date].

2. Catalog components of transgender client's transition: [transgender client's post-transition name] took cross-gender hormones for the purpose of gender transition from [date to present] and underwent surgical gender reassignment in [year].

3. [Transgender client's post-transition name] name was legally changed from [transgender client's birth name] to [transgender client's post-transition name] on [date of name change].

4. [Transgender client's post-transition name] received a [new or amended] birth certificate from [birth state] on [date of new birth certificate] that indicates her/his name to be [transgender client's post-transition name] and sex to be [male/female].

5. [Transgender client's post-transition name] and [spouse name] are listed as [transgender client's post-transition name][male/female] and [spouse name][male/female] on their marriage license from [state].

6. [Transgender client's post-transition name] and [spouse name] were married on [marriage date], in [marriage city and state].

7. At the time of their marriage, [spouse name] was fully aware that [transgender client's post-transition name] was born [transgender client's birth name], and transitioned — including by undergoing hormone therapy and surgical gender reassignment — prior to her/his marriage.

8. [Transgender client's post-transition name] and [spouse name] fully believe their marriage is valid under the laws of the State of [state] and recognize they are bound by those laws.

9. [Transgender client's post-transition name] and [spouse name] understand that [transgender client's post-transition name] will not be able to conceive/sire a child.

10. Neither [transgender client's post-transition name] or [spouse name] will challenge the status of their marriage on the basis of [transgender client's post-transition name]'s prior gender or gender transition.

SPOUSE AFFIDAVIT
PAGE 1 OF 2

OATH AND VERIFICATION:

STATE OF _____]
COUNTY OF _____]

I have read and understand the above statements. Everything I have said is true and correct to the best of my knowledge and belief.

_____   _____
(transgender client's post-transition name)   (spouse name)

WITNESSED BY:

_____   _____

Subscribed and sworn to before me this _____ day of _____ by
(transgender client's current name) and (spouse name), and witnessed by
_____ and _____
personally known or proven to me to be the persons named herein.

_____
Notary Public

SPOUSE AFFIDAVIT
PAGE 2 OF 2

10C. **Partial Will**

LAST WILL AND TESTAMENT
OF
MARY SMITH

I, **MARY SMITH**, formerly known as John Smith, of Boston, Suffolk County, Massachusetts, make this my Will and revoke all wills and codicils previously made by me.

At the time I make this Will, I live with my spouse, **THOMAS JOHNSON**, and have one child, **ZACHERY JOHNSON**.

I am married under the laws of the Commonwealth of Massachusetts to **THOMAS JOHNSON**. If, for any reason, this marriage is not recognized by any competent jurisdiction, and regardless of any change in law, other outcome or subsequent legal event (other than divorce) that invalidates this marriage or converts it to civil union or other pseudo-spousal status, it is my intention that this Will shall nonetheless remain valid and in effect as written and that all bequests to, and appointments of, Thomas Johnson be made as provided hereunder.

ARTICLE I.

FIDUCIARIES

I appoint my spouse, **THOMAS JOHNSON** of Boston, Massachusetts, as Executor of my Will. If **THOMAS JOHNSON** is unable or unwilling to serve, then I appoint my friend, **KAREN LEWIS**, of Boston, Massachusetts to serve as successor Executor.

Any Executor named in this Will shall also serve as Temporary Executor upon application to the probate court with such Temporary Executor to have all the powers granted to the Executor by this Will and by operation of law as if appointed by the probate court.

I appoint my spouse, **THOMAS JOHNSON** of Boston, Massachusetts as guardian and/or conservator of any minor children I may have. If for any reason **THOMAS JOHNSON** fails to qualify or ceases to serve as guardian and/or conservator, I appoint, my friend, **KAREN LEWIS** of Boston, Massachusetts, in his place.

ARTICLE II.

GENERAL PROVISIONS

The following provisions shall govern the administration of my estate under this Will:

(1) **In Terrorem Clause.** If any beneficiary shall contest the probate or validity of this Will or any part of it, or shall institute or join in, except as a party defendant, any proceeding to contest the validity of this will from being carried out in accordance with its terms, not including a petition for instructions for the interpretation of this Will instituted in good faith and for probable cause, then all benefits provided for such beneficiary and his or her issue are revoked and shall pass under my Will as if the beneficiary and his or her issue had predeceased me.

PARTIAL WILL
PAGE 1 OF 3

(2)   **Omitted Family.** My failure to make provisions in this will for my father, **ROBERT SMITH** of Boston, Massachusetts, and my sister, **MARGARET SMITH** of Boston, Massachusetts, is intentional and not due to any oversight or mistake.

(3)   **Relationship.** Adoption of a child who is then a minor shall have the same effect as if the adopted child were born to the adopting parents. Adoptions of adults shall not be recognized. In determining whether any person is the issue or ancestor of a designated person, it shall be assumed that decrees of divorce rendered by a court of record are valid. **ZACHARY JOHNSON** is referred to in this document and is to be treated for all purposes in interpreting and applying this document as the child of me and Thomas Johnson, regardless of whether Zachary Johnson is considered under the laws of any relevant jurisdiction to be the child or issue of either me or Thomas Johnson.

ARTICLE III.

FUNERAL INSTRUCTIONS

I specifically authorize and direct that my organs be donated for transplantation and my remains be cremated. I understand that due to the nature of the cremation process, any valuable materials, including dental gold or other metals with the remains, will be either destroyed or not recovered in their original form, and I hereby authorize the disposal by the cremation service or cemetery of any such material that may remain after the cremation process. I further understand the cremated remains are bone fragments, which will be reduced in size by mechanical means.

During any memorial service, obituary or preparation thereof, I direct all coroners, funeral home employees, health care workers, and participants to refer to me by my legal name of **MARY SMITH** irrespective of whether I have changed my name on any identity documents. During any memorial service, obituary or preparation thereof, I also direct such persons to use the female pronoun in reference to me, irrespective of whether I have obtained a court approved gender change, or changed my gender marker on any identity documents. Finally, I direct such persons to maintain my feminine appearance.

I direct that all other decisions regarding disposition of my remains and funeral and memorial service arrangements be made by my spouse, **THOMAS JOHNSON**, or if he is unavailable, my friend, **KAREN LEWIS** (or if both are unavailable someone designated by Thomas or Karen) in such person's sole and complete discretion.

I, the undersigned testatrix, declare that I willingly sign and execute this instrument as my Will in the presence of each of the witnesses, who also sign below, and that I execute it as my free and voluntary act, this ___ day of _____, [year].

MARY SMITH, Testatrix

PARTIAL WILL
PAGE 2 OF 3

We, the undersigned witnesses, each declare in the presence of the testatrix that the testatrix signed and executed this instrument as her Will in the presence of each of us, that she signed it willingly, that each of us signs this Will as a witness in the presence of the testatrix, and to the best of our knowledge the testatrix is eighteen (18) years of age or over, of sound mind, and under no constraint or undue influence.

Witness Name: _____

Address:

Witness Name: _____

Address:

(i) COMMONWEALTH OF MASSACHUSETTS

Suffolk, ss.

On this _____ day of _____, [year], before me, the undersigned notary public, personally appeared Testatrix, **MARY SMITH**, proved to me through satisfactory evidence of identification, which was a Massachusetts Driver's License, to be the person whose name is signed on the Last Will and Testament of **MARY SMITH**. Also appeared before me the above-named witnesses, _____ and _____, who are personally known to me. This Will was subscribed, sworn to and acknowledged before me by the said Testatrix and witnesses this ___ day of _____, [year].

Notary Public
Name:

My commission expires:

PARTIAL WILL
PAGE 3 OF 3

10D. <u>Healthcare Proxy</u>

MARY SMITH
MASSACHUSETTS HEALTH CARE PROXY

TO MY FAMILY, DOCTORS, AND ALL THOSE CONCERNED WITH MY CARE:

1.   APPOINTMENT

I, **MARY SMITH**, formerly known as John Smith, (the Principal), residing at 100 Washington Street, Boston, Massachusetts, being a competent adult at least eighteen years of age or older, of sound mind and under no constraint or undue influence, hereby appoint the following person to be my HEALTH CARE AGENT (or, herein, "Agent") under the terms of this document:

Name: **THOMAS JOHNSON**
Address: 100 Washington Street, Boston, Massachusetts 02116
Telephone: (617) 555-5555

In doing so, I intend to create a Health Care Proxy according to Chapter 201D of the General Laws of Massachusetts. In making this appointment, I am giving my Health Care Agent the authority to make any and all health care decisions on my behalf, subject to any limitations I state in this document, in the event that I should at some future time become incapable of making health care decisions for myself.

2.   ALTERNATE APPOINTMENT

I hereby appoint the following person to serve as my Health Care Agent in the event that my original Health Care Agent is not available, willing or competent to serve and is not expected to become available, willing or competent to make a timely decision given my medical circumstances, or in the event that my original Health Care Agent is disqualified from acting on my behalf.

Name: **KAREN LEWIS**
Address: 20 Boylston Street, Boston, Massachusetts 02116
Telephone: (617) 444-4444

3.   POWERS GIVEN TO HEALTH CARE AGENT

A.   I give my Health Care Agent full authority to make any and all health care decisions for me including decisions about life-sustaining treatment, subject only to any limitations I state below.

B.   My Health Care Agent shall have authority to act on my behalf only if, when and for so long as a determination has been made that I lack the capacity to make or to communicate health care decisions for myself. This determination shall be made in writing by my attending physician according to accepted standards of medical judgment and the requirements of Chapter 201D of the General Laws of Massachusetts.

C.   The authority of my Health Care Agent shall cease if my attending physician determines that I have regained capacity. The authority of my Health Care Agent shall recommence if I subsequently lose capacity and consent for treatment is required.

HEALTHCARE PROXY
PAGE 1 OF 5

D.   I shall be notified of any determination that I lack capacity to make or communicate health care decisions where there is any indication that I am able to comprehend this notice.

E.   My Health Care Agent shall make health care decisions for me only after consultation with my health care providers and after full consideration of acceptable medical alternatives regarding diagnosis, prognosis, treatments and their side effects.

F.   In exercising the authority granted to him or her herein, my Health Care Agent is instructed to try to discuss with me the specifics of any proposed decision regarding my medical care and treatment if that is possible and if I am able to communicate in any manner, even by blinking my eyes.   My Health Care Agent shall make health care decisions for me only in accordance with my Health Care Agent's assessment of my wishes, including my religious and moral beliefs, or, if my wishes are unknown, in accordance with my Health Care Agent's assessment of my best interests.

G.   My Health Care Agent shall immediately upon signing of this document, regardless of whether there has been a determination of lack of capacity as required under paragraph B, have the right to receive any and all medical and other information necessary to make informed decisions regarding my health care, including any and all confidential medical information that I would be entitled to receive and any and all information or records of any health or disability insurer.   In addition to the other powers granted hereunder, my Health Care Agent shall have the power and authority to serve as my personal representative for all purposes under the federal Health Insurance Portability and Accountability Act of 1996 (HIPAA), and in particular its 2003 Privacy Regulations.

H.   The decisions regarding my health care made by my Health Care Agent on my behalf shall prevail, as my decisions would have if I were competent, over decisions by any other person, including an attorney-in-fact person acting pursuant to a durable power of attorney, except for any limitation I state below or a specific Court Order overriding this Health Care Proxy.

I.   If I object to a health care decision made by my Health Care Agent, my decision shall prevail unless it is determined by Court Order that I lack capacity to make health care decisions.

J.   Nothing in this proxy shall preclude any medical procedure deemed necessary by my attending physician to provide comfort, care or pain alleviation including but not limited to treatment with sedatives and painkilling drugs, nonartificial oral feeding, suction and hygienic care.

K.   Limitations: I do not wish to limit my Agent's exercise of his or her discretion and judgment with respect to any decisions regarding my medical care. I give my Agent full and final authority and unlimited discretion to make medical decisions on my behalf consistent with the provisions of the previous paragraphs. I have executed a living will, which expresses my wishes for end-of-life decision making.   I herby incorporate that document by reference and instruct my agent to honor these wishes.

L.   My Agent shall not be liable to me or to my estate for the consequences of any decision my Agent makes on my behalf in the good faith exercise of the authority given to my Agent pursuant to this Health Care Proxy.

M.   I specifically authorize my Agent to arrange and contract for my admission to a medical, nursing, residential or similar facility, to enter into agreements for my care, to apply for medical insurance coverage, third-party payments or governmental benefits to pay for my care.

HEALTHCARE PROXY
PAGE 2 OF 5

N. I specifically authorize my Agent to employ and discharge medical personnel including physicians, psychologists, dentists, nurses, therapists, and health and personal aides. However, my Agent is directed that I am fully satisfied with the medical personnel with whom I am working at this time.

O. I specifically authorize (but do not direct) my Agent to give or withhold consent to any medical procedure, test or treatment, including surgery, or to order the termination of any such procedure, test or treatment or the withdrawal of any life-sustaining measures (including nutrition and hydration) even if this might hasten my death or be against conventional medical advice.

P. I specifically authorize my agent to receive from any facility or authority all items of my personal property and effects that are in my possession at the time of illness, disability or death.

4. REVOCATION

This Health Care Proxy shall be revoked upon any one of the following events:

A. My execution of a subsequent Health Care Proxy;
B. My notification to my Health Care Agent or a health care provider orally or in writing or by any other act evidencing a specific intent to revoke the Health Care Proxy.

5. GOVERNING LAW

This document shall be governed by the laws of the Commonwealth of Massachusetts in all respects, including its validity, construction, interpretation, and termination. I intend for this Health Care Proxy to be honored in any jurisdiction where it may be presented and for any such jurisdiction to refer to Massachusetts law to interpret and determine the validity of this document and any of the powers granted under this document.

6. PHOTOCOPIES

My Agent is authorized to make photocopies of this document as frequently and in such quantity as my Agent shall deem appropriate. All photocopies shall have the same force and effect as any original.

7. SEVERABILITY

If any part of any provision of this document shall be invalid or unenforceable under applicable law, such part shall be ineffective to the extent of such invalidity only, without in any way affecting the remaining part of such provision or the remaining provisions of this document.

8. WOMAN and CUSTOMARY PRESENTATION

I am a woman and as such it is my desire and expectation that I be treated with the same dignity and grace accorded to any female patient or client. During any period of treatment, I direct my physician and all medical personnel and any other caregivers to maintain my overall appearance and attire in a well-groomed fashion if and when I am unable to do this for myself. This directive includes but is not limited to the performance of such tasks as the continuing of hormone replacement therapy, removal of any and all facial, hand, nostril or ear hair, application of make-up, trimming and polishing of nails, coiffing of hair to maintain style and blond-coloring, bathing at least daily.

HEALTHCARE PROXY
PAGE 3 OF 5

9.   RESPECTFUL RELATIONS

During any period of treatment, I direct my physician and all medical personnel and other caregivers to refer to me by my legal name, **MARY SMITH**. This directive is to be enforced regardless of names that may appear on out-of-date documents. Furthermore, such persons are reminded that I am a woman and as such expect to be related to and addressed strictly as a female, paying particular attention to the use of the appropriate feminine language.

10.   VISITATION

In the event that I am hospitalized or being treated in a medical facility, it is my wish that **THOMAS JOHNSON** be given first preference in being admitted to visit me in such facility, whether or not there are parties related to me by blood or by law or other parties desiring to visit me. It is my further wish that **THOMAS JOHNSON** decide which parties related to me by blood or by law or other parties be allowed to visit me. It is also my desire that **THOMAS JOHNSON's** right of visitation with me extend to visits in any intensive care unit or similar type of unit to which I may be confined.

SIGNATURE OF PRINCIPAL

I sign this Health Care Proxy on _____, in the presence of two witnesses, neither of whom is my Health Care Agent or alternate.

_____
MARY SMITH
Principal

WITNESSES

We, the undersigned, have witnessed the execution of this document by the Principal or at the direction of the Principal and state that the Principal appears to be at least eighteen years of age, of sound mind and under no constraint or undue influence. We have not been named as Health Care Agent or alternate Health Care Agent in this document.

Witness 1   Witness 2

Signature: _____   _____
Printed Name:
Address:

HEALTHCARE PROXY
PAGE 4 OF 5

COMMONWEALTH OF MASSACHUSETTS

Suffolk, ss.

On this _____ day of _____, [year], before me, the undersigned notary public, personally appeared **MARY SMITH,** proved to me through satisfactory evidence of identification, which was a Massachusetts Driver's License, to be the person whose name is signed on the preceding or attached document, and acknowledged to me that she signed it voluntarily for its stated purposes.

_____
Notary Public
Name:
My Commission Expires:

10E. HIPAA Authorization

AUTHORIZATION OF PRINCIPAL FOR RELEASE OF
PROTECTED HEALTH INFORMATION

I, **MARY SMITH**, formerly known as John Smith, intend to comply, now and in the future, with all requirements set forth in the Standards for Privacy of Individually Identifiable Health Information, known as the "Privacy Rule" which implements the privacy requirements of the Health Insurance Portability and Accountability Act of 1996, commonly known as "HIPAA," so that the information described below will be freely available to those described below. All provisions hereof shall be construed in accordance with that intent. I hereby authorize each Covered Entity identified below to disclose my individually identifiable health information as described below, which may include information concerning mental illness (except psychotherapy notes), laboratory test results, medical history, treatment, or any other such related information.

1. **My Additional Identification Information:**
    Name: **MARY SMITH**
    Date of Birth: 1/1/1976

2. **Identity of Person or Class of Persons Authorized to Make Disclosure.**

I hereby authorize all covered entities as defined in HIPAA, and all other health care providers, health plans, and health care clearinghouses, including but not limited to each and every doctor, psychiatrist, psychologist, therapist, nurse, hospital, clinic, laboratory, ambulance service, assisted living facility, residential care facility, bed and board facility, nursing home, medical insurance company or any other medical provider or agent thereof having protected health information (as that term is defined in HIPAA), each being referred to herein as a "Covered Entity."

3. **Description of Information to Be Disclosed.** I hereby authorize each Covered Entity to disclose the following information: All health care information, reports and/or records concerning my medical history, condition, diagnosis, testing, prognosis, treatment, billing information and identity of health care providers, whether past, present, or future, and any other information which is in any way related to my health care. Additionally, this disclosure shall include the ability to ask questions and discuss this protected medical information with the person or entity who has possession of the protected medical information, even if I am fully competent to ask questions and discuss this matter at the time. It is my intention to give a full authorization for ANY and ALL protected medical information to the persons named in this authorization.

4. **Person or Class of Persons to Whom the Covered Entity May Disclose the Above Described Protected Health Information.** The above-described information shall be disclosed to my spouse, **THOMAS JOHNSON**, and my friend, **KAREN LEWIS**, hereinafter referred to as "Authorized Persons."

5. **Termination.** This authorization shall terminate on the first to occur of: (1) two years following my death, or (2) upon my written revocation actually received by the Covered Entity. Proof of receipt of my written revocation may be either by certified mail, registered mail, facsimile, or any other receipt evidencing actual receipt by the Covered Entity. Such revocation shall be effective upon the actual receipt of the notice by the Covered Entity except to the extent that the covered entity has taken action in reliance on this Authorization.

HIPAA AUTHORIZATION
PAGE 1 OF 2

6.   **Re-Disclosure.** By signing this Authorization, I acknowledge that the information used or disclosed pursuant to this authorization may be subject to re-disclosure by the Authorized Persons and the information once disclosed will no longer be protected by the rules created in HIPAA. No covered entity shall require my authorized persons to indemnify the covered entity or agree to perform any act in order for the covered entity to comply with this authorization.

7.   **Instructions to My Authorized Persons.** My Authorized Persons shall have the right to bring a legal action in any applicable form against any Covered Entity that refuses to recognize and accept this authorization for the purposes that I have expressed. Additionally, my Authorized Persons are authorized to sign any documents that the authorized person deems appropriate to obtain the protected medical information.

8.   **Revocation.** I may revoke this authorization at any time by delivering my intent to so revoke in writing to any of my Authorized Persons.

9.   **Valid Document.** A copy or facsimile of this original authorization shall be accepted as though it was an original document.

10.   **My Waiver and Release.** I hereby release any covered entity that acts in reliance on this authorization from any liability that may accrue from releasing my protected medical information and for any actions taken by my Authorized Persons. I also specifically prohibit my Authorized Persons, or any other person designated as any agent in any capacity from filing a complaint of any kind against any Covered Entity that complies with the directions of my Authorized Persons hereunder to the extent that such a complaint purports to charge said Covered Entity with any violation of the Privacy Rules or other Federal or State laws related to disclosure of medical records as a result of their compliance with said directions.

_____

MARY SMITH

Date: _____

COMMONWEALTH OF MASSACHUSETTS

Suffolk, ss.

On this ____ day of _____, [year], before me, the undersigned notary public, personally appeared MARY SMITH, **proved to me through satisfactory evidence of identification, which was a Massachusetts Driver's License, to be the person whose name is signed on the preceding or attached document, and acknowledged to me that she signed it voluntarily for its stated purposes.**

_____
Notary Public
Name:
My Commission Expires:

HIPAA AUTHORIZATION
PAGE 2 OF 2

10F. Living Will and Advance Directives

LIVING WILL & ADVANCE DIRECTIVES FOR MARY SMITH

To my family, my physicians, my attorney and all those concerned with my care:

I, **MARY SMITH,** formerly known as John Smith, presently residing in Boston, Massachusetts, and being an adult of sound mind, make this declaration as a directive to be followed if for any reason I become unable to make or communicate decisions regarding my medical care.

I have executed or will execute in the future a health care proxy pursuant to Massachusetts General Laws, chapter 201D. I understand that, by signing such document, I am giving my Health Care Agent (my "Agent") the authority to exercise his or her best judgment regarding all health care decisions including decisions about life-sustaining treatment. Regarding decisions about life-sustaining treatment, it is my desire that my agent, and all other persons and courts, be guided by the following statement of my wishes, as indicated below.

I do not want medical treatment that will keep me alive if I am unconscious and there is no reasonable prospect that I will ever be conscious again (even if I am not going to die soon in my medical condition) or if I am near death from an illness or injury with no reasonable prospect of recovery. The procedures and treatment to be withheld and withdrawn include, without limitation, surgery, antibiotics, cardiac and pulmonary resuscitation, ventilated respiratory support, intensive care, administration of blood products, dialysis and artificially administered feeding and fluids including nasogastric or gastric tube feeding and intravenous nutrition and hydration. I direct that treatment be limited to measures to keep me comfortable and to relieve pain, even if such measures shorten my life.

I wish to live out my last days at my home rather than in a hospital or hospice, if it does not jeopardize the chance of my recovery to a meaningful and conscious life and does not impose an undue burden on my family. This wish is to be carried out even if it will cause me increased suffering and financial burden.

If, upon my death, any of my tissue or organs would be of value for transplantation, I freely give my permission for the donation of such tissue or organs. I give **[my body] [any needed organs or parts] [or list specific organs or parts]** to **[name specific institution] [the physician in attendance at my death] [or the hospital in which I die]** for the following purposes: **[any purposes authorized by law] [therapy of another person] [medical education] [transplantation] [or research].**

RESPECTFUL RELATIONS

During any period of treatment, I direct my physician and all medical personnel to refer to me by the name of Mary Smith irrespective of whether I have obtained a court ordered name change and/or I have changed my name on any identity documents.

During any period of treatment, I direct my physician and all medical personnel to use the female pronoun in reference to me, my chart, my treatment, etc., irrespective of whether I have obtained a court approved gender change, or changed my gender marker on any identity documents, or have or have not undergone any transition related medical treatment.

During any period of treatment, I direct my physician and all medical personnel that if I am unable to maintain my feminine appearance, to maintain my feminine appearance.

FINAL WISHES

During any memorial service or preparation thereof, I direct all coroners, funeral home employees, health care workers, and participants to refer to me by the name of Mary Smith irrespective of whether I have obtained a court ordered name change and/or I have changed my name on any identity documents.

During any memorial service or preparation thereof, I direct all coroners, funeral home employees, health care workers, and participants to use the female pronoun in reference to me, irrespective of whether I have obtained a court approved gender change, or changed my gender marker on any identity documents, or have or have not undergone any transition related medical treatment.

These directions are the exercise of my legal right to refuse treatment. Therefore, I expect my family, physicians, health care facilities and all concerned with my care to regard themselves as legally and morally bound to act in accordance with my wishes, and in so doing to be free from any liability for having followed my directions.

Signed this ____ day of _____, [year].

_____
MARY SMITH

WITNESSES

We, the undersigned, have witnessed the execution of this document by **MARY SMITH** and state that **MARY SMITH** appears to be at least eighteen years of age, of sound mind and under no constraint or undue influence. We have not been named as Health Care Agent or alternate Health Care Agent in the Health Care Proxy of **MARY SMITH**.

Witness 1   Witness 2

Signature: _____   _____
Printed Name:
Address:

COMMONWEALTH OF MASSACHUSETTS
Suffolk, ss.

On this ___ day of _____, [year], before me, the undersigned notary public, personally appeared **MARY SMITH**, proved to me through satisfactory evidence of identification, which was a Massachusetts Driver's License, to be the person whose name is signed on the preceding or attached document, and acknowledged to me that she signed it voluntarily for its stated purposes.

_____
Notary Public
Name:
My Commission Expires:

LIVING WILL & ADV DIRECTIVES
PAGE 3 OF 3

10G. **Durable Power of Attorney**

DURABLE POWER OF ATTORNEY
OF
MARY SMITH

I, **MARY SMITH**, fka John Smith, of Boston, Suffolk County, Massachusetts, hereby appoint **THOMAS JOHNSON** and if he dies, resigns, or is determined by a physician in writing to be incapable of serving, then I appoint **KAREN LEWIS** instead, to serve as my agent and attorney-in-fact (hereinafter referred to as my attorney), for me and in my name and behalf to control and manage my property and affairs in all respects including full power and authority:

1. **GENERAL GRANT OF POWER.** To exercise or perform any act, power, duty, right or obligation whatsoever that I now have or may hereafter acquire, in relation to any person, matter, transaction, or property, real or personal, tangible or intangible, now owned or hereafter acquired by me, including, without limitation, the following specifically enumerated powers. I grant to my attorney full power and authority to do everything necessary in exercising any of the powers herein granted as fully as I might or could do if personally present, with full power of substitution or revocation, hereby ratifying and confirming all that my attorney shall lawfully do or cause to be done by virtue of this power of attorney and the powers herein granted.

(a) **Powers of Collection and Payment.** To pay my current bills and just debts; to collect, receive, request, demand, sue for, recover, and hold all such sums of money, debts, dues, commercial paper, checks, drafts, accounts, deposits, legacies, bequests, devises, notes, interests, stock certificates, bonds, dividends, certificates of deposit, annuities, pension, profit sharing, retirement, social security, insurance and other contractual benefits and proceeds, all documents of title, all property and property rights and demands whatsoever, liquidated or unliquidated, now or hereafter owned by, or due, owing, payable or belonging to me, or in which I have or hereafter acquire an interest; to have, use, and take all lawful means for the collection and recovery thereof, and to adjust, sell, compromise, and agree for the same, and to execute and deliver for me, on my behalf, and in my name, all endorsements, releases, receipts, or other sufficient discharges for the same;

(b) **Power to Acquire and Sell.** To acquire, purchase, grant options to sell, mortgage (including a reverse mortgage), pledge, lease, transfer, assign, deliver, convey or otherwise dispose of real and personal property, tangible or intangible, or interests therein, on such terms and conditions as my attorney shall deem proper, and in connection therewith to sign, seal, execute and deliver deeds, bills of sale, stock powers, and any other documents necessary or convenient to accomplish such action, and no purchaser, transferee or assignee shall be bound to see to the application of the proceeds; all powers in this provision, including the power to sell or transfer shall specifically apply to the property at 100 Washington Street, Boston, Massachusetts, and any interest in other real property I may own or hereafter acquire, without limitation, as it is my express and specific intention to empower my attorney to sell, transfer or otherwise deal with all such properties;

(c) **Management Powers.** To invest and reinvest, maintain, repair, improve, manage, insure, rent, lease, encumber, and in any manner to deal with any real or personal property, tangible or intangible, or any interests therein, that I now own or may hereafter acquire; to enter any premises leased by me and to care for any such premises and its contents, all upon such terms and conditions as my attorney shall deem proper;

(d)   **Banking Powers.** To make, receive, sign and endorse checks and drafts, deposit and withdraw funds, acquire and redeem certificates of deposit, in banks, savings and loan associations and other institutions, execute or release such deeds of trust or other security agreements as may be necessary or proper in the exercise of the rights and powers herein granted; to open and close checking and savings accounts; to certify my taxpayer identification number;

(e)   **Voting Powers.** To exercise either in person or by general or limited proxy, any voting rights I have in relation to any shares of stock, any interest in any condominium, condominium association, condominium trust, real estate cooperative or other investment or interest of any type, or to refrain from exercising such rights;

(f)   **Business Interests.** To conduct or participate in any lawful business of whatever nature for me and in my name; to execute partnership agreements and amendments thereto; to incorporate, reorganize, merge, consolidate, recapitalize, sell, liquidate, or dissolve any business; to elect or employ officers, directors and agents; enter into or carry out the provisions of any agreement for the sale of any business interest or the stock therein; and to exercise voting rights with respect to stock, either in person or by proxy, and exercise stock options;

(g)   **Investment Powers.** To open any investment accounts and with respect to any investment accounts, whether presently opened or hereafter opened; to make purchases and sales (including short sales); to subscribe for and trade in stocks, bonds, options, or other securities, or limited partnership interests or investments and trust units, whether or not in negotiable form, issued or unissued, foreign exchange, commodities, and contracts relating to same (including commodity futures), on margin or otherwise, for my account and risk; to deliver or surrender securities on my account, or to instruct others to deliver or surrender securities to my attorney on my account; to order payment of monies from my accounts and to receive and direct payments from my accounts; to sell, assign, endorse and transfer any stocks, bonds, options or other securities of any nature, at any time standing in my name and to execute any documents necessary to effectuate the foregoing; to receive any and all notices, calls for margin, or other demands with reference to my accounts; and to make any and all agreements with reference to such accounts on my behalf;

(h)   **Tax Powers.** To prepare, sign, and file joint, separate or single income tax returns or declarations of estimated tax for any year or years; to apply for and receive any refund due me; to receive any communications with respect to any tax, and to appear for me and represent me before any federal, state or municipal or other agency in connection with any tax matter; to prepare, sign and file gift tax returns with respect to gifts made by me or by my attorney hereunder for any year or years; to consent to any gift and to utilize any gift-splitting provisions or other tax election; and to execute any Power of Attorney designation on forms required by the Internal Revenue Service or any state department of revenue or taxation for three tax years prior to the date of this instrument and for all tax years thereafter;

(i)   **Safe Deposit Boxes.** To have access at any time or times to (and to enter by force if necessary) any safe deposit box rented by me, wheresoever located, to remove all or any part of the contents thereof, and to surrender or relinquish said safe deposit box; and any institution in which any such safe deposit box may be located shall not incur any liability to me or my estate as a result of permitting my attorney to exercise this power;

(j)   **Gift Making Powers.** To make gifts from my property to one or more charitable organizations, the choice of such organizations and the amounts of such gifts to be determined in the sole discretion of my attorney, taking into account the desirability of income-tax deductions for the current year and my prior charitable-giving practices; to make outright or in trusts gifts of my property (including gifts of real

POWER OF ATTORNEY
PAGE 2 OF 7

293

property) to or for the benefit of my spouse, **THOMAS JOHNSON**; gifts hereunder need not be made in equal amounts to my Beneficiaries but should be generally consistent with my overall estate plan. Nothing hereunder shall be construed to limit the powers set forth in paragraph (l) below;

(k)   **Powers Under Inter Vivos Trust.** To transfer, convey, and deliver any and all of my property, real and personal, to the trustees of any revocable or irrevocable trust created by me as donor or for the benefit of me or my spouse, **THOMAS JOHNSON** (unless such trust grants my attorney a general power of appointment), and to do all things necessary or convenient to accomplish the same, including without limitation to sign, seal, execute and deliver deeds, bills of sale, and stock powers; to create and fund any trust, revocable or irrevocable that I may have power to create, for the benefit of myself or my spouse, **THOMAS JOHNSON**; provided all actions of my attorney are generally consistent with my overall estate plan;

(l)   **Estate or Benefit Planning Powers.** To take such action or to apply funds in a manner and for a purpose that is in keeping with my estate planning wishes, without petition to or leave of court, to conserve my property, minimize current or prospective federal and state taxes, and maximize entitlement to or availability of federal and state medical, welfare, housing, and other public programs for myself, to make revocable or irrevocable transfers of my property into trusts (whether established by me or my attorney) for the benefit of myself or to increase the funds available to establish the legacy referred to above. Nothing hereunder shall be construed to limit the powers set forth in paragraph (j) above;

(m)   **Power to Make Statutory Elections and Disclaimers.** To make on my behalf any and all statutory elections and to disclaim any interest in property passing to me by gift, bequest, devise or other transfer if my attorney in the exercise of his or her sole discretion determines that such disclaimer is likely to increase the after-tax amount ultimately passing to my family after my decease without materially affecting my well-being;

(n)   **Power to Act in Probate Proceedings.** To assent or to oppose the allowance of any probate or other accounts in which I may be or become interested, and generally to act in any and all probate matters or proceedings in which I may become interested;

(o)   **Power to Act in Legal Proceedings.** To appear, answer and defend, or compromise any suits that have been or may hereafter be commenced against me; to begin, and to prosecute or compromise, any suit that my attorney may deem proper; to waive the client-attorney privilege on my behalf; and generally to act on my behalf in any and all legal proceedings in which I may become interested;

(p)   **Retirement Plan Powers.** To deal with all retirement plans in which I may have an interest, including, but not limited to, individual retirement accounts, Keogh, stock option, thrift, savings, 401(a), 403(b), 401(k), variable annuity pension, profit-sharing or other employee benefit plans, as well as settlement options and distributions, rollovers and voluntary contributions; in regard to these, to exercise in any manner any election or option thereunder and to make withdrawals therefrom; to become a participant in such a plan or to establish an Individual Retirement Account in my name; to change the designation of beneficiary for any such account or plan, provided the new beneficiary is my spouse, **THOMAS JOHNSON**; to waive any rights that I may have with respect to any plan in which my partner is a participant; to contribute to any existing account or plan in my name; and to roll over the proceeds of a lump-sum distribution from any qualified pension or plan into an Individual Retirement Account or another qualified pension or profit sharing plan;

(q)   **Insurance Powers.** To exercise all rights I may have with respect to any life insurance policy (whether on my life or that of another) or any annuity contract, or any interest in any such policy or

POWER OF ATTORNEY
PAGE 3 OF 7

contract, as fully as any owner or beneficiary of the same; to engage in any transaction and to exercise and enjoy all options, benefits, rights and privileges under such policy or contract, including powers to borrow upon the same; to pledge the same for loans; to name a new or additional beneficiary or owner as long as such new owner or beneficiary is my spouse, **THOMAS JOHNSON**; to surrender, assign, exchange or otherwise modify any such policy or contract; elect settlement options, accumulate dividends or have dividends paid out, apply for waivers of premiums or disability income, and surrender the policy for cash value;

(r)   **Motor Vehicles and Boats.** To apply for a Certificate of Title upon, and endorse and transfer title thereto, any automobile, boat or other motor vehicle and to represent in such transfer assignment that the title to said motor vehicle is free and clear of all liens and encumbrances except those specifically set forth in such transfer assignment;

(s)   **Governmental Entitlement Powers.** To deal with any and all state or federal agencies from whom I receive or may be entitled to receive governmental benefits of any description or amount in order to: (i) prepare and file all documents required by such agencies; (ii) apply for any benefits to which I may be entitled; (iii) modify the amounts or terms of such entitlements; (iv) assert my rights against any curtailment or termination of benefits; (v) appeal or compromise any contested claim; (vi) effect a termination thereof.

(t)   **Power to Designate a Substitute.** To appoint and substitute for my attorney any agents or attorney for any or all of the purposes herein enumerated, and to revoke their authority at his or her pleasure;

(u)   **Powers to Provide for My Care.** To make such use of my personal and real property as is necessary to provide for my maintenance, transportation, and necessary medical, dental and surgical care, hospitalization and custodial care;

(v)   **Contracts.** To enter into contracts of whatever nature or kind in my name;

(w)   **Power to Hire and Pay for Services.** To retain such accountants, attorneys, social workers, consultants, clerks, employees, workers or other persons as my attorney shall deem appropriate in connection with the management of my property, person or affairs and to make payments from my assets for the fees of such persons so employed; and

(x)   **Unenumerated Powers.** In addition to the foregoing, my attorney hereunder may act as my alter ego with respect to any and all possible matters and affairs not otherwise enumerated herein and which I as principal can do through an agent.

2.   HEALTH CARE DECISIONS and FUNERAL PLANS. To authorize my admission to any health care facility including any medical, nursing, mental health, residential or similar facility and to enter into agreements for my care and to authorize the release of my medical records in my attorney's discretion including any and all confidential medical information and any and all information or records of any health or disability insurer. In addition to the other powers granted hereunder, my attorney shall have the power and authority to serve as my personal representative for all purposes under the federal Health Insurance Portability and Accountability Act of 1996 (HIPAA), and in particular its 2003 Privacy Regulations; to enter into contracts for my funeral, burial or cremation and to pay in advance for such services; to establish a bank account designated as a funeral account on my behalf. To the extent that this provision conflicts with authority granted under any health care proxy that I have executed and that is then in effect, decisions made and actions taken by my agent under such Health Care Proxy shall prevail over decisions made and actions taken by my attorney-in-fact under this Durable Power of Attorney.

3. COURT APPOINTED FIDUCIARIES. If it is deemed necessary to seek appointment by a probate court of a guardian of my person or a conservator of my estate, I hereby nominate my said attorney, **THOMAS JOHNSON**, or if he is incapable of serving, my said successor attorney, **KAREN LEWIS**, for appointment by such court to serve as such fiduciary and request that surety bond be waived for such appointment. Nothing in this section shall be construed as a direction that such a petition be filed or such appointment be made, and it is my express wish that such action be taken only when and if absolutely necessary.

4. GUARDIANSHIP & CONSERVATORSHIP OF MINOR CHILDREN. I appoint my spouse, **THOMAS JOHNSON**, as the temporary and then permanent guardian and/or conservator of my minor children. In the event and only in the event that **THOMAS JOHNSON** predeceases me or is totally disabled and thereby unable to act as the legal and custodial guardian and/or conservator of my minor children, then in his stead I nominate, on the same terms set forth above, my friend, **KAREN LEWIS** as guardian and/or conservator in her place. I request that surety bond be waived for such appointment.

5. COMPENSATION FOR MY ATTORNEY. My attorney named herein, and his or her successor, shall be entitled to reasonable compensation for any expenses that are incurred and for the time, effort and services rendered as my attorney.

6. THIRD PARTY RELIANCE. Third parties may rely upon the representations of my attorney as to all matters pertaining to any power granted to my attorney, and no person who may act in reliance upon the representation of my attorney or the authority granted to my attorney shall incur any liability to me or my estate as a result of permitting my attorney to exercise any power.

7. VALIDITY OUT OF STATE, GOVERNING LAW, BOND, PHOTOCOPIES. This instrument is executed and delivered in the Commonwealth of Massachusetts, and the laws of the Commonwealth of Massachusetts shall govern all questions as to the validity of this power and the construction of its provisions. Nevertheless, I intend that this instrument be given full force and effect in any state or country in which I may find myself or in which I may own property, whether real or personal or in which my attorney finds it necessary or desirable, in his or her discretion, to exercise this power. I direct that my attorney not be required to give bond for any purpose, and if any bond is required, that no sureties be required. I direct that photocopies of this instrument shall have the same power and effect as the original.

8. NON-LIMITATION ON POWERS. This instrument is to be construed and interpreted as a general durable power of attorney. The enumeration of specific powers herein is not intended to, nor does it, limit or restrict the general powers herein granted to my attorney. For a third party to construe otherwise would be contrary to my intent.

9. DISABILITY OR INCAPACITY OF PRINCIPAL. This Durable Power of Attorney shall not be affected by my subsequent disability or incapacity, and shall be binding not only upon me but also upon my heirs, executors and administrators up to the time of the receipt by my said attorney of a written revocation signed by me or of reliable intelligence of my death. This Durable Power of Attorney shall remain in full force and effect until such time as I execute a written revocation thereof.

10. REVOCATION OF PRIOR INSTRUMENTS. If I have executed any Durable Powers of Attorney prior to the date of this instrument, I hereby revoke any such earlier documents and the powers conferred therein.

11. REFUSAL TO HONOR POWER. Should any third party, including any bank, trust company, insurance company, or any other third party, refuse to accept the validity of this Power of Attorney, and should I suffer any financial or personal damages as a result of such refusal, then I direct my attorney to bring whatever legal action he or she may deem appropriate to compensate me or my heirs for the damages suffered due to such refusal.

12. SUCCESSOR ATTORNEY. Any party dealing with my successor attorney may rely upon his or her representation as to my original attorney's death, incapacity or resignation as conclusively correct. The terms of Article 5 above shall apply equally to those actions taken by my successor attorney and to third parties acting in reliance on representations of my successor attorney.

13. SELF-DEALING. My attorney is authorized to engage in self-dealing in accordance with the terms of this document; provided, however, my attorney is only authorized to take actions to benefit him or herself to the extent such benefit is needed for my attorney's health, education, maintenance or support unless such actions are assented to by a party with a substantial interest that is adverse to that of my attorney. However, notwithstanding any other provision of this instrument, my attorney is not authorized to take any action of any type to discharge any legal support obligation of my attorney under state law, or to otherwise benefit him or herself, his or her estate, his or her creditors, or the creditors of his or her estate, if the authority to take such act would be construed as the grant of a general power of appointment. It is my intent that my attorney-in-fact not be granted or construed as having been granted a general power of appointment or any other power that would require the inclusion of my assets in her or his gross estate for the determination of federal estate tax, if she or he predeceases me. Any provision in this instrument giving him or her or construed as giving him or her such a power is not intended, and shall be deemed to be void.

14. RESPECTFUL RELATIONS. During any activity conducted by my attorney, I direct my attorney and all persons involved with my affairs or my attorney to refer to me by my legal name, **MARY SMITH,** irrespective of the name on any out-of-date identity documents. During such activity or transactions, I also direct such persons to use the female pronoun in reference to me and in my contractual relations and affairs (unless such reference will have negative legal effect on my well-being that my attorney deems to be of sufficient significance) irrespective of whether I have obtained a court approved gender change, or changed my gender marker on any identity documents.

15. SPOUSE. I am married under the laws of the Commonwealth of Massachusetts to **THOMAS JOHNSON.** If, for any reason, this marriage is not recognized by any competent jurisdiction, and regardless of any change in law, other outcome or subsequent legal event (other than divorce) that invalidates this marriage or converts it to civil union or other pseudo-spousal status, it is my intention that this instrument shall nonetheless remain valid and in effect as written and that all references to, and appointments of, Thomas Johnson be recognized and carried out as provided hereunder.

16. VALIDITY DESPITE PASSAGE OF TIME. This instrument shall remain in full force despite the passage of time.

IN WITNESS WHEREOF, I have executed this Durable Power of Attorney this _____ day of _____, [year].

_____
MARY SMITH
Principal

We, the undersigned, have witnessed the signing of this document by the Principal or at the direction of the Principal and state that the Principal appears to be at least eighteen years of age, of sound mind and under no constraint or undue influence. We have not been named as the Principal's agent or attorney-in-fact, or as successor agent or successor attorney-in-fact in this document.

Witness 1   Witness 2

Signature: _____   _____
Printed Name:
Address:

COMMONWEALTH OF MASSACHUSETTS

Suffolk, ss.

On this _____ day of _____, [year], before me, the undersigned notary public, personally appeared **MARY SMITH**, proved to me through satisfactory evidence of identification, which was a Massachusetts Driver's License, to be the person whose name is signed on the preceding or attached document, and acknowledged to me that she signed it voluntarily for its stated purposes.

_____
Notary Public
Name:
My Commission Expires:

POWER OF ATTORNEY
PAGE 7 OF 7

10H. Directive as to Remains

DIRECTIVE AS TO REMAINS FOR MARY SMITH

To my family, my physicians, my attorney, any medical facility in which I may hereafter be, any individual who may become responsible for my health, welfare, or affairs, and to any court having jurisdiction over my person or property:

I, **MARY SMITH**, formerly known as John Smith, of Boston, Massachusetts, being of sound mind, hereby make the following declaration of my carefully deliberated wishes and intentions.

I specifically authorize and direct that my organs be donated for transplantation and my remains be cremated. I understand that due to the nature of the cremation process, any valuable materials, including dental gold or other metals with the remains, will be either destroyed or not recovered in their original form, and I hereby authorize the disposal by the cremation service or cemetery of any such material that may remain after the cremation process. I further understand the cremated remains are bone fragments, which will be reduced in size by mechanical means.

During any memorial service, obituary or preparation thereof, I direct all coroners, funeral home employees, health care workers, and participants to refer to me by my legal name of **MARY SMITH** irrespective of whether I have changed my name on any identity documents. During any memorial service, obituary or preparation thereof, I also direct such persons to use the female pronoun in reference to me, irrespective of whether I have obtained a court approved sex change, or changed my sex marker on any identity documents. Finally, I direct such persons to maintain my feminine appearance.

I direct that all other decisions regarding disposition of my remains and funeral and memorial service arrangements be made by my spouse, **THOMAS JOHNSON**, or if he is unavailable, my friend, **KAREN LEWIS** (or if both are unavailable someone designated by Thomas or Karen) in such person's sole and complete discretion.

It is my intention that my wishes set forth above be honored regardless of whether any of these named people is available and that the funeral home accept direction to implement these wishes from any responsible party. It is my further intention that all references to my spouse, **THOMAS JOHNSON**, be honored regardless of whether, for any reason, this marriage is not recognized by any competent jurisdiction, and regardless of any change in law, other outcome or subsequent legal event (other than divorce) that invalidates this marriage or converts it to civil union or other pseudo-spousal status.

IN WITNESS WHEREOF, I, **MARY SMITH**, have hereto set my hand below and do declare this instrument to be a true statement of my wishes this _____ day of _____, [year].

....
MARY SMITH

DIRECTIVE AS TO REMAINS
PAGE 1 OF 2

COMMONWEALTH OF MASSACHUSETTS

Suffolk, ss.

On this _____ day of _____, [year], before me, the undersigned notary public, personally appeared **MARY SMITH**, proved to me through satisfactory evidence of identification, which was a Massachusetts Driver's License, to be the person whose name is signed on the preceding or attached document, and acknowledged to me that she signed it voluntarily for its stated purposes.

_____

Notary Public
Name:
My Commission Expires:

DIRECTIVE AS TO REMAINS
PAGE 2 OF 2